INFANT

FIGURES

The Death of the 'Infans'
and Other Scenes of Origin

INFANT

FIGURES

CHRISTOPHER FYNSK

Stanford University Press
Stanford, California 2000

Stanford University Press
Stanford, California

© 2000 by the Board of Trustees of the Leland Stanford Junior University

Printed in the United States of America

Library of Congress Cataloging-in-Publicaion Data

Fynsk, Christopher
　　Infant figures : the death of the infans and other scenes of origin / Christopher Fynsk.
　　　　p.　　cm.
　　Includes bibliographical references and index.
　　ISBN 0-8047-3407-0 (alk. paper) — ISBN 0-8047-3408-9 (paper : alk. paper)
　　1. Language and languages—Philosophy.　　I. Title.

P106 .F957　　2000
401—dc21　　　　　　　　　　　　　　　　　　　　　　　　00-056354

∞　This book is printed on acid-free, archival quality paper.

Original printing 2000

Last figure below indicates the year of this printing:
09　08　07　06　05　04　03　02　01　00

Designed by James P. Brommer
Typeset in 10/13.5 and 9/15 Minion and Arial

Acknowledgments and Dedication

Among the many who have supported this project, I would like to give special thanks to Edith Doron, Sue Golding, Susan Hanson, Michael Hardt, William Haver, Mary Lydon, Joan Scott, Helen Tartar, and Elisabeth Weber. Others have helped shape the spirit and insights that guide this work, but the responses and support of these friends enabled me to bring it to completion. I am deeply grateful to them.

It grieves me that I cannot express my gratitude to one more dear friend: Jean-François Lyotard. The words in this volume that were written for him are left now like orphans. But I take solace in the thought that some of those who knew him (and perhaps even some who know only his writings) will recognize a trace of his gift in the many pages he rendered possible here, and I will listen for the sound of his humor in their reactions. I dedicate the volume to his memory.

Contents

Illustrations

INFANT

FIGURES

Introduction

At the heart of this volume is a meditation on two accounts of mortal exposure, two deaths of an enigmatic and haunting character. Each scene is singular in event and presentation, but each points beyond its narrated occasion (the death of a child) to questions of general import concerning the human relation to language. With the strange resonance of the "primal" or the "originary," these two scenes from texts by Maurice Blanchot and Jacques Lacan make comparable claims on thought, compelling claims whose grounds are no less resistant to strict description than is the possibility of response. They call for a mode or modes of reflection (philosophical, ethical, and aesthetic) for which the rule and measure are always to be invented.

The response I will offer in this volume proceeds from an unfolding thought on the "origin" of language. In a form of questioning that respects the topic's own reserve, I will attempt to describe the site from which the two scenes speak as the locus of an "infant figure," naming with these last words an emergent figuration that attends a human subject's birth to language. Only the second section of the volume, the central piece of its triptych, focuses thematically on such a figure. But each section moves back to its site to think the relations that enable or necessitate its birth. On each occasion, it is a question of exploring what the figural conveys of a material relation that is "before" or "otherwise than" Being and inconceivable apart from a human element that exceeds any symbolic determination. At each figural site, it is a question of following a pragmatics (of art, of writing) that seeks the limits of language.

Such an undertaking could not innocently follow the normal line of discursive inquiry or critical commentary—not once it had lost its innocence with the recognition that its topic could never constitute an *object* for research.[1] Nor could it be satisfied with forging in masterly fashion a theoretical neologism or chains of aporetic formulae designed to cancel their own signification and point to an "unsayable." Even presuming it could reach such levels of sophistication, the present endeavor required a different kind of textual density. Or more accurately: this other density became inevitable once it was a matter of bearing witness—however faint—to the disruptions engaged by the forms of research (the art, the writing) that are examined in these pages. I would not hesitate to call this volume "experimental" if that term could evoke the manner in which these texts have sought a *response* to creations of a riveting insistence: a range of images by Francis Bacon, textual figures realized by Friedrich Nietzsche, Maurice Blanchot, and Jacques Lacan (among others, including Serge Leclaire), and a set of "anonymous figures" by Salvatore Puglia.

Structures of counterplay thus gradually urged themselves upon an initial, rather modest attempt to honor in commentary and graphics the haunting presence of a small group of images. If I were to try to account for these developments chronologically, I would begin by noting, first, the strangely recurrent pertinence of earlier work on the motif of cruelty in Nietzsche's later writings, work that was not only relevant to my study of Bacon (even amusingly so), but also called upon by Lacan's meditation on the "second death" in his seminar on ethics (a meditation that illuminates his understanding of the dream of the burning child from Freud's *The Interpretation of Dreams*). I thus chose to "preface" this first section on Bacon with the analysis of Nietzsche's *The Genealogy of Morals* and *Ecce Homo*. But I did not do so in order to provide a defining philosophical paradigm or even a tonality for the readings to follow. (If the text functioned in such a manner, I would be most regretful.) I was attempting, rather, to mark a horizon for what was to come and thereby clear a space of reflection. There was undoubtedly some risk in prefacing the essay on Bacon in this way; a hasty reader could conclude that I meant to promote a sexy version of the will to power under the guise of a fashionable theme and some no less fashionable pictures. I hoped, however, that by disjoining the texts as I did, a gap would open, and that *from that gap* I could evoke something of the strange force of Bacon's practice, perhaps even the material presence of what he calls, in his late, Shakespearean mode, an "essence." From a space of exposure like the one thought by Nietzsche under the name of the Dionysian, Bacon pursued a pragmatics of the image that forces us to rethink the relations between the image and the real. He worked for the sake of an event that is comparable to the one Friedrich Hölderlin saw in modern tragedy: a "forcing" of its participants *back to the*

earth and into a time Hölderlin understood to be irreversible. I read the famous "presence" of Bacon's figures as a mark of that event—a mark of the
fact of existence as taken in a tragic, sometimes tragi-comic apprehension of
reality.

A further development in the counterplay to which I have referred marks
the passage from the first section of the volume to the second. The step involved cannot be summarized in advance of the discussion, so I offer no more
than a formula when I say that the fold that divides the first section is "inter-
nalized" in the second, appearing in a disruption of expository form and a fictive redoubling of the voice (a redoubling that should not be taken as a dialectical opposition—this is where the notion of a "counterplay" reaches its
limit). In the briefest terms, the writing of the second section *suffers* the interruption marked in the first and unfolds from it in two periods of reflection.

This section takes its point of departure from Maurice Blanchot's *The
Writing of the Disaster*, and specifically from Blanchot's assertion (inspired by
readings of Serge Leclaire and D. W. Winnicott) that all human speech and
psychic life are haunted by the death of a child, a being whose passing is the
condition of speech, and who is therefore, of necessity, without speech: *infans*. The dialogue pursues a speculative development of this assertion
through a reading of a brief narrative, "(A Primal Scene?)," that is implicitly
presented by Blanchot as the *ur-text* for his meditation on the death of the *infans*. I use this term "ur-text" as a form of shorthand and only to suggest that
Blanchot's narrative is not taken as the possible illustration for a thesis. In *The
Writing of the Disaster* itself, there is no way of determining whether the narrative responds to the psychoanalytic discussions addressed throughout the
volume, or whether it is the original event of writing that led Blanchot to
those discussions (and the exact meaning of each of these alternatives is already worth consideration). It is clear, however, that the problem of accounting for the nature of its legibility and the relation to which it calls its readers
is indissociable from the questions that guide the meditation here and in the
second half of the dialogue (which addresses Lacan's reading of the dream of
the burning child). Among these questions is the one that introduces the
"fold" to which I referred: that of the possibility of responding to the opening
(an opening *of* language, but prior to any speech) that occurs with the mortal
exposure of that being, in each of us, that is the *infans*.

What is the precise status of this "infans," this figural inscription whose appearance in Freud's research (as it is given to us by Lacan) marks a decisive

moment for his understanding of trauma and the function of repetition in the primary processes? How do we understand the strangely motivated character of this figure, which Blanchot considers necessary to all speech and life (is it a figure?), and how do we evaluate the speculative endeavors in which it is proposed to thought? How, for example, do we assess Blanchot's statement that the fantasmatic phrase he takes from Leclaire, "a child is being killed," cannot be fully heard or even properly spoken by any conscious (or even unconscious) subject?[2] And what do we make of Lacan's statement in reference to something he hears in the phrase, "Father, don't you see I'm burning?," his assertion "that no one can say what the death of a child is—except the father *as* father, that is to say, no conscious being"?[3] Are these statements possible from a philosophical and theoretical point of view? Or do they illegitimately conflate orders of analysis (philosophy of language and psychoanalytic research) via metaphor or fiction, through an infusion of pathos deriving from the normal reaction to the imagined or real death of a child?

The long dialogical meditation that unfolds in the space of these statements will offer no definitive answers. In pursuing a formal account of what I will term "the exigency of the figure" (an account of the structural necessities to which the figure answers), and in attempting to honor the *presence* of that exigency in psychic life (a presence deriving from pathos only inasmuch as the latter marks relation to a more fundamental *pathein*, an immemorial exposure that precedes any subjective affect and is indissociable from the opening to language), I will make a passage between discursive orders (including fiction) that is unjustifiable in strict theoretical terms. I will also refrain from offering anything other than "literary" evidence and even shun some of the substantial empirical findings provided by studies devoted to the traumatic impact of the actual deaths of children. I will rely on textual support no stronger than what psychoanalysts adduce for the notion of a "primal scene" and the psychic relation to what Lacan terms the "real."

I will also try to suggest, however, that there exists another form of evidence for the insistence or exigency of the figure, another kind of "offering" that is indissociable from our relation to language itself, a relation that certain literary and philosophical texts (like the ones read here) take as their "object." For a problematic like the one approached in this volume, I want to argue, we must rethink both the notion of evidence and the idea of an "answering" or corresponding thought of that evidence. We must rethink these notions *from* an experience with language that escapes any conceptual or descriptive grasp (which is why material from the extensive body of clinical studies devoted to the psychic meaning of the death of children will never suffice for the questions raised here).

It will be clear that I cannot provide in this introduction a justification for the shift in method to which I am pointing. But to provide a hint of what I am trying to convey here about my topic and the question of language itself, I would like to turn briefly to a passage from Primo Levi's *Survival in Auschwitz*, a passage that could well be added to the "dossier" treated in the dialogue inasmuch as it evokes an experience of the limits of language and something intimately related to what I have termed the "death of the infans." I will not quell anxieties concerning the legitimacy of my enterprise by citing this text (no quantity of "literary evidence" will suffice in this respect—on the contrary . . .), but I may succeed in communicating part of what I am seeking in pausing over it, and for this reason I will cite at length.

The passage to which I refer comes early in *Survival in Auschwitz*. It recounts a dream that is recognized by Levi's friend and fellow prisoner, "Alberto," as one of his own, and as "the dream of many others, perhaps everyone." It is a dream concerning the impossibility of sharing the very experience of the camp that Levi is in the process of narrating:

> This is my sister here, with some unidentifiable friend and many other people. They are all listening to me and it is this very story that I am telling: the whistle of three notes, the hard bed, my neighbour whom I would like to move. . . . It is an intense pleasure, physical, inexpressible, to be at home, among friendly people and to have so many things to recount: but I cannot help noticing that my listeners do not follow me. In fact, they are completely indifferent: they speak confusedly of other things among themselves, as if I was not there. My sister looks at me, gets up and goes away without a word.
>
> A desolating grief is born in me, like certain barely remembered pains of one's early infancy. It is pain in its pure state, not tempered by a sense of reality and by the intrusion of extraneous circumstances, a pain like that which makes children cry; and it is better for me to swim once again up to the surface, but this time I deliberately open my eyes to have a guarantee in front of me of being effectively awake.
>
> My dream stands in front of me, still warm, and although awake I am still full of its anguish: and then I remember that it is not a haphazard dream, but that I have dreamed it not once but many times since I arrived here, with hardly any variations of environment or details. I am now quite awake and I remember that I have recounted it to Alberto and that he confided to me, to my amazement, that it is also his dream and the dream of many others, perhaps of everyone. Why does it

happen? Why is the pain of every day translated so constantly into our dreams, in the ever-repeated scene of the unlistened-to story?[4]

For the reader who is already familiar with the text by Lacan I will discuss in the course of the dialogue of the second section, the echoes will be strong.[5] But the essential tie concerns Levi's reference to a "barely remembered" affect associated with an experience of the limits of language. If we compare what Levi implies here with other accounts of the need and impossibility of testifying to an experience of affliction or destitution as extreme as Levi's, then we cannot but ask whether Levi is offering something fundamental about the human relation to language and an experience (before experience: "not tempered by a sense of reality") of infancy.[6] And we have further evidence that the latter experience must be thought in relation to the question of the other human being, or *autrui*, to use this term in the manner of Blanchot and Emmanuel Levinas. Blanchot raises this question powerfully in his meditation on the death of the infans in reference to a notion of responsibility. The mortal exposure that is the death of the infans must be thought, in his argument, within a structure of saying or address, and can only be thought from a reflection on the possibility of response. Lacan's own reflection on Freud implicitly foregrounds this question of the relation to the other, and points to the necessity of thinking the structure of exposure as an opening of the ethical relation.

Let me conclude this introduction to the problematic of the second section with a note on the second half of its dialogical meditation. The length of this portion of the dialogue derives in part from an effort to develop fully the terms of Lacan's discussion of the dream of the burning child (a "theoretical" text no less challenging in its mode of writing than the fragments I read in Blanchot's *The Writing of the Disaster*).[7] But I want to observe, also, that I use an explication of the text to return to a question that arises at the horizon of my reading of Nietzsche. Here, I should add that one of my aims in undertaking such a careful and lengthy commentary of the scenes offered in these pages was to push past whatever pathos and whatever forms of identification might be provoked by them. I sought to traverse the "screen" constituted by these moving, even terrible representations, in order to approach the reality that lies behind their insistence. My *supposition* was that this reality involves something more than the subject's relation to the "nihilation" it knows in its assumption of its relation to language (the mortal exposure that gives what Hegel proposed to us as "the life that bears death and maintains itself in it," to use Blanchot's words). A thought of the death drive that proceeds from the latter exposure (the very object of Nietzsche's practice of "cruelty") can carry us to the extreme of the tragic knowledge enunciated by the Oedipus who reaches Colonus: the knowledge Lacan finds in the words "*me phunai.*" And there is no question that one of the paths that crosses the plain on which "we" stand now, at the end of the metaphysics of subjectivity and at the time of the "death of God," leads to this knowledge. But it is also possible to envision other relations to the limit of subjectivity, and thus other configurations of the limit. Other paths open if we think exposure as a structure of relation and think the relation to the other from an originary "yes." "Infancy" is also about such a yes, and I hope that the pairing of the texts by Blanchot and Lacan will help to bring forth its structure and its presence.

The dialogue on the infant figure has appended to it—this is part of the fiction, part of the counterplay—a brief essay on the motif of *philia* in Antigone: "Antigone's friendship." The latter analysis takes up a thread from the preceding discussions (and the discussion itself) in that it attempts to draw forth a dimension of the question of relation that is explored under the rubric of relation to the other, or *autrui*. It is my hope that the notion of *philia* explored here will shed further light on the an-archic grounds of the ethico-political relation. The thought of another "pragmatics" (whose *pragma* is the world, or existence itself) has nothing less at stake. But with this theme of friendship, I also have something a bit more humble in mind that is pursued in the subsequent section on the work of Salvatore Puglia. I consider all of the work gathered in this volume to be inseparable from forms of accompaniment (among them, a form of friendship) that are very much threatened by the economics of the contemporary artistic and intellectual marketplace, including that marketplace referred to as the academy. I am sure that I need hardly argue for the point that critical or theoretical production can compete with any other when it comes to "alienation." Puglia has pursued a mode of activity that modestly and soberly counters such alienation, and it has been my pleasure for almost two decades to work in his company (together with a number of others, some of whose names also appear in these pages). In writing a brief essay for an exhibition held at the Onassis Center for Hellenic Studies in New York, I had the opportunity to honor that working friendship, but I also began to approach something of what was at stake in an artistic practice devoted to the grounds of historical consciousness. To complement what I had been able to articulate in that essay, which was devoted principally to a small number of works, I envisioned a dialogue with Puglia that would bring forth a larger trajectory and testify to the social and artistic practice in which it is embedded. Here again, I sensed that a "thetic" formulation, a critical "presentation" of the work, could not suffice—that different modes and a different graphics would be required. I cannot deny the factitious character of the means to which I have had recourse (the dialogue itself, though faithful to the movement of discussion, is a reconstruction of almost eight hours of conversation), but I hope that they will serve more than an aesthetic purpose. A statement regarding Puglia's work, however lengthy, could never do justice to his own restless search for what he calls a "possible" beyond any statement. Thus, by combining a freely moving dialogue, reproductions, and a brief, focused text, I had recourse to a kind of analogue of his own practices of juxtaposition, shadowing, and overlay. From the density and complexity of the space created, I hoped to evoke a resonance that would capture both the movements in his work and something of its importance for my own very interested inquiry into the possibility of "a pragmatics of the real."

The various texts that make up the three sections of this volume should ultimately bear no more relation to one another than do the images that compose some of Francis Bacon's triptychs. If the volume "works" (and the very meaning of this term lies in the path of its inquiry), then there should be no more than the hint of a necessity to their juxtapositions. Reasoned discourse, of course, normally requires a bit more than a hint; and in this respect, my experimentation in this volume may turn out to be unreasonable (just as it could fail by being reducible to its reasons). I hope, however, that I have provided in the course of these discussions the required conceptual apparatus and sufficient speculative foundation for intelligibility. I also hope that the counterplay of this volume traces some of the limits of the discursively legible.

WHAT REMAINS AT A

CRUCIFIXION

Part One

A Preface on Cruelty
Nietzsche's Self-Examination

Nietzsche begins the preface to *Ecce Homo* with the words "Seeing that before long I must confront humanity with the most difficult demand ever made of it, it seems indispensable to me to say *who I am*."[1] He must say who he is, he explains, because he has not been seen or heard, and would not be confused with anyone else. But he will go on to add in *Ecce Homo* that he has not been heard because he constitutes a beginning, an *event* in the history of humanity that marks a complete break with the past—he *could* not have been seen or heard by his contemporaries. And he will suggest that he is not to be confused with anyone else because his identity is absolutely singular, incomparable; he is absolutely different. This alterity is what Nietzsche proposes to present in *Ecce Homo*. Indeed, his task demands this paradoxical self-presentation because he embodies, in himself, the passage beyond nihilism to which he calls humanity. He is the self-examination he will demand of humanity, and his demand will be inseparable from this self-presentation.

11

What Remains at a Crucifixion

> And let me confess it: I feel instinctively sure and certain that Lord Bacon was the originator, the self-tormenter of this uncanniest kind of literature: what is the pitiable chatter of American flat- and muddle-heads to *me*? But the strength required for the vision of the most powerful reality is not only compatible with the most powerful strength for action, for monstrous action, for crime—it even presupposes it.
>
> We are very far from knowing enough about Lord Bacon, the first realist in every great sense of that word, to know everything he did, wanted, and experienced in himself.
>
> —Nietzsche, *Ecce Homo*

Michel Leiris reports that Francis Bacon would appeal to Nietzsche in conversation, a fact for which he accounts by pointing to a will to power in Bacon's painting.

"*Revaluation of all values*: that is my formula for an act of supreme self-examination on the part of humanity, become flesh and genius in me" (EH, p. 326). After him, he goes on,

> The concept of politics will have merged entirely with a war of spirits; all power structures of the old society will have been exploded—all of them are based on lies: there will be wars the like of which have never yet been seen on earth. It is only beginning with me that the earth knows *great politics*. (EH, p. 327)

It would be easy to pass over hyperbolical declarations like this, were it not for the fact that someone like Heidegger took them seriously, and to the point that he even attempted to engage the "great politics" of which Nietzsche spoke by taking over the task of provoking a general act of self-examination on the part of the German people. Heidegger, of course, spent quite a bit more than a decade trying to come to grips with this deluded gesture, and initially tried to have done with the issue (though he never had done with it) by telling us who Nietzsche's "sovereign subject," the subject of great politics, might be. His answer was: the subject of modern metaphysics. But this answer ef-

The supposition is a bit surprising at first, but it is certainly not inadmissible if we pause to consider what the term "will to power" might encompass in this context—that is, if we recognize in it a fundamental affectability and open it in such a way as to allow the extremes of "self-animal-torment" to co-exist with a creative or inventive drive. Bacon clearly understood such an uncanny turn of the will (and a finitude of the will) to be the condition of his own form of realism, the groundless source of his own active attempt to "translate man back into nature" via art, via a will to power as art. To be sure, there are other compelling reasons for Bacon's interest in Nietzsche: Bacon's profound grasp of everything Nietzsche named with the term "nihilism" (for which phrases such as "we now know that life is a game" can only convey a hint of the historical and philosophical understanding involved), or his abiding attention to what might be at stake in a return to the "birth of tragedy."

fectively disavowed the results of his earlier meditation on eternal recurrence and the will to power ("as art"), on the Dionysian and Nietzsche's contribution to an understanding of the tragic essence of the human Dasein. Everything Heidegger said in the early and mid-1930s about Nietzsche's understanding of the tragic would indicate that he found in Nietzsche's text a meditation on human finitude and not, or not simply, a bringing to completion of the metaphysics of the subject.

In returning to the question of "who" the Nietzschean subject might be (or become) via the motif of cruelty, I will rejoin the substance of Heidegger's first answers concerning the finitude of the will, but will not be seeking a return to the possibility of "great politics" (or certainly not as Heidegger understood the phrase). I may well be touching on the possibility of a politics, if by that last term we intend a practice that proceeds from and answers to an experience of the ethico-political, an engagement with that an-archic ground of the social where the question of political and ethical meaning *opens* in all its historicity and materiality (and if this is in fact part of what Nietzsche meant by "great politics," then perhaps "great" can be salvaged). Michel

But Leiris is perhaps not far from the essential in referring to a will to power in order to account for Bacon's references to Nietzsche—not far if we take the phrase to name what drove Bacon to proclaim himself a "realist": an acutely exposed sensibility transposed by the cruel humor of an exhilarated *amor fati*, a love for what is given (violently), and an active impulse to render it. Something of the passion and sensibility (the same *Stimmung*), in other words, that prompted Nietzsche to celebrate Shakespeare's "truly diabolical cynicism" (Bacon's phrase) to the point of attributing the plays to Lord Bacon and aspiring to no less of a creation.

One last line from *Ecce Homo* by way of transition—but only to set the stage, not to mark a point of reference (my interest lies in Bacon's "realism," not his possible sources; "will to power" does not name the truth of the movement I want to follow). If Bacon knew Nietzsche's words about the "self-

Foucault was clearly attending to such a ground of possibility with his meditations on the question of askesis in his project on the history of sexuality, and I may in fact be exploring one of the essential traits of Foucault's own personal and philosophical practice, one of his own forms of askesis as the subject of an exemplary ethical and political undertaking.[2] Foucault knew well the cruel turn of the will that Nietzsche considered the condition of any "sovereign" exercise in politics or in any other domain, indeed of any invention of the self, of any creative overcoming and self-fashioning. But cruelty, as a dimension of self-reflection (and its disruption), defines no more than a way of access—among others—to that non-ground I have termed the ethicopolitical, and the latter is also the ground of *impossibility* for any rational foundation of the political order (which is not to affirm the "irrational" in politics, but to recognize that any politics, like any political order, however rational or just, is without a final ground). It would therefore be inappropriate to project a determinate politics on the ground of this structure of reflection, or to seek one that might be adequate to the experience to which it opens. It was not through discretion that Foucault made only

animal-torment" of his supposed forebear, then he undoubtedly knew these last words of Nietzsche's self-presentation: "Have I been understood?—Dionysus versus the Crucified" (EH, p. 335). The echo would have been haunting, for crucifixion is Bacon's privileged figure for "self-animal-torment," his primal scene for self-examination. It also happens to be a privileged figure for the exercise of what Leiris termed a "will to power." Where these figures pivot (where the thematic motif becomes a figure for the artistic practice itself), we take a turn even Nietzsche might not have anticipated: it is via crucifixion that Bacon approaches the Dionysian. In the pages that follow, I will try to take this path to Bacon's "realism."

A CRUEL USAGE

First the theme. The motif of crucifixion punctuates Bacon's work from its beginnings through its final period.[1] Its persistence is especially striking for the sparest political assertions from the basis of his meditations on the practices of the self, ancient and modern; for he was seeking in them an *opening* to new forms of political relation, not defined structures. The present, rather modest treatment of the question of cruelty can hardly pretend to be more than the sketch of a possible form of access to the ethico-political.

But it is perhaps appropriate to point to what such a form of experience does *not* allow for political and ethical reflection (and thereby indicate a large measure of its significance): namely recourse to a notion of self-appropriation in the sense of an auto-formation (*Bildung*) or auto-production, any elaboration or stylization of experience directed to its subsumption in meaning or form (either along the aesthetic lines proposed by Alexander Nehemas, or in the more pragmatic mode defined by Richard Rorty[3]). "Becoming what one is" through an art of existence is not an aesthetic elaboration of the self, not a *poiesis* in the sense of the modern metaphysics of production. Likewise, the entity that would proceed from a "war of spirits" is not an organic artifact. There is creation and art in the practice of the self Nietzsche envisions (not to

the fact that Bacon strips it of any Christian resonance, or brutally subverts that resonance by linking the motif to more archaic mythological themes. And since Bacon denies his figures any allegorical significance beyond a rudimentary allusion to the "ways things are," we are cautioned from taking it as merely a grim or bitter parody, an ironic statement of some kind.[2] We are offered a scene, and the more its meaning is undone, the more it insists. This makes Bacon's only two remarks about its significance for him (there are others about its formal possibilities) all the more poignant.

The first of these comes in Bacon's first interview with David Sylvester. In response to a question about Bacon's motivations in regard to the triptych of 1962, *Three Studies for a Crucifixion*, Bacon responds:

> I've always been very moved by pictures about slaughterhouses and meat, and to
> me they belong very much to the whole thing of the Crucifixion. There've been
> extraordinary photographs which have been done of animals just being taken up

Figure 1 Francis Bacon, *Painting*, 1946. © 1999 Estate of Francis Bacon/Artists Rights Society (ARS), New York. Oil and pastel on linen, 197.8 x 132.1 cm. Museum of Modern Art, New York. Photograph © 1999 The Museum of Modern Art, New York, reproduced with the kind permission of the Museum of Modern Art, New York.

speak of style[4]), but it passes by way of a disruption and disappropriation that can never be subsumed. It is a *usage* of the self that involves an exposure of/to a dimension of existence that is properly "useless," resistant to any *work* of meaning. There is a "truth" to be found in such a (dis)appropriating usage, as Foucault suggests in the very beautiful preface to the second volume of the *History of Sexuality (The Use of Pleasure)*, but this is the truth of a becoming that does not conform to any aesthetic ideology (or its political translations), or lend itself to the telos of an *oeuvre*. As Foucault understood (after Georges Bataille and Antonin Artaud, and with quite a few others), sovereignty is not about self-production and self-possession in a totalizing form. Sovereignty, for Nietzsche, presupposes a measure of cruelty toward the self and is therefore constantly disappropriating.

With these words of introduction, I do not mean to overdramatize the notes on Nietzsche that follow.[5] I want merely to suggest that my topic speaks to something more than prurient interest and that this generally neglected motif has significant import for contemporary reflection on the ethics of the self. But let me turn now to

before they were slaughtered; and the smell of death. We don't know, of course, but it appears by these photographs that they're so aware of what is going to happen to them, they do everything to attempt to escape. I think these pictures were very much based on that kind of thing, which to me is very, very near this whole thing of the Crucifixion. I know for religious people, for Christians, the Crucifixion has a totally different significance. But as a non-believer, it was just an act of man's behaviour, a way of behaviour to another.[3]

These words clearly rejoin other references to the link Bacon establishes between an experience of mortality and a knowledge of the flesh—the flesh in its most raw manifestations. Bacon will go very far with such a physical "translation" back into nature—as when a discussion of the cry leads him to speak of the mouth's beauty and reminds him of color plates of diseases of the mouth to which he has turned for inspiration. (Though this is anything but a

Nietzsche's text and his "sovereign subject," namely "Nietzsche," insofar as he claims he is the subject of an accomplished self-examination, "the proud and well-turned out human being who says Yes, who is sure of the future, who guarantees the future" (these are nearly the last words of *Ecce Homo* [p. 335]). This claim implies that Nietzsche's genealogy (of which *Ecce Homo* is in part the presentation) is that of the sovereign philosopher who has emerged from the cocoon of the ascetic ideal, having carried the logic of asceticism to its extreme limit by carrying the value of truthfulness to the point where truthfulness itself comes into question and a creative decision is required concerning the "Why" of existence in its totality. *Ecce Homo* describes the singular configuration of "great health" and some of the forms of askesis that have allowed Nietzsche to become what he is, but his type is that of the "sovereign individual" described in the beginning of the second essay of *The Genealogy of Morals*. To grasp his full genealogy, I would suggest that we need to follow the emergence of this type as it is described in the latter volume.

The sovereign subject, Nietzsche tells us, is one who has achieved the right to a fu-

mere reduction to the physical, since he will immediately refer to his dream of painting a mouth like Monet would paint a sunset [pp. 48–50]).

So crucifixion is in large measure about the exposure of mortal flesh in its most irreducible, but also vulnerable, presence. Its aesthetic analogue, as Gilles Deleuze would say, is the hanging carcass. The passage I have cited also suggests, however, that there is another exposure of the mortal body that is indissociable from this knowledge of the flesh and perhaps its condition.[4] And here we return again to the cry (powerfully latent in Bacon's remarks about the animal reaction to the smell of death). Deleuze is in fact drawing on these remarks, I believe, when he attempts to define what Bacon seeks to paint in the cry: namely the communication of an extreme of bodily affectability.[5] Deleuze proposes that the *presence* so frequently attributed to Bacon's figures derives from what they communicate (as *figures*, in paint) of a quite bodily beture and the right to affirm itself. It is a subject capable of forgetting, and thus capable of a healthy present unburdened by the past (thus the opposite of the creature of *ressentiment* who cannot free itself of painful memories), but also a being capable of a future in that it wills for itself a future and *guarantees* that future. It is a being who commands a *memory of the will* and whose will commands authority. The sovereign subject is one who has the right to make promises—a self-established right because its word stands as guarantee for itself, imposes itself as law. Its word is not empowered by a law that would pre-exist it in any way. Rather, this word freely affirms itself as the law (it is "autonomous and supra-moral," Nietzsche says [GM, p. 59]). It gives the law as it imposes a measure of value—in this sense it is creative—and it *authorizes* itself. The sovereign word *speaks for itself.* Hence it comes like lightning—Nietzsche's privileged image for the creative word that institutes its own authority.[6]

The history that makes possible this development (that is, the creation of a memory of the will, and with it a notion of responsibility, a conscience) is the long history of asceticism: millennia of conscience-vivisection and self-torture: *Selbsttierquälerei*

ing in the world, which Deleuze describes as the affectability of a "being without organs." The latter notion permits a compelling account in material terms of the rhythmic components of the exposure in question—a rhythmic dimension of experience that exceeds what a phenomenological account will allow. But Deleuze also evokes the relation between the body and what he terms the invisible forces of time, or death: a bodily ecstasis. He effectively rejoins a transcendental reflection (though in the manner of Luce Irigaray's attempt to describe a "transcendental sensible") when he proposes that we understand the cry of Bacon's figures from the locution "*crier à*"—these figures *cry at* what is coming in that moment when they apprehend their mortality. The cry thus captures a kind of pure relation to what comes, drawing out in this way its invisible presence (*débusquer* is the word he uses for what occurs in this futural ecstasis). "It is expressed in the formula 'crying at.' Not crying *before*, nor *from* ("self-animal-tormenting"), as Nietzsche puts it near the end of his second essay (GM, p. 95). It is a history that has its mainspring in cruelty—in the sometimes noble, sometimes "sick" pleasures of cruelty. Cruelty, as we will see, is one of the crucial traits distinguishing the philosopher who undertakes the task of self-examination—in fact, a healthy cruelty turns out to be the condition of any sovereign yes-saying. The philosopher, or what Nietzsche calls the "seeker after knowledge" in *Beyond Good and Evil* (§ 229), says "No" where the basic inclination of the spirit would like to say "Yes." He is thus an "artist and transfigurer of cruelty [*Grausamkeit*]"—a concept Nietzsche develops in § 230 by describing how the will of the seeker after knowledge counters what I might call the appropriative drives of the will to power. The spirit, Nietzsche explains here, naturally wants to be master in its own house and feel that it is master: it simplifies, falsifies, and excludes in its dealings with the external world in order to incorporate the other and to grow. The same goals are served by a willful ignorance and a delighted self-deception. Even the will's dissimulating, creative, and form-giving force, its play with masks and with surfaces serves this appropriative drive. But the spirit's simplifications and dissimulations are *countered*, Nietzsche says, by a "sublime inclina-

[it is not a matter of relating to an object, some*thing* that is terrible], but crying *at* death [*crier à la mort*], in order to suggest the coupling of forces, the sensible force of the cry and the insensible force of what makes cry out."[6] Bacon does not paint in his cries a violent reality that causes the cry; he paints the *relation* to reality of an agonized and sometimes ecstatic body. The cry that Deleuze attempts to describe captures that relation at its purest—though the relation in question is a material one.

We are undoubtedly only "very, very near this whole thing of the Crucifixion" if we grasp the full movement of the passage from which we started—from the reference to meat through the apprehension of death—and conceive of the way Bacon links a relation to flesh in its most brutal presence (and transfigured beauty) with the extreme of relationality that he portrays in the cry. And we can perhaps only grasp this relation in something other than a

tion," a will in the seeker after knowledge "which is a kind of cruelty of the intellectual conscience and taste" (*Beyond Good and Evil*, p. 161). He continues:

> Every courageous thinker will recognize this in himself, assuming only that, as fit, he has hardened and sharpened his eye for himself long enough and that he is used to severe discipline, as well as severe words. He will say: "There is something cruel in the inclination of my spirit"; let the virtuous and kindly try to talk him out of that.

Nietzsche goes on to suggest that it might be in the philosopher's interest to let this cruelty go under the name of "extravagant honesty" (*Beyond Good and Evil*, p. 161); but I suspect that even this term would stand convicted of what Nietzsche terms in the third essay of the *Genealogy* a "tartuffery of words" (GM, p. 138). We psychologists are "still 'too good' for our job," Nietzsche exclaims there. Honesty dictates that honesty be called cruelty.[7]

  The Genealogy of Morals thus explores the original manifestations of the trait that is "spiritualized" in the philosopher—that trait by which the will turns against itself, interprets itself, and creates for itself a temporality and a conscience. Cruelty is in fact the

narrative or logical manner (where the hanging carcass would translate something like the meaning of "crucifixion" via its result) if we grasp it in the unity of an experience, taking this last term in a very large sense. Bacon offers it in this manner in the second statement to which I have referred (which is also where we will find the most significant formal statements). Sylvester asks, "In painting a Crucifixion, do you find you approach the problem in a radically different way from when working on other paintings?" (p. 46). Bacon: "Well, of course you're working then about your own feelings and sensations, really. You might say it's almost nearer to a self-portrait. You are working on all sorts of very private feelings about behaviour and the way life is." Crucifixion, in other words, is Bacon's privileged scene for portraying his own experience of being in the world, his scene of "self-animal-torment." To be is to be exposed at this extreme limit of suffering. From here, from this evocation one thread (though it is hardly a *single* thread) that ties together an extraordinarily complex and perhaps even willfully contradictory piece of speculative history-writing.[8] It serves, first of all, to account for the possibility of that primitive form of exchange by which punishment comes to serve as an equivalent for an unpaid debt. At the beginning of the second essay, Nietzsche explains that promising and memory have their possibility in a long mnemotechnics by which a memory to pay what is due is burned into the subject—first the legal subject and then the political subject, the member of a community. Nietzsche argues that if punishment is allowed as satisfaction for an unpaid debt, it is because the cruel pleasure taken in punishment is seen to be sufficient compensation for material loss.[9] It is an *active* pleasure, Nietzsche argues:

> It seems to me that the delicacy and even more the tartuffery of tame domestic animals (which is to say modern man, which is to say us) resists a really vivid comprehension of the degree to which *cruelty* constituted the great festival pleasure of more primitive man and was indeed an ingredient of almost every one of their pleasures . . . something to which the conscience cordially says Yes. (GM, p. 66)

of experience, Bacon can add, after another connection to the butcher shop and "this great beauty of the color of meat": "Well of course we are meat, we are potential carcasses. If I go into a butcher shop, I always think it's surprising that I wasn't there instead of the animal" (p. 46). Bacon's surprise is what should be retained here—his surprise at the uncanny presence of the hanging carcass.

To be, for Bacon, is to know an exposure like that of a crucifixion—a pain of exposure, we must add, that is inseparable from guilt, for the violence to which the existent being is delivered seems almost always to take a vengeful form (hence the frequent presence of the Erinyes). I would not presume to judge this experience of existence *without justification* by rushing to link this with a Christian notion of original sin; for, once again, Bacon is occupying a limit where the Christian experience resonates with archaic echoes as it

Shortly after these words, he speaks of the manner in which primitive men were "unwilling to refrain from *making* suffer and saw in it an enchantment of the first order, a genuine seduction *to* life" (GM, p. 67). But we might pause to ask here whether a pleasure in watching the other suffer is not tinged with a certain passivity.[10] Moreover, there is little question that such pleasure is fueled by ressentiment (or is caught up in that turn) if it is part of an economy and a direct function of the punisher's social position: "The enjoyment will be the greater the lower the creditor stands in the social order," Nietzsche asserts (GM, p. 65). In the next section he speaks of it again as "a genuine *festival*, something which, as aforesaid, was prized the more highly the more violently it contrasted with the rank and social standing of the creditor" (GM, p. 65). Nietzsche appears to recognize the problem when he adds: "This is offered only as a conjecture; for the depths of such subterranean things are difficult to fathom, besides being painful" (GM, p. 65). Should we presume that if things have gotten a little out of hand here at the outset, it is because Nietzsche is enjoying the pain? But "genealogy," in any case, is not concerned with essences. We should not look to cruelty as a unitary phenomenon over time.

reaches its end in nihilism. I would merely pick up here Bacon's oblique reference to "man's behaviour, a way of behaviour to another" as part of "the way life is" and note that the exposure to which I have referred cannot be thought outside its ethico-political dimension (which does not make the exposure in question any less material, or any less acute—on the contrary). But I would emphasize that crucifixion is hardly one conduct among others for Bacon, for it appears to touch on the very grounds of human relation, on its limits: at the site of an irreducible experience of affliction. That we might identify this as an essentially human, essentially "social" experience of the pain of existence does not belie a reference to "self-animal-torment" or deny that we reach here a zone of "indiscernibility" between the human and the animal, an animal presence of the suffering body. Because at this point we are touching on something like the relation between the human and language,

Let us move from these ambiguities to the second historical account: Nietzsche's description of that historial perversion he names "bad conscience." I speak of a second history because it starts catastrophically, even though it overlaps with the first, since it is part of that history by which humankind is tamed through such devices as punishment. But here the punishment is not part of an economy, at least originally. Rather, it comes suddenly, and with such a fateful character that it precludes all struggle and all ressentiment. This is an important point: in both of the histories from the second essay to which I am referring, ressentiment has no place (or so Nietzsche claims—we have seen how problematic this claim is in the first case). Cruelty, Nietzsche tells us, is originally the expression of an active, joyous will, even when it initially turns upon itself and opens the paths of bad conscience. Of course, this latter turn can only have occurred insofar as there has been a lapse of the will of some kind—the will does not struggle with an external force, it folds, so to speak. But nevertheless, even in turning upon itself it remains active. Nietzsche figures the catastrophe that produces this turn as a conquest. A "conqueror and master race" (GM, p. 86) lays its claws upon a formless or nomad pop-

which is all that distinguishes the human from the animal. Which is to say, also, that we are at the limit of the human and the animal, or what Nietzsche called the Dionysian.

I introduce language now because of the second way in which crucifixion figures in Bacon's remarks, namely as a means of representation and ultimately as a figure for representation or figuration itself. To evoke in the broadest sense what I would like to develop here, I would draw an analogy with Georges Bataille. For just as we can say that writing *is* an act of sacrifice for Bataille,[7] we could say that painting, for Bacon, is crucifixion.

First, for Bacon the cross is a frame, an armature, as he puts it, for "hanging all sorts of feeling and sensation" (p. 44). He evokes in this context a special resonance afforded by the history of the motif: "Perhaps it's only because so many people have worked on this particular theme that it has created this

ulace and imposes upon it a tyrannical "state" machinery that molds and forms that populace. The latter is described as an "artistic" process, a kind of natural poiesis. The blond beasts of prey are "artists of violence and organizers who build states," Nietzsche says, and these states are described as organic social formations where every part has its meaning in relation to a *living* whole (GM, pp. 86–87). The primitive state is a work of art formed by a violent, appropriative will to power.[11]

The *same* will to power is at work in the populace, whose "instinct for freedom" has been repressed. But here, it works internally (this is the origin of human depths, of the "soul"): the inhibited will turns upon itself. Nietzsche's figure for this process is a caged animal that maltreats itself for want of any external discharge, turning itself, Nietzsche says, "into an adventure, a torture chamber, an uncertain and dangerous wilderness" (GM, p. 85). But this self-torture takes on in its turn an artistic character:

> Here the material upon which the form-giving and ravishing nature of this force vents itself is man himself, his whole ancient animal self—and *not*, as in that greater and more obvious phenomenon, some *other* man, *other* men. This secret self-ravishment,

armature . . . on which one can operate all types of level of feeling" (p. 44). But as a formal device it works most essentially to raise, isolate, and suspend the figure, offering the flesh in the manner Bacon so admires, for example, in the painting by Degas entitled *After the Bath* (p. 46). Of course, one of the predominant traits of Bacon's work is the use of such an armature; the cross is just one example to be linked to all the chairs, cages, and rails that prefer the figure in the way I have noted. But the crucifixion motif also lends itself in a striking way to Bacon's conception of the act of figuration itself.

This dimension of the motif appears furtively in a passage in the *Interviews* that follows a powerful evocation by Bacon of the link between sexuality and death. Sylvester remarks that Bacon tends to dwell on the behavior of friends in extreme situations and adds, "It seems to me that that preoccupation of yours is very relevant to your work, overtly or implicitly. Overtly when you

Figure 2 Francis Bacon, *Figure in Movement*, 1976. Oil on canvas, 198 x 147.5 cm. © 1999 Estate of Francis Bacon / Artists Rights Society (ARS), New York. Photograph reproduced with the kind permission of the Photo Galerie Claude Bernard.

this artist's cruelty, this delight in imposing a form upon oneself as a hard, recalcitrant suffering material and in burning a will, a critique, a contradiction, a contempt, a No into it, this uncanny, dreadfully joyous labor of a soul voluntarily at odds with itself that makes itself suffer out of joy in making suffer—eventually, this entire active "bad conscience"—you will have guessed it—as the womb of all ideal and imaginative phenomena, also brought to light an abundance of strange new beauty and affirmation, and perhaps beauty itself.—After all, what would be "beautiful" if the contradiction had not first become conscious of itself, if the ugly had not first said to itself, "I am ugly"? (GM, pp. 87–88)

Two points should be underscored here. First, a *self-interpretation* is identified as the origin of the will (both moral and "supramoral") that is capable of the promise.[12] It begins with the howl of the frustrated animal and then takes shape in a process of self-contradiction that is finally directed and interpreted by the ascetic priest. The caged beast suffers from its own strength, its own affects, and turns this strength upon itself as the cause of its suffering ("Thus began the gravest and uncanniest illness, from which humanity has not yet recovered, man's suffering *of man, of himself*—the result

paint the scream . . . and the Crucifixion, and people violently coupling on beds, and single figures in convulsive attitudes, and nudes injecting drugs into their arms" (p. 78). Bacon, as though to interrupt any suggestion that his interest lies in the portrayal of extreme situations and an evocation of the pathos associated with them, reacts abruptly in formal terms. He responds:

> I've used the figures with a hypodermic syringe on beds as a form of nailing the image more strongly into reality or appearance. I don't put the syringe because of the drug that's being injected, but because it's less stupid than putting a nail through the arm, which would be even more melodramatic. I put the syringe because I want a nailing of the flesh onto the bed. But that, perhaps, is something I shall pass out of entirely. (p. 78)

The syringes may have been a passing fancy (though they lasted at least a decade, to my knowledge), but the nailing certainly was not; and the link

Figure 3   Francis Bacon, *Two Studies for a Portrait of George Dyer*, 1968. © 1999
Estate of Francis Bacon/Artists Rights Society (ARS), New York. Oil on canvas,
198.1 x 147.3 cm. Sara Hildén Museum, Tampere, Finland. Photograph reproduced
with the kind permission of the Sara Hildén Foundation.

of a forcible sundering from his animal past" [GM, p. 85]). The ascetic priest merely interposes a concept of sin and gives a figure to the desired transcendence of that suffering. Secondly, and I am again reiterating a point I have made, this self-contradiction does not originally take the form of ressentiment. In ressentiment, a will suffers passively what it cannot fight off or digest. It suffers from its inability to rid itself of what affects it, and proceeds to negate that which it considers the cause of its affliction. It *suffers* the other and proceeds to define itself in relation to that other, positing the other as evil, and itself as good.[13] Bad conscience takes, originally, the opposite form. It does not negate the other in order to posit itself (mediately). It negates *itself* and posits an other. "I am ugly, therefore there must be a beautiful." Ressentiment will eventually develop out of this uncanny process. And it may simply be the product of a will that does not have the strength for this process—a kind of supplementary development of the will's turn against itself and its self-interpretation. Bad conscience and ressentiment have the same origin: there is an inhibition and lapse of the will. At a certain moment, the will is not able to affirm itself against the other; but the caged beast

made here between these motifs was clearly not a casual one, because we find an explicit evocation of the intention Bacon describes in a canvas of 1968, *Two Studies for a Portrait of George Dyer*, where one of the two images of Dyer—the one of Dyer in the flesh, we might say—is nailed to a surface over against a seated Dyer, with the gaze of both figures powerfully drawn to the right side of the canvas.

So what is the function of, or what occurs with, this "*fixion*" of the image? He used the hypodermic syringe, he said, for purposes of "nailing *the image more strongly into reality or appearance.*" Reality or appearance. We could spend pages with this conjunction and its onto-phenomenological implications. It names, first of all, what Bacon claims frequently to be reporting: a presence whose force seems almost to require on occasion that he render it after the fact (*après-coup*), but that gives itself *as fact*—at however many returns upon itself—and this is the origin of the ascetic priest who actively interprets—whereas the man of ressentiment turns against the other, economizes on his pain by biding his time and cultivating his revenge.

The ascetic priest, as Nietzsche describes him in the second and third essays, is one who controls and channels ressentiment. In fact, the priest is said in §11 of the third essay to embody ressentiment himself to an unparalleled degree, and in the succeeding section of the same essay, the sickness treated by this sick doctor turns out to be ressentiment. Nevertheless, the perverse interpretive craftiness of the ascetic priest has its origin in an *active* bad conscience—the will's cruelty toward itself. And the priest's active will to power is said to be the condition of man's self-overcoming. "The ascetic priest," Nietzsche writes, "is the incarnate desire to be different, to be in a different place and indeed this desire at its greatest extreme, its distinctive fervor and passion" (GM, p. 120). The ascetic priest works out of bad conscience—he *works* ressentiment. But ressentiment is a will that has lapsed and become reactive. The ascetic priest has an active will and is pregnant with a future.

moves of meaning and representation—in what Bacon most frequently terms an image,[8] an image whose facticity or "objective value" frequently derives from a poignant juxtaposition of tensions like those Bataille attributes to the "tragicomic oppositions" defining the "real presence" of a flower.[9] The portraits hold the status of an exception here by reason of the insistence of their referent (particularly where we are dealing with the presence of the gaze[10]). But where a *scene* is constituted in such a way as to define what Deleuze terms a "matter of fact," the referent of this portrayal cedes to a "reality" or appearance that is proper to the painted figure.[11] And this is undoubtedly the principal direction of Bacon's words when he speaks of nailing the image into reality or appearance. He nails it down (the implication being that it will "drift off" otherwise—namely, into illustration), and thereby nails it *into* reality or appearance—transitively, we might say. He nails it down to bring it forth in

The wicked philosopher, in turn, is nothing but the priest's own self-overcoming. He is a healthy priest (therefore something other than a priest). While the priest tends the sick (and is therefore sick himself), the philosopher, out of his fundamentally healthy nature, takes his distance from the herd. He knows what's good for him. And unlike the priest, he does not want to become different: he embraces his fate, as Nietzsche says in *Ecce Homo*. I will return to this claim shortly, but I want to complete my overview of the theme of cruelty in *The Genealogy of Morals* by noting simply that the philosopher's health manifests itself initially in a heightened form of cruelty. The philosopher overcomes asceticism by pushing it—cruelly—to its limits. Nietzsche explains that this animal begins in asceticism and under the garb of the priest, not only in order to acquire the power and respectability of the priest, but because he must turn against his own natural impulses. The philosopher began "with an evil heart and often an anxious head" (GM, p. 115) and had to fight against his own initially healthy instincts. "As men of frightful ages," Nietzsche writes, "they did this by using frightful means: cruelty toward themselves, inventive self-castigation. . . . " They entered the

such a way as to produce the "that" of Being—the "that" of "that there are beings rather than nothing." The nail itself (or the syringe) figures this act of figuration, this in(x)scription by which the figure is brought into emergence and "reality" is ex-scribed (to use Nancy's term[12]) in such a way as to produce the "that" (*Dass*) that a work of art *says* in its createdness, according to Heidegger. All of Bacon's figures, as Deleuze recognizes, have a certain presence, more or less of the presence that conveys the "that" of existence. But the nail also remarks the cruci-fixion or ex-scription by which existence is given in Bacon's paintings.

Bacon employs other forms of "nailing" than the ones we have seen. Figures are worked by surfaces (flattened, for example, as against the photographic plate of an x-ray machine), refracted or even divided by walls, mirrors, and canvases, thereby fixed in representation in a manner that is perhaps

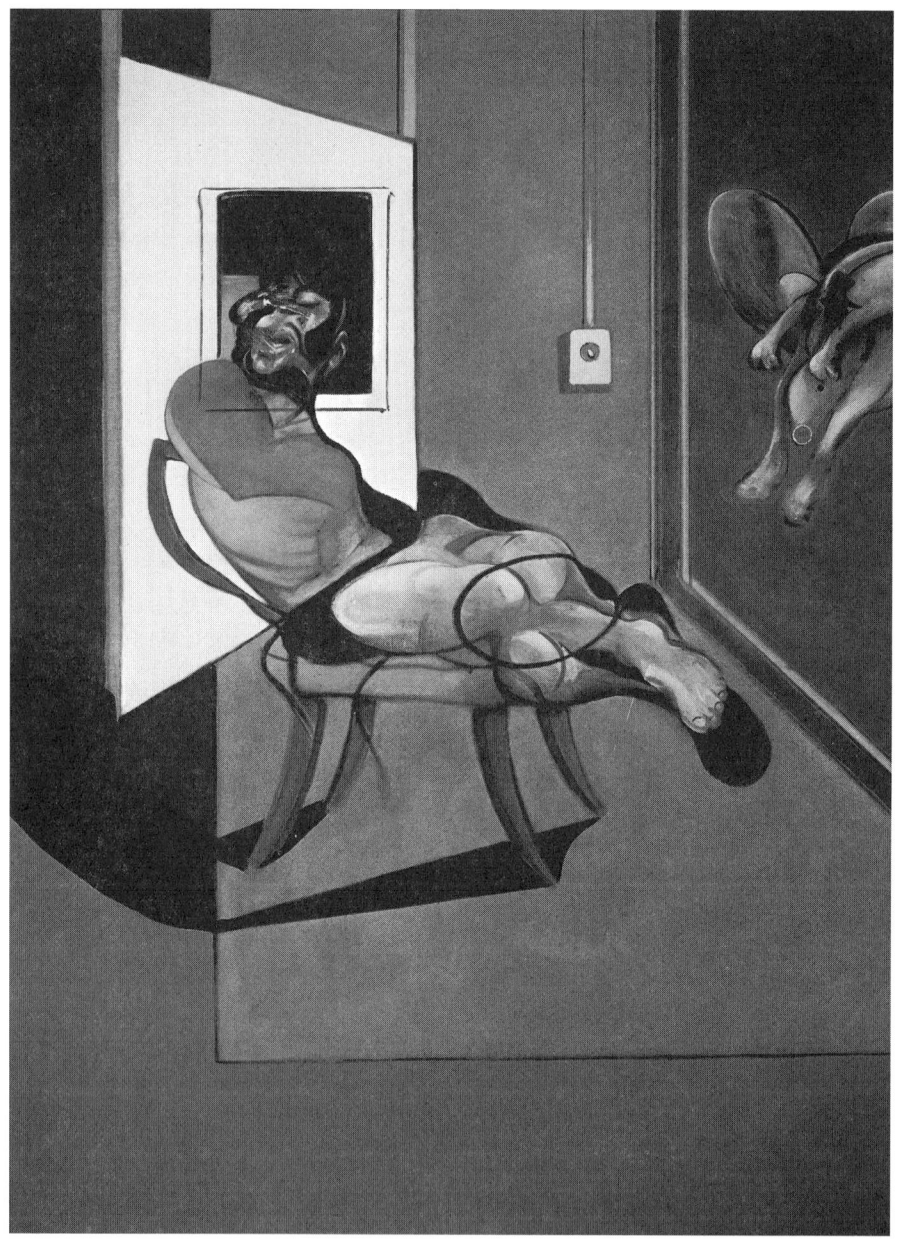

Figure 4 Francis Bacon, *Seated Figure*, 1974. © 1999 Estate of Francis Bacon /
Artists Rights Society (ARS), New York. Oil on canvas, 198 x 147.5 cm. Private
collection. Photograph reproduced with the kind permission of the trustees
of the collection.

cocoon of the priest, cultivating everything that makes of the priests "interesting ani-mals"—their depth and evil ("The two basic respects in which man has hitherto been superior to other beasts" [GM, p. 33]). But then, out of "sublime wickedness, an ulti-mate, supremely self-confident mischievousness in knowledge that goes with great health" (GM, p. 96), they take their flight. They turn away from the ideal, and by a su-perbly perverse gesture, wed bad conscience to any ideal aspirations. In their extrava-gant honesty, they attempt to translate man *back into nature*, as Nietzsche puts it at the end of the long passage from *Beyond Good and Evil* with which I started. This turn, this translation, is not the turn of science. *The Genealogy of Morals* ends with an unmask-ing of the scientific ideal as the final avatar of the ascetic ideal. The scholar and the sci-entific laborer, even when they appear as "hard, severe, abstinent, heroic spirits" (GM, p. 148), heroes of intellectual cleanliness, remain nevertheless captivated by a faith in the absolute value of truth and in the grips of a contempt for humankind. They refuse interpretation inasmuch as "forcing," "adjusting," "falsifying" are "of the *essence* of in-terpreting" (GM, p. 151—as in the case of this willful piece of history-writing), and

consonant with the nailing we have seen. (Twisting is another way of intensi-fying the image, forcing it into reality or appearance. All of these motifs, in cluding an evocation of the Erinyes, appear in *Seated Figure*, 1974). "Nailing down," or fixing and piercing in representation, is a constant preoccupation with Bacon. And I would be tempted to draw a link here with the figures of sexual coupling. But before pursuing other dimensions of this brutal usage, this rough trade with the image, I want to pause a bit more over the jump I have made from the reality (or appearance) of the referent to the reality of the figure.

The jump is Bacon's, and it is made in a veritable assault on his own talent for illustration. If there is a "will to power" in Bacon's treatment of the image, it passes by way of a willful disruption in which Bacon suspends his attempt to capture the reality of his subject (or the "image" he has in mind) and gives his

inasmuch as interpretation is always an act of the will to power, always a function of drives and affects. They still suffer from their own affects, we might say, and seek an escape of some kind. Or they lack the conviction of their affects, the will of their affects (the will to will); they do not create values and cannot bring into question the value of "truth." The presupposition of this movement, again, is great health, and the courage that goes with it: a resurgence of affect and the courage of a sublime wickedness by which the will *turns against itself* in such a way as to open the possibility of a creative deed. *Ecce Homo* describes that movement and its conditions.

The passages in *Ecce Homo* in which Nietzsche describes his "health" and his practices for its cultivation are among the most delightful in his work (I refer principally to "Why I Am So Wise" and "Why I Am So Clever"). To be sure, he knows sickness, as he tells us, and in this he has the experience of decadence. This is the gift from his father. But this gift is also accompanied by an enlightenment about ressentiment. Because he has "one foot beyond life," he is not predisposed against others or against himself; he does not allow injury to fester but responds with either sweets, thanks, or

efforts over to chance. It is not simply that he welcomes accident with the brush or a toss of paint. Rather, the *need* to render the reality in question ("the fact you are obsessed by") at the level at which it strikes the "nervous system" prompts a desperate passage through what Deleuze aptly names after Maldiney a "catastrophe."[13] In fact, this disruption is anything but willful (though Bacon seems to have learned to modulate it), as we see from Bacon's regular use of words like "exasperation," "hopelessness," "frustration," "despair," "impossibility," and "abandon" to describe what drives him to this passage. He must *destroy* illustration to release the image latent in sensation or offered to "instinct" in this moment of passage by what may be not quite the limit-experience portrayed in the crucifixion, but certainly an exposure to a presubjective dimension (a rhythm perhaps?—in any case, a kind of spatio-temporal opening wherein an entirely different measure opens and a visage can offer it-a rude response. And when his vital energies are at their lowest ebb (this is the very definition of sickness in Nietzsche's case), he instinctively practices what he calls Russian fatalism: he avoids all the stimulation of reactive affects that the ascetic priest uses to manipulate the herd. When weak, he accepts himself as fated; at such moments he knows a kind of quiet *amor fati.* And because he has one foot beyond life, he tells us, he never postures, is never tempted by the poses that accompany pragmatic interests. Never having striven for "honors, women, or money" (!), never having prematurely interpreted what he calls his task with a pragmatic goal of any kind, Nietzsche is free of all false posturing—all of the postures of the ideal which he describes as "pathological" (EH, p. 257). This is why he says, "Life was easy for me." He has never wanted anything to be different. And out of this profound self-love and "disinterest" (with one foot beyond the pragmatic concerns of life, accepting his fate), he has allowed his multiple, normally irreconcilable, capacities to grow and join in a unity that is not the product of an organic synthesis, but nonetheless such that these singular traits of the will mutually condition one another.[14] No-saying and yes-

self like a landscape or a mouth like a sunset). Nietzsche, as we have seen, would suggest that only one who has known the extremes of self-animal-torment can practice such an interruption by which the image is as much created as discovered—invented, let us say. As for Bacon, if we can say that he is practicing a cruel usage of the image, it is only via a cruel usage of his own will—a usage, in fact, that one can barely call "his," and by which any ownership of the image is suspended.

A number of motifs lead me to draw on this Heideggerian notion of "usage" to address Bacon's practice as a painter, starting with the interruption of the will we have considered—the exposure to which Bacon delivers himself in disrupting his considerable illustrational talent. Bacon lends himself to the birth of the image in such a way as to enable precisely the kind of "free use of the proper" Heidegger describes in his essays on language when he speaks of

saying, for example (perhaps this is the preeminent example), are indissociable. And great health names not only the possiblity of this coexistence, but the condition of the passage between them, their articulation—or better, the opening of one to the other.

Nietzsche tells us near the end of *Ecce Homo* that he chose Zarathustra precisely as a figure of the self-overcoming of morality: "The self-overcoming of morality, out of truthfulness, the self-overcoming of the moralist, into his opposite—into me—this is what the name of Zarathustra means in my mouth" (EH, p. 328). In the immediately succeeding section, he writes, "Negating and destroying are the conditions of saying yes" (EH, p. 328). Once again, the dialectic of morality, pushed to its extreme in a joyous and extravagant cruelty, is the condition of Zarathustra's affirmation. But it should also be emphasized that the "no" is not simply an uncompromising critique of ascetic ideals (a destruction of "idols") and a form of self-discipline (as Nietzsche's words might suggest when he defines the task of translating man back into nature in *Beyond Good and Evil*). It involves an extravagant cruelty that allows an opening onto what Nietzsche terms the abyss or the terrible, also the forbidden—an exorbitant form of

a "use" of the human in what is proper to it *bodily* for the advent of language—a use that is not attributable to any subject or to language, but that belongs to an event (*Ereignis*) from which language and any subject proceed, and which defines the (non)ground for all human usage or "handling"— that is to say, *all praxis and poiesis.* That Heidegger ascribes an erotic dimension to this ground of relationality and recognizes a form of violence in it (the step Bataille makes in linking usage and *jouissance* is anything but abusive[14]) only makes it seem more pertinent for describing the "handling" to which Bacon submits the image once it appears in the process of creation. This handling itself seems to recover the unity of praxis and its object that Heidegger grasps in Pindar's use of the term *pragma* (a unity of an aletheic comportment of unconcealing—*prattein*—and that which is unconcealed). Indeed, *pragma* may be the perfect term for defining the "matter of fact" con-

critique that is something quite other than a "scientific" knowledge of *homo natura* (cf. *Beyond Good and Evil*, p. 161).

Nietzsche points to this dimension of cruelty and its intimate relation to creation in the fourth section of the chapter in which he explains why he is so clever. While discussing Heine's "divine malice," he remarks: "I estimate the value of men, of races, according to the necessity by which they cannot conceive the god apart from the satyr" (EH, p. 245). He then goes on to compare himself to Byron and to Shakespeare, of whom he says, "The great poet dips *only* from his own reality—up to the point where afterward he cannot endure his work any longer" (EH, p. 246). Nietzsche cites here his experience with *Zarathustra*, and then returns to Shakespeare:

> I know no more heart-rending reading than Shakespeare: What must such a man have suffered to have such a need of being a buffoon? Is Hamlet understood? No doubt, *certainty* is what drives one insane.—But one must be profound, an abyss, a philosopher to feel that way.—We are all afraid of truth. And let me confess it: I feel instinctively sure and certain that Lord Bacon was the originator, the self-tormentor [*Selbsttierquäler*] of this uncanniest kind of literature. (EH, p. 226)

veyed in Bacon's paintings. Most importantly, this "handling," governed, as Heidegger emphasizes, by the essence of the hand, is directed to the essence of what is addressed—it *answers*, and in such a way that its hold is not a utilizing but a delivering. It is from this basis, I believe, that we should understand the "injury" Bacon does to his subjects. The notion of injury seems to cause Bacon some discomfort (p. 41), but only because there is a profound fidelity behind this usage, not to speak of love.[15] If we do not grasp this ground of Bacon's "cruelty" and his devotion to the object, we will not grasp his realism.

Deleuze emphasizes a kind of *technical* moment in the genesis and development of the image that emerges from the violent interruption we have considered, and this too may be an important component of Bacon's usage (as of the notion of usage itself, which must be linked to a notion of custom, but

Selbsttierquälerei: we are back to the very origin of moral humanity. But this particular cruelty toward animals (indulged in by the great poet or great philosopher— any great realist) does not lend itself to an ascetic turn. If the will is "interpreting" in this "uncanniest kind of literature," this "theater of cruelty"[15] by which it maliciously turns its suffering back upon itself, it does so not in order to burn a form into itself, but rather in order to translate itself (in an almost transitive sense) back *into* nature and to know further the pain of existence. It does not open itself to a charge of guilt, it exposes itself to the terrible and the questionable (EH, p. 331)—what Nietzsche called in *The Birth of Tragedy* the "Dionysian." This is what Nietzsche means when he speaks of striving for the forbidden (*nitimur in vetitum*). Such striving, Nietzsche says, requires courage and strength (cf. pp. 218, 272, 290): the measure of a spirit's value, Nietzsche reiterates, is how much of the abyss (what he sometimes calls "truth") it can dare and endure—how far it can go in opening to what is strange and questionable in existence, how far it is capable of a Dionysian affirmation.

This does not mean simply recovering the "natural" strengths of the ugly primitive

also to a thought of instrumentality or operativity). If the latter interruption is translated by a free movement of the hand, the constitution of the image itself proceeds from Bacon's elaboration of the *operative* character of traits left by this involuntary manual movement, traits that belong to a kind of schema or graph.[16] As Deleuze argues in a powerful passage on aesthetic analogy that develops his sense of the link between Bacon and Cézanne, the work of painting lies in the fluid interplay of hand and eye that elaborates the "factual possibilities" suggested by the "operative ensemble" of line and color. The argument is compelling for Bacon and for an understanding of the haptic character of the painted figure in general. It accounts beautifully for the strange poise and power of Bacon's figures, particularly in the sculptural compositions, and it opens an invaluable access to Bacon's lyricism. But Deleuze may be too rapid in suggesting that this understanding of the "pictural fact"

affects (lust for power, sexual drives, joy in cruelty, etc.) for the purpose of sublimating them and using them in a more powerful, higher deed of the creative will than what Christianity has allowed hitherto. Nietzsche does in fact have frequent recourse to a model of sublimation or spiritualization, and the majority of Nietzsche's readers have felt comfortable with Nietzsche's cruelty (when they recognized it) because they have understood it as leading to a kind of *Aufhebung*: one taps the evil in oneself in order to become stronger, if only spiritually. But Nietzsche goes farther. This is precisely why he speaks of the terrible, the sublime, the questionable, the strange, and the forbidden. What the cruel will of the philosopher does in translating the will back into nature is to force the will to undergo a meaningless suffering. This is what makes the philosopher's will so uncanny, so wicked. The will not only punishes itself, it pushes itself into a void where willing becomes impossible—and that, according to Nietzsche, is the cruelest suffering of all (if not simply intolerable). As he says at the beginning and end of the third essay of *The Genealogy of Morals* (the lesson was obviously important): the will would rather will nothingness than not will. This latter tendency is what made

should carry us beyond the reality evoked so insistently by Michel Leiris, for between the fact for which Bacon "grasps" in Leiris's account and its virtual sublation in the figure constituted by the "haptic" vision described by Deleuze, there is something that Bacon persists in seeking to *capture* in his subjects—what he calls a residue of reality, or an "essence." I believe we need to hold to this residue if we are to appreciate Bacon's "realism," and for this purpose I will attend by way of conclusion to Bacon's *operation* on this image and consider a last avatar of the formal meaning of crucifixion.

I speak of "operation" on the basis of Bacon's explanation of the way he uses cages or frames to isolate the image and fix it: "I use that frame to see the image—for no other reason. . . . I cut down the scale of the canvas by drawing these rectangles which concentrate the image down. Just to see it better" (pp. 22–23). And if I am struck by the insistence of this motif of trapping, it

possible the ascetic ideal; this is what ultimately allowed the suffering animal to lend itself to the interpretations of the ascetic priest and to turn its earthly life into a hell in the name of a desired transcendence. To reverse the direction of bad conscience as it has unfolded thus far—to punish the will by destroying all ideal goals, all mystifications, to turn the will upon its own interpretations (in general), is to push itself back into a meaningless suffering and to make it experience again its "basic fact," its foundation—a *horror vacui* (GM, p. 97). The cruelty of the philosopher consists in pushing the will back to its originary exposure, to a becoming that offers no meaning, no telos. The reference to Hamlet in *Ecce Homo* is telling in this regard if we think back to his appearance in *The Birth of Tragedy*. Indeed, Hamlet's problem is not doubting, it is certainty: he knows the abyss. The philosopher's (or poet's) divinely cruel turn of the will involves forcing the will to confront the impossibility of willing something beyond a meaningless becoming, in making it suffer the pain of unjustified existence. We could speak here, perhaps, of an ecstatic "being towards death" inasmuch as the confrontation in question is a confrontation with mortality. But we would have to add that this

may well be in recollection of that "cage" that holds the self-lacerating animal that Nietzsche describes in *The Genealogy of Morals*, that figure of animality at the threshold of "moral" humanity. But trapping, as Bacon uses the figure, is generally not about "self-animal-torment"; it defines the entire process of capturing a "living" reality by "artificial" means.

Let me cite just two passages regarding this capture—two passages that will convey something of *what* is captured. Referring to the difference between film or photography and painting as regards the capture of "fact," Bacon remarks:

> What can you do [as a painter] but go to a very much more extreme thing where you are reporting fact not as simple fact but on many levels. Where you unlock the areas of feeling which lead to a deeper sense of the reality of the images, where you attempt to make the construction by which the thing will be caught raw and

is also a being-between-two-deaths, an experience of the real that exceeds any tragic subsumption.

But how could the will drive itself into the impossibility of willing in this cruel devotion to its "truth" (its "basic fact")? And how could such an experience be the condition of a creative affirmation, of a Yes-saying? How would the experience of the *nihil*, or even more radically perhaps, the Dionysian inseparability of life and death (the void is still somehow more comforting, in a philosophical perspective, than the Dionysian), *release* the will to an affirmative act? How does the event of such ex-posure *free* the will? Must not great health (which is Nietzsche's only answer in the pages we are reading—his only way of accounting for the passage into the No and into the Yes), harbor a "Yes," a Yes to the will's finitude, even to that extreme of exposure that is its "basic fact"? The will must know (have known) its "truth" to turn upon itself as it does—only a knowledge of finitude could make this turn possible. But at the same time, it can only know its limit experience in affirmation, only as it affirms its existence as an opening, a reiterated opening to what exceeds its hold. The No is indissociable from a Yes. But

alive [obviously, we are not far from crucifixion] and left there, and, you might say, fossilized—there it is. (p. 66)

"There it is"—Bacon may be punctuating, but he also seems to be saying something about what happens when he captures the thing "raw and alive . . . fossilized." He is talking about the surprise of appearance, the "magic" or "alchemy" of the act of rendering, but also about the *character* of the presence involved, a presence Bacon attributes to the special texture of paint in its address to sensation. "Fossilized" expresses what he elsewhere terms "endurance" (p. 58), a quality he links to a certain materiality, a sedimented character that belongs to the painted trait (all the more inevitable and enduring the more arbitrary and non-illustrational it is). There it is—he means by this "life," "reality or appearance" as brought forth in the medium of his "operation": the medium of a usage that does not sublate its material base in a process of sig-

the Yes does not subsume the No, precisely because the affirmation of eternal recurrence is also an affirmation of the finitude of the will. Yes and No are joined as the two poles of a passage that is at once the opening to an alterity and the creative affirmation that proceeds from it, the latter leading back into this alterity even as it overcomes it. The will of "great health" is *cruel and creative*, and in its creation it is cruel. It is of its nature to carry itself into an encounter with alterity, to open to the other, and to draw out this otherness in a creative act: to draw it out in such a way that the creative act is an ongoing exposure to that otherness. And because the will is cruel even in its creation (Nietzsche repeatedly characterizes Zarathustra in these terms), the will's creative transfiguration cannot be thought as a subsumption of that to which the will opens. The terrible, the forbidden, the uncanny, is not overcome. It becomes more terrible; this is why the Dionysian affirmation is tragic and why its affirmation is ecstatic.[16]

I started by suggesting that Nietzsche posits himself in *Ecce Homo* as the sovereign subject he describes in *The Genealogy of Morals*. He claims to embody the type of the philosopher who is the master of a free will, who has the right to make promises and

nification, but rather brings it forth in its physical character, *arresting* mediation for the sake of another mediality, another communication. The "that" of Being, as Heidegger demonstrated in his meditation on art and poetry, is conveyed by the fact of language itself (taking language in a very broad sense). Deleuze has perhaps captured the essential character of Bacon's language with his notion of aesthetic analogy, but I would add that part of the force of Bacon's painting, of his "pictural fact," lies in his presentation of the fact of this language.

A second citation will underscore that what is communicated here is not simply "language," as my last words could suggest. In the course of a discussion of realism in the eighth interview with Sylvester, Bacon's focus turns to the arbitrary or artificial means of the trap, and Sylvester alludes to the structure of the triptychs. He says:

stand guarantee for its future. He is the subject with "sufficient will of the spirit, will to responsibility, freedom" (GM, p. 116) to emerge from the cocoon of asceticism and create new values. *Ecce Homo* leaves no doubt, in fact, that Nietzsche considers himself the first sovereign subject. As he says in his description of *Twilight of the Idols*, "I am the first to hold in my hands the measure for 'truths'; I am the first who is *able* to decide" (EH, p. 315). And it is clear that he stakes this claim on the basis of his creation of Zarathustra. The "supreme deed" that is *Zarathustra* represents a new determination of Being. Everything he says about the linguistic nature of this event (beings, he says, offer themselves to his language, and they offer themselves as language, whereby his language returns to the original nature of imagery), everything he says about the experience of rhythm, about the measure opened with this event ("Till then one does not know what is height, what depth; one knows even less what truth is" [EH, p. 305]) and about its absolutely singular character ("There is no moment in this revelation of truth that has been anticipated or guessed by even *one* of the greatest" [EH, p. 305])—all of this points to the eventful character of this creative act. If Nietzsche insists hyperboli-

—It seems to me from all you've been saying that in the end what matters most to you is not an immediacy in the work's reference to reality, but a tension between juxtaposed references to different realities and the tension between a reference to reality and the artificial structure by which it is made.

—Well, it's in the artificial structure that the reality of the subject will be caught, and the trap will close over the subject matter and leave only the reality. One always starts work with the subject, no matter how tenuous it is, and one constructs an artificial structure by which one can trap the reality of the subject matter one has started from.

—The subject's a sort of bait?

—The subject is the bait.

—And what is the reality that remains, the residue? How does it relate to what you began with?

—It doesn't necessarily relate to it; but you will have created a realism equivalent to the subject matter which will be what is left in its place. You have to

cally on his singularity and greatness, it is because he is claiming to have achieved a radically new determination of the Being of what is: no prior creative act can compare to his precisely because his act is incommensurable and sets entirely new standards. Everything Nietzsche says about this solitude and about the fact that he cannot be heard follows from his sense that he is, as he says, a destiny. Something *happens* in his text, he tells us: a new law is given that speaks in his word.

We may well balk at such a claim (would this be the place to confess my reservations about *Zarathustra?*). But the important point for my purposes is that it is predicated on the possibility of a radical suspension of all prior interpretation—indeed, on a reopening of the question of the meaning of existence in its totality. It is predicated on a transcendence, if only in the manner of an ex-posure to the nothing named in Blanchot's phrase: "Nothing is what there is, and first of all nothing beyond."[17] Cruelty, as I have traced it here, is the enactment of this exposure. But I would also add immediately that Nietzsche thinks this exposure as inseparable from an experience of the Dionysian. I am hesitant to fill in this term as enthusiastically as Bataille does in his

> start from somewhere and you start from the subject which gradually, if the thing works at all, withers away and leaves this residue which we call reality and which perhaps has something tenuously to do with what one started with but very often has little to do with it. (pp. 180–82)

Bacon is clearly attenuating to an extreme degree the referential character of the process of mimesis, despite his insistence throughout the *Interviews* that he is painting after the fact, recording the fact. But then, the point, as Leiris notes, is not to paint the thing, but its "fact," the fact of its existence (which for Bacon frequently becomes the experienced fact of existence itself). When he says elsewhere that his aim is to record the essence,[17] he means essence in the sense of how a thing is *given* in its materiality. He is thinking the mode of essence to which Heidegger refers with his meditation on the phrase *es gibt* or *il y a* (once again: "there it is . . . "). That this thing is already

"Nietzschean Chronicles" in referring to the chthonic powers called up in communal religious experience,[18] but I believe we do well to attend to Nietzsche's insistence on the relation of death and sexuality when he returns to the notion of the tragic in *Twilight of the Idols*, and to recognize that the experience of the Dionysian is a bodily experience of alterity, a translating of the human *back into nature* that is not a simple dissolution of the human in forces that exceed it (though it becomes problematic to speak of subjective experience, and indeed of a "psychology of tragedy" [EH, p. 273]), but the baring of another "basic fact" where the human will is concerned: the bodily affectability of human existence and its singular materiality, what Haver has named so powerfully "the body of this death."[19]

In short, Nietzsche's sovereign creative act (and in general any self-styling or self-invention) is creative because it entails exposure to a dimension of experience that is irreducible to any work of meaning or totalizing initiative, even in the "aesthetic" form of giving a shape to one's existence. "Self-examination" and the "revaluation" that proceeds from it constitute an open-ended, an-archic play of creation that constantly en-

lost to illustration (or simply signification) forces us to speak of no more than a residue, the trace of a reality, so to speak. But the trace is compelling enough, material enough, to oblige us to recognize this "referential" dimension of the image—its force in *drawing out* existence as it is given in its fact. It does so, again, *après-coup*, after the fact, and via considerable transformation. This fact—this "that" of what is in all its facticity—has never really *been* before its ex-scription; it is both singular and originary. But "that it is" marks relation, the fact of an event. It trails relation, so to speak. This relationality is part of what "touches" our gaze and carries it back constantly in a reference to "reality."

So the residue of these paintings—"this residue that we call reality"—is what Leiris calls "the sheer fact of existence," ex-scribed in a singular presentation. In the fixed density of Bacon's images and in the fixing tension of their

gages what of the human is resistant to any ideological formation (or "idolization"). It is "cruel" not simply by virtue of a cruelty latent in the very structure of the will's self-affection, but because it undoes any surety of identity, exposing the self constantly to the exigency of new initiatives. Of course, since this exigency can only be truly known in affirmation, the task is a light one. And since the exposure in question *communicates* itself (as Bataille understood), it does not have to be undertaken alone. But here we reach a dimension of the ethico-political (its an-archic ground) where Nietzsche, in his icy solitudes, is of relatively little help, or even inhibiting: the thought of the pathos of distance as a relationality. The task that opens here is one that Foucault might have embraced as a "queer politics" of a kind. But even with that joyful epithet, we philosophers may still be too good for our job.

reference, we have existence written apart and asunder (*auseinander-geschrieben*, to borrow Paul Celan's term), or splayed and nailed to appearance in such a way as to offer this existence. What is left is reality. If we are to read in our seeing, *that* is what we must learn to read in such figuration.

INFANT

FIGURES

Part Two

(A primal scene?) You who live later, close to a heart that beats no more, suppose, suppose this: the child—is he seven years old, or eight perhaps?—standing, drawing the curtain and, through the window pane, looking. What he sees: the garden, the wintry trees, the wall of a house: while he sees, no doubt in a child's way, his play space, he tires and slowly looks up toward the ordinary sky, with its clouds, the grey light, the day pallid and without depth.

What happens then: the sky, the same sky, suddenly open, absolutely black and absolutely empty, revealing (as though the pane had broken) such an absence that all has since always and forevermore been lost in it, to the point that there is affirmed and there dissipates there the vertiginous knowledge that nothing is what there is, and first of all nothing beyond. The unexpected in this scene (its interminable feature) is the feeling of happiness that immediately submerges the child, the ravaging joy to which he can bear witness only by tears, an endless streaming of tears. He is thought to suffer a childish distress; attempts are made to console him. He says nothing. He will live henceforth in the secret. He will weep no more.

—Maurice Blanchot, *The Writing of the Disaster*

(Une scène primitive?) *Vous qui vivez plus tard, proches d'un coeur qui ne bat plus, supposez, supposez-le: l'enfant—a-t-il sept ans, huit ans peut-être?—debout, écartant le rideau et, à travers la vitre, regardant. Ce qu'il voit, le jardin, les arbres d'hiver, le mur d'une maison: tandis qu'il voit, sans doute à la manière d'un enfant, son espace de jeu, il se lasse et lentement regarde en haut vers le ciel ordinaire, avec les nuages, la lumière grise, le jour terne et sans lointain.*

Ce qui se passe ensuite: le ciel, le même ciel, soudain ouvert, noir absolument et vide absolument, révélant (comme par la vitre brisée) une telle absence que tout s'y est depuis toujours et à jamais perdu, au point que s'y affirme et s'y dissipe le savoir vertigineux que rien est ce qu'il y a, et d'abord rien au-delà. L'inattendu de cette scène (son trait interminable), c'est le sentiment de bonheur qui aussitôt submerge l'enfant, la joie ravageante dont il ne pourra témoigner que par les larmes, un ruissellement sans fin de larmes. On croit à un chagrin d'enfant, on cherche à le consoler. Il ne dit rien. Il vivra désormais dans le secret. Il ne pleurera plus.

I.

Infans. Our language seems to render the figure almost unavoidable, but then immediately shrouds it. The being that accedes to language is by definition, prior to this accession, "infans." And if we accept that the opening of language is indissociable from an experience (before experience) of a kind of death, there must be in our speaking, if only as a trace, the death of a child. The dying assumes other figures, for it is never finally accomplished—the "human," in its vulnerability, remaining in excess of any appropriation, required in every act of speech (this is the finitude of language). But the figure of the dying child insists in psychic life and in language; as though the interminable, immemorial dying in question must have a temporal figuration. No one can say fully, intelligibly, what the death of this child is, for all saying proceeds from such a death. But all saying is also haunted by it.

So he began, but it was not long before he declared he could not sustain a discourse on this topic.

It was not that he lacked something to say, it was that discourse was failing. "Insufficient" was his word. And then there was a hesitation concerning what he called the "legitimacy" of his undertaking.

—There are some topics for which speculation seems almost unseemly, though only speculation can approach them. Or perhaps it's a question of legitimacy. Even commentary seems unwarranted.

I replied—too lightly, I'm afraid—that he risked fetishizing his topic with that hesitation. Fearing his response, and before he could speak, I suggested that he was running the risk of literalizing what could only be a figure.

His question, he replied, concerned the necessity of the figure. Not just its force or insistence, but its necessity.

I asked him what had prompted this work, now.

—There's a text by Maurice Blanchot I've lived with for a very long time. A brief "récit" I saw first in 1976 and that was republished in *The Writing of the Disaster* in 1980. You know it, I think: the "primal scene." I thought perhaps the time had arrived for me to read it, particularly since I've been meditating on another, related "scene" from *The Interpretation of Dreams* that was discussed by Lacan.

I knew of his preoccupation with the text by Blanchot, and I had heard him refer to the dream of the burning child; I knew that this could not be the first time he had attempted a reading. Before I could renew my question he continued.

—And then recently, or some years ago, a friend who had proposed some "readings" around the topic of infancy said to me, "I sense you're very close to this infancy." Imagine, I found that satisfying! It was during the same visit that he said, "I fear the death drive in you."

I realized now that the matter was a bit more grave than I had anticipated. Not that our conversations were normally frivolous. But there was always a great deal of theory, or "speculation," and I had anticipated that the evening would go in that direction, especially after he had started reading to me. I realized now, however, that in speaking of "legitimacy" he was addressing the question of his relation to an experience of some kind, and that his problem, the "gravity," came from the fact that he was not speaking about some specific occurrence, be it as profoundly shattering as the death of a child. I had no idea what deaths he had known and could associate with the theme of the infans *he was drawing from Blanchot, but I knew this was also something else.*

—I'm not sure I'm *not* talking about the death of a child, or of children. There's more than the dreams I've had. . . . But I fear the pathos in such a topic, and I fear it all the more for the fact that it threatens to be no more than another speculative turn in a meditation on the origin of language. And what is the significance of the fact that it seems impossible, or rather *absurd*, to posit any kind of thesis on this question and attempt to *demonstrate* its validity?

—Didn't you start with a thesis?

—A thesis for which there could be no conclusion, no demonstration—more the definition of a site than a statement to be weighed. I find the figure of the *infans* compelling in a very strong sense, and I suspect that its "death" has more than a figural or metaphorical status. But I'm describing an event of a "quasi-transcendental" character that resists any thetic statement, any documentation.

—You're pointing, I gather, to a kind of crossing between the "transcendental" and the "real"—perhaps at a level you haven't known before. Clearly, you'll never find the peace of the concept or the satisfactions of a thesis at such a site. It can only be *passed through*, or touched in some kind of passage, and the "results" of the engagement will never be more than pale reminders. Why don't you leave aside the exigencies of discourse? Or let's try negotiating with them a little. Read what you've written—I see a sheaf of pages there. Let's talk them through.

He was clearly fighting with something and was slow to respond; as though his thought *were slurred, but he continued.*

—There is at least the question of the status of a text like Blanchot's "primal scene." I continue to think (call me traditional) that the struggle to open a place for such texts is an important one. "Literary thought" starts when the strangeness or force of a text obliges us to start asking questions about language, fiction, and so forth. This one does in part through its context. In the pages preceding its presentation, Blanchot argues that the death of the *infans must* be figured. It's immediately after that statement that he offers the "primal scene." The challenge for me bears on the relation between that assertion and the language of the text that follows.

—But clearly, there is far more here for you than a literary question—else you wouldn't worry about "legitimacy"; this is not a topic in criticism. Nor is it even a philosophical topic—for again, you wouldn't experience that problem with legitimacy. No, I believe you think this text *says* something, and the question has to do with the status of that saying. Because it concerns you—you wouldn't have the burden of that responsibility otherwise. The real question has to do with that concern.

—I suppose that's why I was starting to speak of a literary *thought*. But you're right to recall me to the real "object," the real matter. Let me propose the following: let me back up and approach the question of the necessity of the figure, the infant figure. Then we can attempt to consider together the "scene"; perhaps we'll find the real object of this meditation along the way.

He didn't need my accord to begin, though he wouldn't start without a sign, a kind of formal agreement. A renewed pact.

—You remember that Blanchot considers two figures of the *infans* in those first pages on the topic in *The Writing of the Disaster*. The first is from D. W. Winnicott, who posits an infant who cannot know the primal agonies that overwhelm it, a state before the development of any self that would be capable of schematizing its experience. A "memory without memory," retaining the mark of traumatic events that have never taken place, would thus constitute a childhood that a fissured, adult ego must reconstitute for itself via an act of rememoration: "a fictive application designed . . . to furnish a representation of the unrepresentable, to allow one to believe that one might, with the help of the transference, fix in the present of a memory (that is, in current experience) the passivity of the immemorial unknown" (WD, p. 109/66).

Closer to home, in Serge Leclaire's *On tue un enfant* (*A Child Is Being Killed*), Blanchot finds another figure of a menacing past that one has never known or lived in Leclaire's meditation on a "primary narcissistic representation" that is formed of the "dreams and desires of those who made us and saw us born (parents, all society)" (WD, p. 110/67). The *infans* here is a figure, or more properly, a "stand-in for representation"—what Freud, and Lacan after him, called a *Vorstellungsrepräsentanz*. Its hold on the psyche must be dislodged if desire is to come to speech—a terrible task inasmuch as this representation is unconscious. The child must be destroyed, Blanchot says: "In order not to remain in the purgatory of the *infans* and on the hither side of desire, one must destroy the indestructible and put an end (not suddenly, but constantly) to that to which one does not have, has never had, and will never have, access—a matter, in other words, of the impossible necessary death [*la mort impossible nécessaire*]" (WD, p. 111/67).

—"The impossible necessary death." Is that Leclaire or is it Blanchot?

—I want to try to get back to Leclaire at some point because I'm not sure Blanchot drew as much from *On tue un enfant* as he could have. But your question is well founded. The last words evoke powerfully the dilemma addressed by Leclaire, but they also point to a motif that is more properly Blanchotian and signal that Blanchot is assimilating the figures offered by both Leclaire and Winnicott to one that appears furtively in the ironic leitmotif of his early essay "Literature and the Right to Death." Spirit, he told us there in a marvelous parody of the Hegelian dialectic, is "la vie qui porte la mort et se maintient en elle"—it brings death [*elle porte la mort*] and sustains death, both confronting and accomplishing it. But as the work of the writer demonstrates, it also *carries* a death ("elle porte la mort") that it cannot fully subsume—a death that becomes the obsession of literature as it explores the limits of the negative at work in language. Even casual readers of Blanchot's fiction will be familiar with the theme of a death that is the impossibility of dying. Blanchot's meditation on Leclaire's title returns us to the site of that impossibility and to the problem of its necessary figuration.

So, a necessary figuration. We glimpse the psychic grounds of that necessity in Blanchot's appeal to Winnicott and Leclaire, and I want to return to them before long. But Blanchot also refers to a necessity of a logical order, a necessity of language, let us say, that is ultimately inseparable from an ethical claim. This logical necessity appears in a rapid evocation of the aporia that lies at the heart of the Hegelian dialectic for the fact that the experience of death that puts the dialectic underway also arrests it.

> I will not go into detail about the way in which, from the early philosophy onward, and through a prodigious enrichment of thought, the difficulty was overcome. This is well known. It remains, however, that if death, murder, and suicide are put to work, and if death dampens itself in becoming powerless power and then negativity, there is, each time one advances with the help of *possible* death, the necessity of not passing over the death without phrasing, the death without a name, outside the concept, *impossibility* itself. (WD, p. 112/68)

It is *necessary*, Blanchot says, not to pass outside or avoid a passing that represents an *impossible* for the concept—necessary because the concept itself constantly exposes what it forgets as it subsumes the "impossible" death in a self-appropriating negativity. If language proceeds from the power of negation, it also marks—even as it effaces—relation to another death, opening thereby another responsibility.

To put this logical imperative directly and abruptly, shifting into a register that is more Heideggerian than Hegelian (though this shift is also always occuring in Blanchot's text), language must mark its finitude. Or better, since such a formulation risks turning language into a kind of subject, we could say that by virtue of its finitude and what I shall call, following Benjamin, its "communicability," language has already marked its relation to an origin that exceeds its hold—it cannot (not) say it in the movement by which it "communicates" itself, or "speaks" (as Heidegger would put it). This necessity belongs to the trace structure thought by both Heidegger and Derrida, a structure to which Blanchot alludes at the heart of this meditation on the "infant figure":

> "A child is being killed." Let us not be mistaken about this present: it signifies that the operation could never take place once and for all, that it is not accomplished

at any privileged moment of time, that it operates inoperably and thus tends to be none but the very time that destroys (effaces) time, an effacement, or a destruction, or a gift that has always already avowed itself in the precession of a Saying outside any said, a word of writing whereby this effacement, far from effacing itself in its turn, is perpetuated without term even in the *interruption* that constitutes its mark. (WD, p. 116/71)

The infancy of the concept, we might say (to play with Hegel a bit more)—its time being a violent offering of time (an offering *of time* that does not sublate it, but rather suspends or interrupts it, marking the limit—and this is already language, already a "saying"—from which a conscious life can temporalize itself and come to speech). But the figural transposition of this event in the phrase "A child is being killed" also invites us to ask a bit more pointedly: who or what is offered up in this gift of time and language? If the phrase says the *time* (before time) of this event, it seems to refer as well to its material site, what authors such as Heidegger, Lacan, and Levinas name, in their respective ways, "the human." (Lacan, you remember, speaks repeatedly of the "human that suffers the signifier"—a "human" factor that is something like a "medium" between language and the real, as he puts it in his seminar on ethics.) Once again, by virtue of its finitude (language is not an infinite logos), and by virtue of its "communicability," language cannot but (not) say the limit that is its origin, and thus its relation to what I'm calling the human.

I'm sure that when Blanchot declares, in the lines immediately before the passage I just cited, that "we know nothing of the child . . . except this, that the possibility of speech and life depend, through death and murder, on the relation of singularity established fictively with a mute past, on the hither side of history, thus outside any past, and for which the eternal *infans* becomes a figure, at the same time as it slips away there" (WD, p. 116/71), he is evoking an exigency proper to the structure of memory and "self"-relation. He is also saying something about the irreducible place of fiction in this constitution of subjectivity, and perhaps something about the very opening of fictionality (and the possibility of fictive "supposition"); when he evokes the re-marking of saying in the subsequent lines, he is touching upon the possibility of the "récit" and the "primal scene"(?) to follow. But I want to capture something more about this exigency of the figure and the place of what I called "the human."

Let me return to my formulation. I said that language cannot but (not) say the relation from which it proceeds as it "speaks" or is brought to language. Of course, language cannot "speak" without an act of enunciation of some kind. Hence language's "need" for human speech, as Heidegger describes it. But humankind would not be capable of such originary "usage" were there not a prior assignment of the human being to language—an assignment, Heidegger tells us, that is a bodily appropriation, a "use" of the human (his term for this, once again, is *der Brauch*). In short, language cannot come to language, cannot "speak," without an act of enunciation on the part of a being whose own always prior exposure to language offers language its material site. This account excludes nothing of the "psychic" exigencies we have touched upon thus far (for we must think, in turn, the conditions of enunciation—conditions that prompt me to retain this term "subject," at least provisionally). It simply suggests that there is a more fundamental exigency—that the speaking subject must have been *given to language* in a bodily exposure that precedes its own emergence, and that when language is brought to speech, this prior exposure is also marked in some way.

—Is that what Heidegger means by "birth" in *Being and Time*?

—I wonder whether he doesn't indeed approach the structure we are trying to think with that motif. But the exposure we are describing also seems inseparable from a kind of passing that is difficult to think together with that temporality Heidegger names a "historizing." How could we think the passage from Blanchot we heard a moment ago with Heidegger's thought of the temporality of existence? But perhaps Heidegger was always seeking to think just such an interruption as he approached the horizon of time. I think I read it in the essays on language and the dialogue on "*Gelassenheit*," for example. If we were to carry that thought back to *Being and Time*, we might have the means to radicalize considerably that "hermeneutic" structure by which the *Dasein* announces to itself its own possibility. The "birth" of the *Dasein* would then be inseparable from the mortal exposure he associates with the advent of language in the later essays, that appropriation of the mortal body that he takes to be the condition of the event of "saying." And thus it would be inseparable from the death of the *infans*, a figure that would emerge only to disappear in that *hermeneuin* by which the *Dasein* says the opening of the "signifiability" that belongs to the structure of "world." The *infans* would appear and disappear in the "circle" whereby the *response* in which humankind appropriates itself to the call it *brings to speech* must of necessity re-mark a relation between language and humankind that precedes the advent of language itself.

Of course, the figure of the *infans* (or "human weakness," as Blanchot puts it elsewhere) is given, in its effacement, only in and by language. But this is not to say that the "the child" or "the human" are merely proleptic figures of an unpresentable, prior condition, as some of our friends might phrase it. Such a formulation can end all too easily by reiterating the movement of the concept in a rhetorical celebration of impossibility, occluding the saying of the event and denying what language avows of a *real* exposure; it risks, once again, effacing the *necessity* of the figure, the exigency of the figure. To be sure, what is said is no more than a figure, but this "primary" figuration speaks to the fact that there opens in language a relation that exceeds its hold or its power, that language proceeds from an exposure (the condition of all linguistic articulation) that language cannot but (not) say. The necessity of the figure speaks to the finitude of language in its inseparability from something like human finitude and the opening of conscious thought itself.

—I'm remembering now the avowal Blanchot describes in the essay on Camus's *L'homme révolté* in *The Infinite Conversation*. You've cited this passage yourself in an earlier work, I think—it's the one containing the meditation on Kaliayev's expression of his failure to murder the Grand Duke Serge in the presence of his children. It's the same avowal as that of "a child is being killed," save its acknowledgment of the impossibility of the deed it is already carrying out. Let me read it again; it will help me keep my bearings:

> We sense that the recoil of violence, its arrest in front of the children's weakness, Kaliayev's "*I cannot*" coincides with the moment at which violence lays bare the visage and makes man this extreme destitution before which death draws back because it cannot reach it, because this weakness is this arrest, this drawing back itself. The children and the wife, their innocence, are nothing other than the visage of the grand duke . . . nothing other than the nakedness that is man in proximity with death's revelation, nothing other than the "*second at which you will look at him.*" What we are left with is this second. This is the *time* of the word, the moment at which speech begins, lays bare the human visage, says the encounter that is this nakedness and says man as the encounter with the extreme and irreducible limit. "*Understand, I could not, and now, too, I cannot.*" "*I cannot*" is the secret of language where, outside all power to represent and to signify, speech would come about as what always differs from itself, and, as difference, holds back. It does not merge with the moral interdiction against killing, nor with the fact that one cannot really kill. "*I cannot*" is death speaking in person, an allusion that death formulates when, in the act of killing, it comes up against the evidence of the visage as though it were its own impossibility; a moment that is death's own drawing back before itself, the *delay* that is the site of speech, and where speech can take place. (*Infinite Conversation*, p. 279/186)

—Yes, there is what must be thought: that moment left to us, language's "se-cret," and then the encounter it holds. Of the many questions I would raise now in regard to that extraordinary passage, two seem especially pertinent to me for the "scene" from *The Writing of the Disaster*. In brief: 1) Who—or what—lies under this death sentence, this arrest of death (and let us note that this "who" is inseparable, as Blanchot's passage emphasizes, from the arrested act, the "I cannot" that already effects what it defers, already announces the death that it cannot assume); and 2) For whom is the secret? To restate: Who exists in this second before any "we"?—what existence is exposed in and to this avowal of destruction?, and who can *say* "us": who retains the avowal (who can speak of what is left)? In the difficult passage between these questions lies what I hesitate to call the problematic of "(A Primal Scene?)."

—Blanchot says somewhere, I believe, that the secret is one only for those who refuse the avowal; but I presume you would say that the avowal "refuses" itself, and that "we" appear somewhere in that movement. But is it even possible, in both (or all) of these questions, to speak of a "what" or a "who," let alone "we"? The first question is the most difficult in this regard: is it possible to speak of the being of what lies in the secret?

—We know at least that *theory* will provide no answer, since what we are try-ing to think does not exist outside or prior to the avowal that exposes and ef-faces, and this avowal is itself prior to any signification. To the question "who?"—or "what?"—there can only be a speculative answer that speaks to the exigencies we have noted: the presumption that *there must be an encounter* figured in the powerless urgency of the phrase, "I cannot," or in the haunting recurrence of "a child is being killed," that *there must be such a figure*, and the further presumption, also "ethical," that spoken there is *the imperative of a re-lation* to the event other than that of the concept.

I'm using the term "speculative" in a sense I'll have to develop shortly, but I recognize that it may say too much (or too little) in that it can connote a form of reflection that inevitably denies its material grounds, whereas the point is to address precisely the material grounds of reflection: the site of exposure ("en-counter," Blanchot insists) that de-fines both the finitude of language and hu-man finitude. I'm also using it in a different sense from the one that is sug-gested by the scene (the speculative[?] fiction) that stages the death of the *infans* in *The Writing of the Disaster*. But perhaps I should start from precisely that point, since it leads us directly to the questions I enumerated a few moments ago. The problem I mean to indicate is the following: Blanchot hints strongly that "(A Primal Scene?)" participates in, "mimes" perhaps, or at least takes its source in, that form of figuration that he describes on the preceding page as "necessary to any speech and life." The figural status of the narrative is thus comparable (at some level) to that of the phrase "a child is being killed"— a phrase Blanchot declares "unpronounceable" since it is unavailable to any conscious or even unconscious representation (its figuration attending the very constitution of any subjectivity). Just as "a child is being killed" cannot be spoken in any mode of expression or representation, Blanchot tells us, the child's experience cannot be "seen" as an event taking place in any time or place whatsoever (WD, p. 176/177). At some level beyond the most manifest (as it is read casually), the "primal scene(?)" offered to us is unavailable to representation; so unavailable, in fact, that the question mark that accompanies this introductory designation marks a hesitation about the presuppositions of the designation itself, presuppositions that bear in part on the use of the term "scene." And yet, while it points to an event that exceeds any conscious or unconscious relation, it inscribes in its fiction a form of reflection, or a kind of knowledge, a thought. My suggestion would be that Blanchot is inscribing in that figuration, which he claims to be essential to speech and life, a form of reflection that is the abyssal origin and possibility of any speculation, as of any specular relation.

Once again, Blanchot himself hesitates before the word "scene." The question mark accompanying the "devolved" title that introduces the passage— "(A primal scene?)"—points as much to Blanchot's respectful uneasiness in regard to the language of psychoanalysis as it does to his concern over the figural status of what a reader/auditor is asked to "suppose" (as though he himself were not quite certain of the character of the passage). As one of the commentators on this scene . . .

—Commentators?

—I'm referring to the voices that appear later in the volume, in the dialogue addressed explicitly to the scene in question. There are also other, unmarked modes of commentary, I believe.

—I remember. But if *The Writing of the Disaster* is composed of fragments, what status does an intertextual reference have? And for that matter, what is the relation between, for example, the discussion of Leclaire's title and the scene itself, which seems to figure in the series of fragments on the *infans* and yet also *ends* that series in an entirely liminal fashion.

—I'll take that as a word of caution. There's no question that if we're to draw widely from *The Writing of the Disaster* to develop the speculative construction to which I referred—and I'm convinced that it invites such usage—we must do so in a way that respects the text's heterogeneity. In short, we have to read the text; and the question of what that means is intimately bound up with our problematic.

Anyway, as one of the commentators who appears later in *The Writing of the Disaster* remarks, the word "scene" is inappropriately applied because what appears in and by this supposition escapes "the figurable" as it does fiction: it is not a scene, it is "a shadow, a faint gleam" (WD, p. 176/114). "Scene," the commentator tells us, merely helps to recall that what is presented cannot be taken as an event happening at a moment in time. For what occurs is an a-temporal interruption, or a "fold" in time of the order of what Heidegger names *Ereignis* —a term that Blanchot holds at some distance in this same volume, ostensibly by reason of the etymological connection Heidegger draws with the archaic German word *Eräugnis* and its reference to a seeing (I say "ostensibly" because I think his real concern is to protect the "disaster" from any easy assimilation to a Heideggerian vocabulary). Blanchot is suspicious of the ancient link between Being and light, just as he is wary of the metaphysical privilege accorded to sight. But, as I've tried to suggest, this "scene" that Blanchot hesitates to term "primal" stages precisely the mortal appropriation of the "human" to speech that Heidegger meditates on via the terms "Ereignis" and "Brauch," and it appeals to the metaphorics(?) of light and seeing no less than does Heidegger. One may well call this accession to the "secret" of language, its sudden fulguration, a blinding of sorts, or understand it as the opening of what Hölderlin thought as a "third eye." It is also the awakening to a watch that will never be watchful enough, that can never penetrate the night to which it opens. But the figure of seeing only insists all the more, as we recognize when one of the commentators explicitly refers to the child's *specular* relation to its own death.

We need to follow this closely, for the reference to a seeing is introduced via a singular fold in the dialogical commentary to which I have referred. The voices suggest that what we are to read in the scene (to the extent that we are prepared to read it, or to hear, in Blanchot's terms, "the echoless of the voice" [WD, p. 178/116]) is inseparable from what the child, *who also figures in the scene*, sees.

> —But who is recounting?—The story.—The pre-story, the "flashing circumstance" whereby the dazzled child sees—he has the spectacle of it—the happy murder of himself that gives him the word's silence. (WD, p. 177/115)

Bracketing for a moment the question of the voice that addresses us, we might conclude from this passage that what recounts, what Blanchot's narrator names the "pre-narrative" or "pre-story" ("avant-récit"), is nothing other than the saying to which Blanchot refers in the passage preceding the presentation of "(A Primal Scene?)": the avowal of the disaster ("always already avowed"), the saying of the gift of time that is also the gift of death and language. What "relates," what "reflects" the child's death to it, would be the interruptive writing by which language opens to itself in a mortal appropriation of the human and by which thought opens to this appropriation—an event, in other words, that is at the origin of both language and thought.

—Slow down. If I follow you, you are suggesting that this text somehow *speaks from* the event to which you referred earlier, that event of "writing" or "saying" that unfolds in a structure of repetition (remember the "always already avowed"). Is that what is meant here by "recounting"? And how are we to attribute a voice to that saying? I can follow the idea that the child's ecstasis has something to do with the "origin" of language. But on what basis are we to ground the narrated sequence on that "saying" prior to any said? I'm playing the devil's advocate now, but some might allege that you're taking the commentators a little too literally and forgetting their own "fictive" status in the process. Why should we read this sequence as more than a mere staging of the speculative notions you are pursuing? Fascinating, to be sure. But why should we understand this to be something more than a kind of "philosophical fiction"? Do you remember Heidegger's description of the "pure night of anxiety" in "What Is Metaphysics?" and his account there of the gift of language? Are we possibly reading a counter-story of sorts, where Heidegger's "that there are beings and not nothing" is replaced by a more radical, "that nothing is what there is, and first of all, nothing beyond"? One could well summarize the essential in this scene (I know there would be more, but I just want to make the point) by asserting that Blanchot is pulling the thought of nihilation toward Heidegger's later meditation on the *es gibt* and toward his own development (with Levinas) of the notion of the *il y a*, thereby further "weakening" the negative and reinforcing (is that the word?) Heidegger's assertion that nihilation is prior to any negation. I'm going fast, I know; these references don't translate so easily into one another. But you see where I'm going. Is this a fictive casting of another "primal" philosophical scene?

—That would already be something, I suppose. And if I were to continue in those terms on my own right (I've tried it), I would want to ask why Blanchot even has recourse to a term as philosophically loaded as "nothing." Shouldn't the notion of the *il y a* connote more a "non-positive affirmation" than any negativity?—For if the negative cannot negate itself, then we must have something like an affirmation. Or is a relation to the "nothing" still somehow a condition of a relation to the *il y a*? Weigh that question; its implications are considerable. But enough, I don't want to translate this text into philosophical terms. Even if it's not so clear, in fact, what the status of a "philosophical fiction" might be, and even if the question of "translation" poses some intriguing problems in itself, I'm far more interested in a different kind of reading. I'd prefer to entertain what the text offers (all of it: the scene, the fictional commentary, the fragmentary writing adjoined to them in *The Writing of the Disaster*) and attempt to think through the statements of the volume from its own terms. I'd like to start by piecing together the meaning and possibility of the commentators' remarks (among other things). I'm well aware that there is some risk of getting caught up in the language and thereby "miming" the text. But I've heard these warnings before from critics and philosophers who are impatient for a "translation" and require a rapid conclusion (or a map and clearly indicated guideposts). I'm more concerned about the risk of weaving a meaning where a disjunction should be honored. Of course, it's not a matter of running everything together—the interruptions, the boundaries, the breaks are also part of what must be read. But the drive for meaning is seductive; it infiltrates even the discourse on interruption. At the same time, however, I'm wary of those forms of complacent surrender that invoke "multiplicity," "fragmentation," and so forth, as soon as things get a little strange or difficult. I say let us try to suffer the disjunction by entertaining as much of the text as possible and by attempting to think it through. I don't think we should assume too quickly the meaning of disjunction itself, even while we attempt to honor it. And if we're at all attentive, it will come. We'll hit a wall of some sort, and I believe we'll have learned much more in the process (and from the encounter) than we would from any labor of philosophical translation, however sophisticated.

As for your discomfort about the reference to a "recounting," well, I share it: "recounting" cannot possibly mean narrating if what recounts is the "prestory," the "avant-récit." To approach this question seriously, we'll have to return to the status of the "scene" as a form of representation. For the moment, though, I want to follow a bit more the claim that this "récit," this "scene" proceeds from what you just called an "originary writing"—that the "primal scene" does not just recount the event (the event of "writing") as its "object," however inaccessible, but rather unfolds from the recounting of the event. A fiction, perhaps, but I want to entertain the supposition.

—No problem—we have all night. But now I want to ask: is it perhaps the child who "recounts" in a kind of spectral return?

—I'm not really sure how to respond as yet. The voice speaks *from* the space of fiction (the possibility of fiction) we noted earlier. It's almost a fictionalized voice of conscience, isn't it? But the fact is, I don't quite know how to account for the address and its almost obliging intimacy. What prompts it or, better, why does it prompt? Whose prosopopoeia is this? I'm just not sure. Let me begin by trying to construct this scene as the commentators give it to us.

So, what recounts, one of the commentators says, is the "flashing circumstance," by which the child, in a kind of illuminated ec-stasis, knows the nothing, the nothing beyond that is the *il y a*. What recounts, what "writes," let us say, before any account or even any invitation to an imagining or a "supposition" is a kind of illuminating reflection, an *originary* reflection that offers the child knowledge of its mortal accession to language (the commentators also evoke knowledge of its "pouvoir-mourir") in and as knowledge of relation to an infinite alterity. The opening of language is *for* the child (he sees his death, the commentators tell us—there is necessarily the advent of a kind of self here), but in and as the opening of a relation language cannot subsume. If what recounts is the originary inscription, the interruptive writing Blanchot calls a saying, then we might understand that the saying spells the child's death in the fold of its suspensive tracing. Or better: we might say that the child comes to its death in that wave of light, that accidental conflagration (I think of the Aristotelian *tuché*), or that burning constellation of circumstance that is the mortal exposure of its vulnerability and thus spells its death with the words, "Nothing is what there is. . . . " It awakens to its death and "survives" henceforth in that knowledge: "He will live henceforth in the secret." The commentators implicitly gloss this line as follows:

> The ever-suspended question: having died of this 'ability to die' that gives him joy and ravages him, did he survive?—or rather, what does survive mean then, if not to live by acquiescence to the refusal, in the drying of emotion, withdrawn from self-interest, dis-interested, extenuated to the point of calm, expecting nothing. Consequently, waiting and watching, because suddenly awakened, and—knowing this full well henceforth—never wakeful enough. (WD, p. 179/116)

Death, we see now, is a kind of death in life, or something else. The *jouissance* of the moment gives way to a reserve of being by which exposure, as I have referred to it, is perpetuated in limitless acquiescence to an exigency that is forever withheld, perpetuated in a non-expectant but ever-renewed watch. The source of that exigency, knowledge of an impossible relation, or relation with the impossible (the *il y a*), refuses itself; but acquiescence maintains what cannot be held by maintaining itself in a passive, dis-interested waiting that knows itself to be infinitely required, infinitely responsible.

—I'm not sure I can grasp that survival (though I suppose that if there is any ground to the appeal to suppose, any reason for the appeal to be *compelling*, there must be such a thing). You seem to be suggesting that a consciousness of sorts opens in the passage between birth and death that occurs in the fold of saying. I follow the notion that we are witnessing the birth of a kind of thought in this very radical account of an experience with language. We are told that in the "flashing circumstance" the child sees the black void of pure loss, an absence so profound (and what is that measure, exactly?—"such an absence," "to the point that"), so profound that a "vertiginous knowledge" forms, only to dissipate in the same instant, presumably because the relation to the *il y a*—nothing that is—cannot be "held." But how could this opening of thought be maintained—and then offered to some reflection or some memory?

—I don't know if consciousness is the word at all. As you've put it, the child's passing is the birth of thought (or of *a* thought—think of the figure that haunts the latter part of Blanchot's *Death Sentence*), the opening of relation, in saying. *There is what remains to us*: an exposure prior to any meaning that is both a kind of unending fall (in relation to the *il y a*) and the accession to a day (the power to die) that is eclipsed in its very opening. I'm not sure how to think that remaining, that acquiescent "subjectivity" Blanchot's commentators describe, but we must remember that this exposure occurs in and with language. The "reflection"—we are straining the term now beyond what it can bear in a philosophy of reflection—belongs to language, or rather to the "avowal" that has always already occurred. The passing, the passage of the *infans* cannot be thought outside this avowal. As you put it earlier, I think, its birth and death are coterminous, "spaced" only by that speech of writing. If the relation to alterity is somehow maintained in an exigency, it is only through language's saying. The survival is in language.

—So it is language that "recounts." And if *the child* somehow speaks its death, it is as the subject *of* that saying.

—That would not exclude this other formulation: that what recounts is the saying *of* a mortal exposure. We must find a way to describe this event that preserves the encounter to which Blanchot referred in that passage on Kaliayev's "I cannot." "A child is being killed" (if we may take this phrase as a figuration of the event in question) and "I cannot" are the saying of the singular relation *from which* language opens. But I am not averse to calling the opening of this relation "language." In fact, I believe we must: if it is not already language, then we cannot respond to what I called earlier the necessity of the figure, an exigency that is no less ethical than it is logical, and no less an exigency for a finite thought. We could not know something like a responsibility—*we could not know it at all*—were there not the inscription of that relation, an inscription that "perpetuates" the interruption and already partakes of the communicability of language.

—Why do you use the word "ethical"?

—That was perhaps too quick, at least for the moment. But isn't there something of an ethical dimension to the speculation we are undertaking and to the assumption of the notion of finitude itself (since this notion can only be assumed in some kind of praxis and can never be demonstrated)? The thought of usage to which I have referred (*der Brauch*—*brauchen* is to need and to use) is an extraordinarily complex elaboration of the *lack* of a ground for thinking something like the relationality implied in the finitude of Being and human being. But what incites to such a thought in all its rigor (and it is nothing if not rigorous—step by step) if not an "ethically" motivated desire to try the limits of language (in Wittgenstein's sense—the "Lecture on Ethics") from the ground of something like the experience we are attending to here, a *need* to which Blanchot refers in this fragment from the opening pages of *The Writing of the Disaster*:

> We constantly *need* to say (to think): something (quite important) happened to me there. By which we mean at the same time: this could not possibly belong to the order of things that happen, or to the order of the important, but is rather what exports and deports. Repetition. (WD, p. 20/9)

I don't believe Blanchot is describing a merely psychic reality (in the everyday sense of the term—above all the one that lies behind so much of the confessional drive in our culture). I suspect he is addressing the same thing that prompts Heidegger to use terms like "lack" and "solitude" in thinking that usage of the human for the advent of language he names *der Brauch*. I know this is a little vague, and I want to return to it later if we get a chance to approach Lacan, but I want to suggest that the act of writing from the need or exigency to which Blanchot refers here—an exigency that exceeds any psychological imperative—is a practice with an irreducibly ethical dimension—though it will never provide an "Ethics."

But let me add another point that will make this term "ethical" a little less strained and also help us rejoin the question of language. We must not lose sight of the fact that when Blanchot names the advent of thought in the mortal passage of the *infans* the opening of "responsibility," he is drawing on Levinas, and thereby linking his words on the opening of a relation to alterity to the thought of *autrui*—to the ethical relation as Levinas understands it. He is also linking the thought of *autrui* to his own thought of difference; he is commenting Levinas in an active, transformative fashion. The relation between Blanchot and Levinas deserves more sustained attention, as Paul Davies has reminded us over the years. But I want to underscore the point that Blanchot never dissociates the question of difference (nihilation, the *il y a*, all of it) from that of *autrui*. The "primal scene" gives us little to work with in this regard. Of the death of the *infans*, it gives only the opening of a relation to alterity. But if, as I'll want to suggest, the event must be understood in a structure of repetition, then nothing excludes the ethical relation as Levinas understands it. Now, for the purposes of our discussion here, we should remember that Levinas understands the relation to the other as a saying and as a *signification*. The motif appears throughout *Otherwise Than Being*, the text that Blanchot comments most immediately in *The Writing of the Disaster*. Blanchot takes over that notion in terms that point toward the notion of saying to which he has recourse in the pages preceding the primal scene. Here, for example:

> When *autrui* is no longer the remote, but the neighbor who weighs upon me to the point of opening me to the radical passivity of the self, then subjectivity—subjectivity as wounded, accused, and persecuted exposure, as a sensibility abandoned to difference—falls in its turn outside of being. Then it signifies the beyond of being, in the very gift—in the giving of a sign—which its immeasurable sacrifice offers up to *autrui*; it is, in the same capacity as *autrui* and as the visage, the enigma that troubles order and cuts into being: the exception of the extraordinary, exile outside the phenomenon, outside experience. (WD, p. 43/24)

This exposition, this signifying, he tells us, is responsibility:

> Where passivity unworks and destroys me, I am at the same time pressed into a responsibility which not only exceeds me, but which I cannot exercise, since I can do nothing and no longer exist as myself. It is that responsible passivity that is Saying. For, before anything said, and outside being. . . . Saying gives and gives response, responding to the impossible, for the impossible. (WD, p. 37/20)

The death of the *infans*, in other words, takes the same structure as the relation to *autrui*. In each case, the exposure to the other is a "signifying," the giving of a sign. Not yet articulated language, but already relation, or the trace of relation: an opening to the other that is also, somehow, open to the self we would normally understand as "responsible."

—So you want to think the awakening of subjectivity, the "survival," as a structure of response and responsibility.

—That would conform, it seems to me, to Blanchot's statements to the effect that the awakening is never sufficient to itself, that passivity is never passive enough, etc. It might also help us understand the nature of the initial address: "You who live later. . . . "

—I'm following your steps, but I'm beginning to lose a sense of the questions from which we started. Is it the child who awakens to this passivity? If so, what does this child have to do with the *infans*? I'd like to take you back to those two questions you laid out earlier, and maybe add one now: Who dies in that saying? Who lives in that saying? And for whom is the exigency?

—Let me try to summarize, and let me begin with the theme of the *death* of a child. It seems to me that much of the complexity lies in the multifold meaning of that term. We have been turning around the questions of subjectivity, reflection, and survival because it is said that the child *knows its death* in seeing the irremediable loss of immanence that is spelled in the knowledge that affirms itself and dissipates in the event—that knowledge of finite transcendence that is the condition of any language and any thought. But "to know its death" means, I believe, at least two things (*at least* two). On the one hand, there is the knowledge of the gift of language, the capability of death ("le pouvoir-mourir"). We are very close here to the Hegelian dialectic, as Blanchot acknowledges in the pages before the "primal scene" and elsewhere in *The Writing of the Disaster*. What differentiates this staging of the opening of thought to itself in an encounter with death is the unsublatable character of the relation to the *il y a*, the passivity of that relation. And *this* dimension of the mortal exposure constitutes what Blanchot will sometimes describe as *another dying*.

Who or what dies, we might ask, if the child knows some passing whose "truth" is not wholly contained in the accession to meaning? The *infans* names something more than a prior immanence where being and nothing are the same. To be sure, any self-relation presupposes some relation to loss (to loss itself, and also to *a* loss—I'm sure we'll come back to that). But if the figure of the child, or rather the *infans* insists, one of the reasons may lie in the fact that what suffers the opening of relation is not a simple passivity, but rather another kind of immanence. Blanchot develops, in fact, two forms of such an immanence in *The Writing of the Disaster*, and does so fairly prominently. The first is Narcissus, the second the anonymous "subject" of the death drive.

The first is a figure of a relation prior to any "mirror stage." Narcissus, Blanchot tells us in a beautiful meditation on Ovid's myth—a meditation accompanied by the same non-title as the récit "(A primal scene?)"—does not see himself in the watery image that captures his gaze. Lacking any relation to the other, he has no self-relation, and therefore loses himself in fascination before an elusive form that resembles no one and nothing, being nothing more than the "pure resemblance" of the image (a notion that carries us back to Blanchot's extensive reflection on the image, in texts such as "Two Versions of the Imaginary," or "Literature and the Right to Death"). For us, Blanchot says, stressing the mythic character of this figure, he is a "divided same, death in life"—the "essence," Blanchot surmises, "of the secret" (WD, p. 204/134). But he does not know this death; he dissolves without knowledge. The figure of Narcissus would thus evoke a "relation without relation," to speak like Blanchot—an imaginary relation that is, in some sense, "prior" to the subjectivity we have approached thus far.

The second figure has a provenance that is perhaps no less mythic, but it is without a name. This is the figure of a *bodily* suffering that Blanchot repeatedly (sometimes explicitly, sometimes obliquely) links to Freud's notion of the death drive. The most forceful evocation of this figure (not the most explicit) comes fairly early in the volume and in terms that will help me reinforce my statement about the passivity of the relation without relation that is the relation to the *il y a*:

> Passivity is not a simple reception, any more than it is formless and inert matter *ready* for any form—passive, the impulses of dying [*les poussées de mourir*] (dying,

silent intensity; that which cannot be welcomed, what is inscribed wordlessly, the body in the past, the body of no one, of the interval: suspension of being, a seizure like a cut in time which we cannot evoke except as raw history, unnarratable, having no meaning in any present). Passive: the non-récit, that which escapes citation and that memory could never recall—forgetting as thought, that is to say, what could not be forgotten since it has always already fallen outside memory. (WD, p. 49/28)

Needless to say (and the severity of the fragmentary writing in this passage almost suffices to convey the point that has to be made here), we are very far from a thought of appropriation or any notion of a "body proper" that would be used for the appropriative movement of *Ereignis*. The anonymous, material relation that is traced with the death of the *infans* utterly disrupts this dimension of Heidegger's notion of usage. Blanchot carries this disruption very far—to the point, I would say, where it becomes extremely hard to think together the subjectivity we located earlier with reference to a specular movement in the event of usage and this silent bodily dying that gives itself to no narration or recitation, and whose only proximity to itself or to a self lies in what Blanchot calls "forgetting": "forgetting as thought." To what extent could the latter "thought" have ever given itself to the formation of a subjectivity, even that disinterested subjectivity before subjectivity that is said to survive the event? What is the relation between the silent "subject" of the death drive (truly *in-fans*), and the subject whose dying consists of an awakening to the *il y a* and an accession to the silence of language? I know you are no partisan of unity, but if we cannot think them together, then even the motif of the death of the *infans* threatens to come apart; and along with it go any number of statements concerning the relation without relation that is responsibility.

—Well, of course, everything depends on what you mean by "together." You are trying to think a *passage*, aren't you? If you are trying to think it as the unity of an experience, then we have a problem; but if you can understand the passage as open-ended, if you can understand the mortal exposure as opening upon (and from) the silent intensities of dying in a way that does not subsume the (non)exposure of the death drive (that "wordless inscription"), then "together" does not have to designate the hold of the concept. It seems to me that the death drive always poses this problem to thought.

—Yes; as you put it, there must also be that (non)exposure of the exposure, a point beyond the specular redoubling. Blanchot's words in the passage I have cited and elsewhere make it clear that there can be no figure for this "body" of the death drive. They help us understand why the *infans* does not appear in the "scene" we are invited to suppose—why it cannot appear.

The last point is important, because we need to underscore the very obvious fact that "the child of seven or eight" who figures in Blanchot's scene cannot be immediately identified with the *infans* of the phrase "a child is being killed." This child of seven or eight, after all, has already entered the order of language and is well underway in his oedipal adventures.

—Are you sure it's a boy?

—Well, that's what I hear in the insistence of the *il*—but it does remain ambiguous. I suppose there are questions to be raised there too (starting with nothing less than that of sexual difference). But for the moment, I want to emphasize the distinction between the "child" of the phrase from Leclaire and *l'enfant* of the passage. And I think we should observe, too, that however arresting Blanchot's scene might be, however much it seems to follow the moving force of the preceding words on Leclaire's title, we nevertheless hear little in it of the *infans* evoked in the prior discussion on Winnicott and Leclaire. Only the strange temporality of the event (an "unexpected joy" that forms an "interminable feature" and is accompanied by an "endless streaming of tears," an "absolute dissolution" [p. 177/115] that is sublimated—is that the word?—in a form of survival [p. 179/116]) suggests to us that the child in the scene has known, again, something like the death of the *infans* as his "own" death. Freud's notion of *Nachträglichkeit*, the delay by which a traumatic event can first be experienced, could help us understand the character of the repetition that is perhaps recorded here. And this would help us honor the devolved title. Blanchot did, after all, borrow the psychoanalytic concept and presumably something of the structure that authors such as Leclaire or Jean Laplanche have brought forth in their readings of that notion.

But there are still problems. Can we say confidently that the *same* child will live in the "secret" as the one who experiences *après coup* the death of the *infans,* if the secret is nothing other than the interruptive saying that is the noncondition of speech and life? Is the one consoled (the child of seven or eight) the *same* as the one who will survive? Or is the subject of that survival not irreducibly some other? If we can identify them (and Blanchot's masculine pronoun also seems to indicate in its insistence a continuity of being of some kind), then perhaps we could generalize from the scene we are reading here and entertain the notion that it is possible to see in certain forms of a child's distress (something that is like a mourning or a melancholy) the trace of a relation to the *infans*. It would be possible to connect *infans* and *infancy*. I must say that I am inclined to this hypothesis, and I would add that if it does not hold, then we have to halt the interchanges between *infans* and child that mark the discussions of both Leclaire and Blanchot. Or we have to recognize that to use the term "infancy" to name a state where there is some relation to the *infans* is also to employ a kind of metaphor, and be prepared to say something like "children also know infancy," or "children are close to infancy."

—I don't have so much trouble with that last phrase, for we should also be able to say: "adults also know infancy." But let me interrupt you just to suggest that this is no small point for our discussion. I too am inclined to think that children, certain children anyway, are close to the *infans*. Have you seen Jacques Doillon's "Ponette"? That film could not have worked as it does were it not for the fact that the very young Victoire Thivisol brought that trait to the camera in scene after scene. I don't believe we could account for her "acting" otherwise. And that could well return us to the question of the imaginary. Remember Blanchot's words in "Two Versions of the Imaginary" concerning the proximity of children to the imaginary? Or think of Freud's comments on the question of play and the compulsion to repeat.

—No, I have to agree, it's no small point. And I don't think I would have undertaken this topic did I not have other experiences of what you are describing in that film. But let me continue the point I was making. The death of the *infans* does not really figure in the scene that we are to suppose. To be sure, the absolute dissolution evokes Narcissus—a figure, Blanchot tells us, who is "very close to the marvelous child, always already dead and nevertheless destined to a fragile dying, of which Serge Leclaire has spoken to us" (WD, p. 193/126). Moreover, the child of seven or eight may not be far, in the boredom of his play-space, from the imaginary dissolution wherein Narcissus founders; he may be entering a space of the imaginary, as Blanchot tries to think it, that is a kind of threshold for the effraction to come. But it seems hardly a matter of chance that Blanchot has so removed the discussion of Narcissus from the earlier commentary on the death of the *infans* (sixty pages or so separate the discussions in the French). For the mythic figure remains just that: too mythic, too much a figure for the passing that must be thought. Blanchot's "scene" can tolerate no more than the trace of this figure, since the dying of the *infans* is ultimately unrepresentable, like the death known(?) by the unconscious under the form of the death drive "for a certain Freud" (WD, p. 182/118–19).

Perhaps the instantaneous passage we are trying to think involves a *kind* of continuity—one that shows a child fading into a dissolution of the imaginary (Narcissus) before the final, unfigurable stage of the *infans* who suffers the death drive. I can't quite find the word for such a "time-lapse" effect of regression in and by the image. Blanchot evokes a continuity in the opposite direction on a few occasions, a continuity of default whereby passivity slips into form. We see an example in *The Writing of the Disaster* regarding forgetting:

> Forgetting would efface that which never was inscribed: the erasure by which the non-written seems to have left a trace that must be obliterated, a slippage that comes to construct for itself an operator by which the subjectless *il* [he—but there is also the *il* of the *il y a*], smooth and without substance, thickens and gets caught up in the divided abyss of the evanescent, simulated I, an imitation of nothing that will congeal in the certain self whence all order returns. (WD, p. 135/85)

How's that for the birth of the subject? The crucial point, in any case, is that the death of the *infans*, at the level we are trying to think it, cannot be brought to any representation or figuration—it is an unfigurable figure. And I think we can appreciate better now the full (im)measure of Blanchot's reflection on this death. For we must think the *syncope* of being that occurs in the writing of the disaster as *both* (a) an interval that *takes bodily* in throes of dying that are no more than a "silent intensity"; and (b) the fold by which a thought comes to itself in its originary response to what calls it and "spells" its knowledge of the *il y a*. We must think a bodily suffering that is immemorial and perhaps irreducible even to the formal unity of a "subjectivity without subject" *together with* the perpetuation or the survival of the relation of responsibility that opens as this interruption. We must think, in effect, a structure of exposure—a writing, let us say—that *perpetuates exposure* both as a reiterated, unsatisfiable exigency, and as the constant presence of an unfigurable material suffering. Perhaps a notion of rhythm could help us think together the body of this interval and the "wave of light" that awakens the body suffering saying. Perhaps rhythm is the true infant figure. But there is no visible or verbal figure that could capture the death of the *infans*. The saying of this death cannot be "said" (or represented) in any mode of signification. Not even a phrase such as "a child is being killed" says this event. Or if it can say it in the mode of a *significance* prior to any representation or signification, the phrase itself remains unpronounceable: "For it is outside consciousness and unconsciousness that the phrase would draw us, each time we would be given, other than ourselves and in a relation of impossibility with the other, to pronounce it, unpronounceable" (WD, p. 117/72).

—Which brings us back to the question of the figural status of "(A Primal Scene?)," since the latter follows immediately upon those last words.

—It's obvious enough that we can't read this liminal "scene" at the end of the sequence on the motif of the *infans* as some form of *illustration* of what has preceded—certainly not after those words. If there is a "miming," as we said earlier, it takes the form of allegory: the secret of the text's saying remains, as the commentators put it, "unsayable" as "narrated," "proferred," or "said." If the saying "figures" in this passage, it does so only in its interrupted character, its arrhythmia (translated, for example, by an odd play of colons). And most importantly, I think, it does so only for one who "supposes" in the manner called for, only for one who supposes the fiction.

Let's return to the opening scene. Its readers/auditors (the French indicates the plural) are invited to receive, to entertain, perhaps even to enact (in a kind of performance) a death that cannot be represented. "Supposition" seems to say all of this, though Blanchot gives us little help with the term in *The Writing of the Disaster* (or elsewhere, to my recollection). I've noticed, though, that he does use the word discreetly on a few occasions. It seems to name both a displacement of the self that is undone by the inscription of the other, and the hypothesis of such an always already sup-posed self (and this is the kind of supposition Heidegger makes, it seems to me, when he speaks of the primordial interpretive act of the *Dasein* . . .).

—That puts a bit of a twist on the "*sujet supposé savoir*," doesn't it?

—Perhaps we'll get back to that. But let me cite two relevant passages. First, in a long statement on the motif of "responsibility," we read:

> For if I can speak of responsibility only by separating it from all the forms of present-consciousness (from will, resolution, interest, light, reflective action; but perhaps also from the non-voluntary, the unconsented, the gratuitous, the unacting, the obscurity that derives from the relation consciousness-unconsciousness), if responsibility is rooted where there is no foundation, where no root can lodge itself, if it cuts across every base and cannot be assumed by anything individual, how then, otherwise than as response to the impossible, and through a relation that forbids me to posit myself or only to pose myself as always already supposed (which delivers me over to the utterly passive) will we sustain

the enigma of what is announced in this term that the language of ordinary morality uses in the most facile way possible by putting it into the service of order? (WD, p. 46/26)

We could pause over the question of who is to do the posing, but I think we can presume that Blanchot is not falling back into the metaphysics of subjectivity by positing some self-positing in the structure of passivity or responsibility. We could also speculate on the elided verb that enables the posing (the French reads: "par un rapport qui m'interdit de me poser moi-même, mais seulement de me poser comme toujours déjà supposé"), but I think the meaning is more or less clear. And then the second passage (WD, p. 50/28) brings home the point that this posing must itself be a "supposing." It's dense—shall I go ahead and read it?

—If you want to. But it seems to me that these two references to a supposition don't quite capture what is called for in the scene we are trying to read. Shouldn't we understand the voice as saying something like "imagine, imagine this"—and as calling, in that repetition, to an act of fictioning? The voice itself is already presupposing some relation to the scene that is offered, some receptivity, perhaps some responsibility on the ground of the fact that the ones addressed are said to live "close to a heart that no longer beats." Already something of the scene is set. But if the "non-event" cannot be represented, then the supposition to which the readers/auditors are called would seem to involve something more; it cannot be a simple spectating. Aren't they called to *suppose* the non-event, beyond the description, so to speak? Aren't they called to at least the patience and forgetting Blanchot attributes to the act of writing? He evokes such a writing at the very opening of the sequence on the death of the *infans*, after all.

—I believe you are right. Those who answer the interpellation are enjoined to a form of reading/listening, a form of reception that is beyond mere "entertainment"—be it of a hypothesis or a fiction. You raised the question earlier as to whether I was taking the "fiction" a little too seriously. I can't *justify* this response, but it does seem to me that with the motif of "supposition" Blanchot is appealing to the possibility of a *fictive engagement of responsibility*, by which I mean the possibility of a relation with the non-event "recounted" in the scene. "Supposition" would name, yes, an engagement of that writing to which he refers at the very outset of the pages he devotes to the death of the *infans*:

To write is not to place in the future the death that is always already past, but to accept suffering it without making it present and making oneself present to it; it is to know that it has taken place, though it has not been experienced, and to recognize it in the forgetting it leaves, a forgetting whose fading traces call upon one to *except oneself from the cosmic order*, there where the disaster renders the real impossible and desire undesirable. (WD, pp. 108–9/66)

If supposition is such a writing, then it indicates a different relation to the fiction than any "literalization" of the figure. It is more like an engagement of the imaginary in the sense that Blanchot develops in "Literature and the Right to Death." "Supposing" the child, we enter the space of the infant figure, a space of the imaginary that must have opened if there is to be any speech and life, and that *is there* inasmuch as we live "close to a heart that no longer beats."

—But there's the *infans*, isn't it, already posited in its death before the scene we are asked to suppose? One could almost miss it in its enigmatic, furtive appearance in that first line.

—I don't know if we can identify it so quickly—that's not the only appearance of an arrested heart in Blanchot. I think I would say rather that the figure of a death marks the *site* of the infans. But nothing, in any case, allows us to identify in an immediate manner the one whose heart has stopped and the one who survives the *jouissance* of its mortal exposure: the subject of the last lines of the "scene." Indeed that gap interrupts the figurative coherence of the scene in an irremediable manner—*alters* it somehow (Blanchot sometimes speaks of a kind of torsion in space—that would be the case here). The most we can say, perhaps, is that the "supposition" to which we are enjoined asks us to join in some way the effaced other—the other of the heart that no longer beats— via the space/time of the *récit* and under the unappearing guise of the one who survives.

But that vague "join" may be too much. I believe we must in fact think "supposition" here as repetition (a kind of "resuscitating" repetition) and avoid positing any simple continuity between the dead *infans* of that first line and the one who "survives." Perhaps the "infant figure" as it is supposed in this scene unfolds only in the unbridgeable distance—the proximity—of the non-relation between the one who is asked to suppose and the anonymous other. There is a fragment where Blanchot names the other—the one who does not accompany —"the non-concerning":

The non-concerning (in the sense that the one—I—and the other cannot hold together, or come together in one and the same time—be contemporaneous) is first of all *autrui* for me, then I as other than myself, what in me does not coincide with me, my eternal absence, what no consciousness can recover, what has neither effect nor efficacy, and which is passive time, the dying that I have in common, without sharing, with all. (WD, p. 42/23)

What I am proposing is that the fictive supposition to which we are enjoined represents a kind of "measuring" of a distance that can never be fully bridged.

—To which *we* are enjoined? I've followed you thus far, but now I must ask: Who exactly is it that is supposed to live "close" to that heart that no longer beats? Is this interpellation supposed to concern *me*? Perhaps the line is informing me of a relation we would normally ignore as conscious subjects (the non-concerning relation described in the passage you just read). Perhaps any reader is supposed to find a place in that address and suddenly becomes the one called. Or perhaps it calls another who lives closer to the *infans*. But who's to say? I can't help wondering whether I belong here at all.

And why are you smiling now?

—I was just remembering the opening dialogue/récit from *The Infinite Conversation*. It's about the non-concerning, among other things, and about the unavoidable need to assume the event in common, or as more than one (since there is no *common* ground and it cannot be shared). One of the interlocutors plays the straight man, while the other speaks from a relation to the event that he cannot quite define. I was beginning to wonder if we were gradually assuming our places in something already scripted. Mind you, I can't claim the other role—the part of the one who also knows an arrest of the heart. I too feel like the straight man.

—All the usual puns allowed, I'm sure. But my question stands: Who is the text's addressee? What, in "us," is addressed?

—I was going to suggest the following. I don't know how to express this exactly, but I think that the initial address has a kind of arresting effect in its strangeness—that in the suspension of that arrest the fictioning has somehow already begun, the space already opened. I don't know—I can't justify that impression. There's something about that mode of address. But the same should perhaps be said of our conversation—that there's no warrant for the positions we're occupying. That's my second thought, and perhaps my real reason for smiling. Nothing legitimates our words or even the fact of our exchange, our "factitious" exchange—beyond the need for it, which both of us seem to feel clearly enough. But I don't mean to be complacent about that situation, just as I don't know how to be quite "responsible" for it. We're back to the question about taking the fiction "seriously." But the question has spread now to the bases of our own exchange and any attempt to engage the alterity that is the death in the other or in ourselves.

—We've also reached the last of the questions from which we started: "For whom is the exigency?"

Let me try to recoup. We've covered a lot of ground, and I'm not fully sure where we stand now. You started with the "speculative" assertion (predicated, as I understand it, on a rather severe notion of the finitude of Being and human being) that language cannot but (not) say the "usage" of the human from which it proceeds, the mortal exposure that you take to be figured by the death of the *infans.* You added, I believe, that a subject cannot speak without this "experience" with language (before phenomenological experience) that is also a knowledge of the *il y a;* that such a transcendence must have opened if there is to be anything like thought and anything like language as we know it, the use of an "is." And you entertained Blanchot's assertion that this experience before experience must be figured in psychic life, that some figuration attends the trace of the experience and that the *necessity* of this figuration constitutes at least the opening of an imaginary, the space of the infant figure. From that basis, you've proposed that a fictive "supposition" might engage, in repetition, the encounter that lies in that exposure that language "cannot but (not) say." Now, I understand that there's no *demonstrating* that such a repetition has any purchase on the real of the death we are trying to think; and as regards the scene we have been reading, nothing guarantees its authenticity. But still, it seems to me you've made a very significant step in entertaining the possibility of a fictive "supposition." For even if we remain in the realm of the imaginary . . .

—"Even" is too restrictive since it connotes the usual divorce of fiction and reality. The imaginary, as Blanchot thinks it, opens with language itself as a constitutive part of its possibility.

—OK, but my point is that with this notion of supposition you have posited the possibility of responding in some way to that prior response to and for the "impossible" that Blanchot and Levinas name "responsibility." You spoke near the outset of "the exigency of another relation." Isn't supposition such a relation, isn't it a form of "response" and "responsibility" on the part of one who reads and writes?

—I certainly didn't say it better. But I admit that with this question of responsibility I grow a little uncomfortable. I fear that the word says too much, or assumes too quickly the relation we are considering now: the supposed relation between an "us" and the anonymous other. It's awfully hard to remember that the so-called responsibility cannot be translated into anything we normally understand by that term in a political or ethical context. And thus it's all too easy to bridge the impossible relation and thereby give everything away in perfect conscience and with no small measure of satisfaction. Blanchot himself puts it categorically. If responsibility is as he has described (involving the exigency of another relation, infinite passivity, etc.), then: "I can certainly call it responsibility, but only abusively, and just as well by its contrary . . . just as, declared responsible for dying (all dying), I can no longer appeal to any ethics, any experience, any practice, whatever it might be—save that of some counter-living, which is to say, some non-practice, which is to say (perhaps) a speech of writing" (WD 46–47/26)). From this basis, Blanchot will evoke the (ultimately untenable) necessity of two languages: the one a language of responsibility in a more traditional sense (and I think his commitment to this discourse cannot be questioned), the other infinitely more uncertain and always "indirect" as regards the exigencies of social justice—a language "that we speak without justification . . . never written, but always to be prescribed" (WD, p. 47/26), and which, in its "supposed extremity" (WD, p. 126/79), opens momentarily onto another relation. But the distinction always breaks down, the language of the concept always undermined by an "imaginary" dimension it cannot be rid of, the "other" language always afflicted by a "becoming-concept" that is fueled by a thoroughly justified "political impatience" to which he alludes at the start of the passage I just cited. The "affliction" to which he refers—the need to answer to immediate ethico-political imperatives—will inevitably lead us to cheat with the word "responsibility."

—But if anything we have supposed regarding the structure of exposure claims our adhesion, then we must also recognize another "immediate ethico-political imperative" in the necessity of responding to the saying that is the gift of that mortal exposure. "The exigency of another relation" comes im-mediately in the saying itself. If we understand that this latter saying also involves relation to the other, to *autrui*, then I have no trouble with this word, "responsibility." I fully accept the idea that any definition of responsibility in the usual political or ethical sense *proceeds* from that more original relation as from its an-archic ground; if we forget that "prior" responsibility, then we are left with ideology (however compelling it might be).

—"Supposition" remains a tenuous measuring of the relation without relation.

—We've been concentrating on a mode of fiction in an effort to read "(A primal scene?)," but we haven't *restricted* supposition to fiction, have we? When we read about responsibility and the "pre-scription" of another language in which that term might have meaning, I assumed that prescription and supposition were related. In each case, there would be a "futural" casting of a relation to the immemorial—"futural," but without a future in the sense of a projected temporality, since the other will never come to an appointed meeting (at least we can't count on it). I have understood that what is at stake in the fictive supposition we are entertaining is the always uncertain possibility of a relation to the real of the mortal exposure. I don't see why the "writing" in question can only be "fictive"—why an engagement can't unfold in a language that might be considered more one of thought. Of course, we should remember that there are any number of material practices of engagement— there is no reason whatsoever to presume that only a linguistic or artistic practice can engage the "im-memorial im-mediate." And perhaps we should pause to consider whether these practices too involve some form of "supposition," at least in their manner of opening to the other (I think, for example, of Avital Ronell's work on "*politesse*," or Sue Golding's on the technologies of otherness). But if we hold only to the question of thinking and giving testimony to the relation, then it seems to me that we must entertain other modes of supposition.

—I agree, and I'm sure I won't surprise you if I hark back to Heidegger. I alluded earlier to a form of sup-position in the existential analytic. There is a lot left to say about the writing of *Being and Time*, the performative character of that text. But I think more, in this context, of the later meditations on language. In *On the Way to Language*, he suggests—and he performs the suggestion—that only a mode of "presumption" (his term is *Vermutung*—my translation emphasizes the dimension of daring), only a mode of presumption can bring thought to language in such a way as to engage that origin that is the relation of thought and language. What is "presumed" in those texts is in fact a relation between thought and poetry, but that doesn't make the presumption "poetic" or "literary." For Heidegger, it seems, there is a "supposition" proper to thought that is undoubtedly close to poetic "daring" (as in Rilke), but nevertheless specific in character. Following Heidegger, I believe, we may presume that there are multiple paths of "responsible" engagement, because language itself is multiple in its paths. And we may presume, I think, that they are always singular (there is no "supposition" in general, no "presumption" in general: there are singular acts of supposition, presumption, etc.). But I think that this question of supposition demands much broader treatment. *I think it's demanded of us.* Our question earlier was: For whom is the exigency? The answer lies in this problematic: it is the one who "supposes" responsibility, the one who performs the supposition without the comfort of any grounds.

—Is the speculative construction of the topic of the *infans* such a supposition?

—I'm certainly not ready to proclaim this the writing of another language. For the most part, we're still at the level of commentary. And yet . . . If what I started to say earlier about the "ethical" character of the kind of research we are undertaking has any purchase, then I think this research also participates in the "supposition" to which you were pointing—at however many removes from a textual event like the one we witness in *On the Way to Language.* I want to come back to this as we approach Lacan. But perhaps we should pause, since we're about to leave Blanchot's scene.

—Before we leave it, may I ask one last question? You said earlier that Blanchot does not seem to draw everything from Leclaire that he might have. To what did you refer?

—That's hardly a small question, but it may be a good point of transition. It's in relation to Leclaire, you remember, that Blanchot voices his reticence regarding psychoanalytic theory: his reticence concerning its properly theoretical dimension, and then his respect for a language whose meaning ultimately cannot be divorced from the risk of its practice. I believe Blanchot is especially sensitive, in this respect, to Leclaire's own reticence regarding his devotion to the concept. The latter part of *On tue un enfant* contains some very beautiful pages on his reason for being a psychoanalyst, on love and transference, and on the psychoanalyst's relation to the *infans* in a psychoanalytic situation. He is quite clear about the traps of institutionality (linguistic or professional) that menace a vital relation to what we are attempting to think with this figure of the *infans,* and I am sure that he would not object, in this very respect, to my reservations about his appeal to the concept of the phallus throughout his volume. But let me cite his own words. His reason for being a psychoanalyst, he says—you'll like this, I think—may be formulated at this point "as an interest in the origin of speech (castration, primal scene, death drive)." Whatever conceptual labor he may produce, he says, from Oedipal schema to Lacanian algorithm,

> I remain an analyst only insofar as I listen to the analysand from that breach through which speech and the space of desire are born and reborn ceaselessly. It is only in this place that the syncopated voice of the subject can make itself heard and in which the singularity of the "primal scene" of the analysand can be said: his "origin," that is to say, the particular modalities of his capture in the order of words, the singular arrangement of his relation to the silences of the first objects. (p. 99)

And what is that breach? It is a place of exposure that I would compare (though again . . .) to the one we have tried to think via Blanchot's notion of saying. Leclaire theorizes it, as you may glimpse in these words, as the gap of desire, that separation from the signifier (in Lacan's sense of this term: what Leclaire terms the "représentant inconscient") wherein the subject relates to the cause of its desire. There is no "speech" of desire but for the subject's relation to the order of unconscious signifiers, but desire, when it "speaks," engages the subject's transcendence of this order in its relation to the object (a) of its desire. The subject speaks only to fade, but it speaks of an order that exceeds the hold of the signifier and engages the body. The child, in Leclaire's presentation (throughout most of it, that is) is an "unconscious representative," a pre-eminent one: the primary narcissistic representation focalizing the desires that constitute the subject's heritage. This child must be killed as the condition of any speech in the "true" sense, for any strict conformity of desire to the unconscious heritage is an effective silencing, a death of another kind. If the psychoanalyst encounters so many fantasms of the order of "a child is being killed," it is because desire, under the impulsion of the death drive (which in Leclaire's presentation is nothing other than the subject's response to the dark imperatives of the phallic reference), seeks to destroy the tyrannical hold of the figure of the *infans*. When Leclaire suggests that the impossible necessary death is required for speech and life, he means a speech and life that would find some measure of freedom in relation to its own origin and over against the order of the symbolic (as governed by societal structures); a speech and life that would find another relation to the *infans*, namely one that would assume the castration that the "marvelous child" occludes in its tyrannical, imaginary figuration. The child must die, in other words, if we are to recover access to a speech that engages the object.

We are far from Blanchot here. Never mind the insistent reference to the phallus, which seems to contain the an-archic possibilities of his words. . . .

—Never mind?

—Well, I do of course. I am willing to entertain some of these logical formulations (out of respect for mathematics). But the deifying references to this supposed principle of order, this "extreme transparency" (cf. p. 91), coupled as they are with a classic account of the discovery of that little difference between boys and girls, leaves me wondering what is being protected. Does the phallus perhaps close the breach that Blanchot attempts to think with the *il y a*? Does it help order the death drive itself into a kind of phallic economy? Compare Blanchot's account of the death drive with Leclaire's; consider the *unworking* Blanchot tries to think in his account of those "poussées du mourir." And that brings me to precisely the point I wanted to make. The child, in Leclaire's account, the *primary unconscious representative*, must be destroyed or murdered inasmuch as it represents an obstacle to any "true" speech of the subject of desire (something close, as I have suggested, to what Blanchot names "saying"). Blanchot seems to allow for such a construction (he cites Leclaire on this point without pausing to qualify), but the child that must die in his account is another. The *infans* whose passing is required for speech and life is the one who "is" only in the exposure of that saying. Blanchot's child is the one who suffers endlessly the unworking of the death drive. How different from Leclaire's account, where the death drive names the difference at work in the signifying order to which the child belongs as one of the first signifiers and preeminent representatives of the phallus.

And yet, in the pages on transference and love to which I have referred, another figure of the *infans* appears. I'll cite at some length, because these words touch in their way the resonance I have heard between "a child is being killed," as Blanchot evokes it, and "Father, don't you see I'm burning?" from the dream read by Lacan. I've just discovered these words, but I believe they say something of what has brought me to this question of the infant figure—my reason for being here, if you will. The context is a discussion of Leclaire's relation with an analysand who is also an analyst (too appropriately named "Sygne"). His topic is the relation of love and transference, and a frank admission of his (necessary) involvement in his analysand's perspicacious deciphering of the indices of his own fantasmatic life:

It is in my oedipal age that she would have wanted to know me; before the image of me at four which she has reconstructed and projects, I cannot *resist*. Letting the last shards of my doctoral respectability fall to the ground, I rediscover, in a smile without a mask, the seriousness of that age where one understands avidly what it is to desire out of love and what it is to suffer. Through that smile, whether it is brightening the eye or the voice, there opens another ear to which there can finally be said, before the pathetic mode, and in a voice of truth, the affliction of being, of being born, from never anything but nothing. Between two traits, two words, what says not a word—*infans*, rather than adorable cherubin—gives a *place*, finally, to what could not be said. That is where the transfer takes form. Sygne says it figuratively: your smile on your face, my pain on your face, your pain on my face, my smile on my face.

I don't believe in the neutralizing illusion of the impassive mask, and I find no need to defend myself in this regard from what might be imputed to me in the way of seduction. Analytic listening passes by way of the putting into play of this point of silence that constitutes the site of the transference; what is given there is the space of a *real* act of intelligence regarding the logic of exclusion, the space for a passage beyond the weave of representatives, a path for traversing the mirror. Presence, goodness, neutrality, the silence of the analyst; all of these are inadequate or approximate ways to mark this point of non-resistance which the psychoanalysis of the analyst must confront him/her with *sans retour*. Whether we call it, paradoxically, a becoming conscious, whether we describe it as the advent of the subject or as recognition of castration, what is absolutely to be required of an analyst is that he or she have the experience of *what speaking means*. (pp. 96–97)

I could go on with Leclaire's words regarding the necessity of perpetrating, from this point of exposure or "non-resistance," the "murder" of the "word-image," of undermining the unconscious signifier, but I do not want to stray too far from Leclaire's reference to the appearance of the *infans* that lies *beyond* the "oedipal" image of the child of four and who speaks from the opening of a smile, in a voice or a gaze, saying without saying the affliction of being "from never any more than nothing." The child's desire and suffering, regiven in a loving address, are like a conduit, a place of passage, on whose threshold appears the *infans*; no more than the spectral figuration of the very site of speech (before "language," before signified meaning): the ghostly, the angelic trace of a constantly re-born, constantly dying engagement with language. That this opening comes *in relation*, in the absolute non-resistance of love (Blanchot would speak of passivity, weakness, or fatigue; Haver has spoken recently of vulnerability in the erotic relation), reminds us again that the opening in question touches the ground of sociality and can perhaps *only* be thought from that relationality (even the solitary act of writing would proceed from a touch . . .). The psychoanalyst's "acte d'intelligence réelle"—I only wish I could translate that phrase: it says so beautifully a *thinking usage*—is fundamentally an act of engagement with the presence of the human (or with whatever might suffer the signifier, to use Lacan's expression), the alterity of the other. It is the only "real" act of thought, wherever it occurs.

—I wonder if you are not going too far. Must all thought engage the "origin," must all thought touch the ethical or the "ethico-political"—that site of exposure and what is known there (even unto the death drive)?

—Perhaps I am going too far. But I would say that any "science" that does not in some way confront *what it means to speak* is less than science.

—Perhaps every science is less than science.

—There's a comforting formula.

II

When he stirred again (the smoke having long since ceased to rise from the ash-
tray poised on the arm of his chair), I proposed we consider adjourning. It was to
acknowledge what I took to be fatigue, but I also wanted to reflect on our conver-
sation, record something of it while it was still fresh in my mind. I knew how
much would be lost as the day reclaimed its rights. I mumbled something about
that loss: its inevitability, the tricks it had played on us. I think I even tried to say
something about an honorable acceptance of that loss—that it stemmed from the
object itself (not an object, but a relation, an engagement). Sure we had trouble
remembering our advances, and sometimes even our very topic. But that proved
the worth of our undertaking! Didn't loss, even a certain futility, prove the well-
founded character of our assumptions?

I offered those words to his irony, but he left them aside. He made a gesture with
his hand that effectively cleared the space, and then pronounced words that were
visibly a quotation. The French startled me less than the ambiguity of the address.

Puisqu'il faut
Que dis-tu là—
Ne m'interromps point

Do you know Mallarmé's poem on the death of his son Anatole? I was recalled
to it recently by a critical analysis proposed by Luc Kinsch. Here is Auster's
translation of those lines:

Since it is *necessary*
What are you saying there—
do not interrupt me—(p. 95)

I think I would have tried to use "must." In any case, Mallarmé has his own exigencies, doesn't he? But I believe I hear a guilt in the need to record—stage—

those words, a guilt stemming from an irritation that involves something more than the clamor of a grim form of the everyday, be it in the form of a mother's preoccupation or the child's feverish agitation—something more even than a life that persists despite the father's effort to write a sentence for death. What is it that interrupts his efforts at burial? What is it if not more or less what Blanchot suggested from the very start of his critical work concerning Mallarmé's encounter with a death that is the impossibility of dying?

I find it especially striking that when Mallarmé attempts to write the tomb for Anatole, he seems to presume that the relation is entirely *his* task; for the burden of that terrible event, as he understands it, lies in the fact that Anatole does not know his death. The very character of the void confronted by Mallarmé seems to inhere in the child's lack of relation to his own death.

sentir éclater	to feel it burst
{le vi} en nuit	{the vo} in the night
le vide immense	the immense void
produit par ce	produced by what
qui serait sa *vie*	would be his *life*
—parce qu'il ne	—because he does not
le *sait* pas—	*know* it-
qu'il est mort	that he is dead
éclair?	lightning?
crise	attack
douleur	pain (p. 31)

"Vent de *rien / qui souffle*" ("Wind of *nothing / that breathes*" [p. 59]), this death. A flash. Mallarmé blames himself for it ("ainsi c'est moi / mains maudites" (thus it is me / cursed hands) [p. 25]), but also assumes responsibility for its spiritual enactment. He will even occupy the tomb with him. For Mallarmé, this idealizing is the *father's* role, it seems ("mère a saigné et pleuré / père sacrifie et divinise" (mother has bled and wept / father sacrifices—and deifies) [p. 154]). It is not without its poignancy, this task, and at moments Mallarmé seems even loath to accomplish it—loath to accomplish the "necessary death," as he understands it, for it means nothing less than the death of the figure, the transmutation of the traces of destruction into an ideal, the child's "being":

que veux-tu, douce	what do you want, sweet
vision adorée—	adored vision—
qui viens souvent	who often come

vers moi—te	towards me and lean
pencher—comme	over—as if
écouter secret [de	to listen to secret [of
mes larmes]—	my tears]—
savoir que tu es	to know that you are
mort	dead
—ce que tu ignores?	—what you do not know?
—non je ne	—no I will not
te le dirais	tell it
pas—car alors tu	to you—for then you
disparaîtrais	would disappear (149–50)
vision	vision
sans cesse épurée	endlessly purified
par mes larmes	by my tears (151)

But despite such hesitations, or even the interruption (which, if it is by Anatole, could well derive from the child's sense of the father's reserve and even expresses a fear of abandonment), Mallarmé's purpose is clear: he will *accomplish* his son's death (perhaps give him his name through those tears?). The presumption is extraordinary. What are the conditions of his assumption concerning the child's knowledge of his impending death or even mortality in general? Not to speak of what the child may know of another death. In any case, it is clear that the fatherly duty, as Mallarmé conceives of it, falls short of another responsibility. If Mallarmé is to "accomplish" the other's death for him, he cannot avoid responsibility for the death of the *infans*. Wasn't that the implication of what we were saying—that one cannot think the one (one cannot *think*) without remarking a relation to the other? In any case, I suspect, once again, that he was driven to accomplish the speculative task as he understood it precisely because of his relation to the death of the *infans*, a dying which he cannot dissociate from the child's agony, even if he denies to Anatole any knowledge of his impending death. He heard something in the child's suffering that doomed his undertaking from the outset.

—You're prompting me to look back at any number of scenes representing the death of a child. Mallarmé has his own obsessions, of course, but is it possible that questions like the ones you're asking are applicable in any scene involving such a death? After all, we all know the death of the *infans*, at some level. Is that "knowledge" an essential part of the overpowering force of some of those scenes? Think of Goethe's "Erlkönig," for example. What is speaking to us there? I'm sure that some would consider this theme of the death of the *infans* to be no more than a mere metaphor—even, possibly, an offensive one in relation to the actual event (though it's not clear what "metaphor" means here if we are talking about the infant figure and the very birth of the possibility of the proper). Lawrence Lerner's recent and, I gather, quite successful *Angels and Absences: Child Death in the Nineteenth Century* will give us some idea of what to expect in this area: a treatment of theoretical issues so uninformed as to express disdain (and no mention of Mallarmé, by the way). But I don't want to dwell on what is invested in such an attitude. I would simply say that if there is anything legitimate in the link between death and language that Hegel established for us, then I believe we have the grounds to pursue this problematic of the *infans* throughout the vast literature devoted to the death of children, and that such a reading would be "responsible" in the deepest senses of the term. I'm sure I don't need to add that it could not possibly be a matter of *reducing* that literature to the problematic in question. But I must also acknowledge that I am a long way from taking the full measure of the literature involved. Has anyone defined the scope of this genre? Is it a matter of a genre?—so vast a body of references. And then there is the question of sexual difference that we glimpsed already in Mallarmé; Gisela Brinker-Gabler mentioned to me that German women gained access to literature in the early seventeenth century via an "occasional" form, a *Gebrauchsliteratur*—"Gebrauchs*literatur!*—that frequently involved poems to accompany the burial of children.

—There's not just literature—think, for example, of Gustav Mahler's *Kindertotenlieder*, another common reference. I don't see why we couldn't look to each of the arts, even photography, for the trace of the *infans*; every art potentially goes to that unrepresentable "origin" of language that is the site of the figure of the *infans*. But our scope still may be too limited—so many massacres of innocents have been commemorated in art and ritual.

—But to narrow the focus again, and to return to my first example, Goethe's "Erlkönig" (almost the standard one today): I'm especially struck, where the question of the *infans* is concerned, by the haunting force of those texts that give expression in some way to the child's experience. Take the poignancy of the address in Goethe's poem, or the presence of that poignancy in Mallarmé's fragments—in each case, there is a vain appeal to the parent. How do you account for the force of that appeal? Is it the prosopopoeia, the way a voice is given to the dying of the other, and the responsibility that speaking engages?

—The death of the *infans* is always the death of an other. As you have been speaking, I've been recalling pages from Paul de Man's "The Rhetoric of Temporality," pages on Wordsworth's "Lucy Gray" poems that I read many years ago. His reading is powerful in many respects, but I believe that what has most haunted me is his observation that Wordsworth could actually have been writing about his own death. I'll pass over what de Man means by "death" here (the fact is, it doesn't seem to be much of a problem for him—not enough of a problem, that is). His point is that the "allegorical" character of the poem he cites resides in the disjunction between the temporality engendered by the language of the poem and that of subjective experience; the former temporality allows us to suspend the question of the actual identity of the one who has died. De Man's point is a logical one; it's not based on empirical proof of any kind. But to introduce it, he appeals to philological evidence. This is where we find the words that I recalled just now:

> Wordsworth is one of the few poets who can write proleptically about their own death and speak, as it were, from beyond their own graves. The "she" in the poem is in fact large enough to encompass Wordsworth as well. More important than the otherness of the dead person is the seemingly obvious fact that the poem describes the demystification as a temporal sequence. (p. 225)

Wordsworth's poem is *about* a failure to hear or see the other (or something of the self), about a waking sleep that closes off relation. So it would be especially inappropriate to press too heavily a point outside of de Man's purpose. Above all, I don't want to fall into the usual complaint about his appeal to what I have termed a logic, a complaint about what we might call, with a more positive tonality, de Man's sobriety. The question deserves far more space. But it remains true that I have never forgotten these lines, and my question is: just how much less important is the otherness of the dead person for the allegory in question? I wholly accept de Man's argument as far as it goes; but I wonder if he hasn't foreclosed a dimension of his problematic? Let us think of Anatole's death. Is Anatole's death really the "origin" of the Mallarméan meditation (in the sense that we could say that Mallarmé truly writes in response), and if so, in what ways? I don't think the question is an easy one, despite our immediate moral assumptions and even common sense—it's especially difficult, in any case, where the *infans* is involved. In evoking the notion of "responsibility," Blanchot, for his part, does not seem to distinguish the death of the other from the death "in us." Of course, he also suggests that we have no relation to the death "in" us, the "other death," except by way of our relation to *autrui*—that there is no responsibility, ultimately, except in relation to *autrui*. I'm not sure he really resolves the question for himself, but I believe that that anonymity of the *infans*, or the impersonality of "a child is being killed," has to do with the fact that the distinction is impossible, and that the child is in fact always "in us" as soon as we speak. That death, as we saw, is the condition of speech and life.

But this brings me to the other scene to which I have been referring—that dream of the burning child recorded by Freud in *The Interpretation of Dreams*, which Lacan calls before us so unforgettably in *The Four Fundamental Concepts*. Cathy Caruth finds in Lacan's discussion powerful testimony to the address of the other as *autrui*, and I'd like to try to approach Lacan's text with that argument in mind.

—Before you begin: Is there any link between these texts, Blanchot's and Lacan's? And while you're at it, didn't Lacan write *The Four Fundamental Concepts* around the time Jean-Pierre Richard was preparing to publish his edition of Mallarmé's notes to his unfinished poem?

—There's an interesting coincidence there, but I think the answer could do little more than satisfy our curiosity. Hasn't the point of thinking the death of the *infans* as a kind of structural necessity "for speech and life," a "quasi-transcendental," been precisely to acknowledge the *fundamental* character of the questions we are addressing? Isn't that what interests us in each of the texts, whatever their relation? But to answer your first question, at least, let me say simply that I find it unlikely that Blanchot was unaware of Lacan's discussion (which dates from 1964) when he wrote *The Writing of the Disaster*. As I've said, the latter volume may be read in part as an engagement with psychoanalysis, and Blanchot had already published comments on Lacan when he began writing it (though Lacan's name is not mentioned, if I'm not mistaken). But we can also turn things around. When Lacan introduces the motif of the unconscious, he addresses the gap it manifests—a gap, he says, in which "something happens" ("il se passe quelque chose" [p. 25/22]), or "something comes about" ("se produit"—in the full sense of the term, he adds [p. 27/25]), something that is of the order of the "non-realized," waiting in the realm of the "non-born." (Of repression, he says in this context: "it's the abortionist's relation to limbo" [p. 23]). He speaks also of the way the unconscious "knocks" or "strikes" us first of all ("frappe d'abord"—and that would be from Mallarmé's preface to *Un coup de dès*: a reference to the problematic of chance or *tuché*, not to speak of generations and dying children) and of the way in which what presents itself in the "gap" presents itself as a rediscovery, and always in withdrawal. The analyst's relation to the subject of desire in its movement of *significance*, he says, is the relation of Orpheus to Eurydice. I cannot but hear Blanchot there; and Eurydice, I might note, is not without relation to what Blanchot means by the *infans*. So if we must speak of influence, we could perhaps say that Lacan brings the motif of the child to Blanchot *après coup*.

Still, I am as wary of this kind of speculation on sources as I am of any attempt to *synthesize* the scenes we are examining or translate them into some theoretical statement. A theoretical presentation that would attempt to read Blanchot from Lacan or Lacan from Blanchot would lose precisely what is at stake, whatever it is that lies in the resonance of those two phrases ("a child is being killed," and "Father, don't you see I'm burning?") as they are brought to sound in the respective texts. The task, it seems to me, is not to translate, but rather to "supplement" (in Benjamin's sense of this term when he talks about the relation between translation and original), and to honor thereby the gap between.

—And then there's Freud's "A Child Is Being Beaten." Forgive me for perpetuating the interruption, but I'm surprised you haven't alluded to that text yet. Could it be one of the subtexts for these meditations on the "deaths" of the child?

—It is certainly difficult not to hear the phrase (or phrases) from Freud's text behind Leclaire's title, and I wouldn't exclude a connection with the phrase from the dream, however differently it's structured. (Definitely not on the grounds that the latter appears in a dream; as Laplanche and Pontalis point out in their famous essay, "Fantasme originaire, fantasme des origines, origine du fantasme," dreams and material from diurnal fantasies may themselves bear the stamp of the "originary.") But I've hesitated to appeal to Freud's essay because I don't know how to avoid a full engagement of the psychoanalytic apparatus in which it is embedded. A proper discussion of it, I think, would require an entire rethinking of the sketchy summaries offered by Freud, who gives us more "conclusions" than material. For a start, however, I suppose we could draw on the masterful reading of the text that Jean-François Lyotard proposed in *Discours, figure*—all the more so as I'm in full sympathy with his guiding assumptions and conclusions. His aim, in that book, is to demonstrate that the fantasm partakes of what he calls the "figural" in that it cannot be reduced to any structural or formal articulation, any logic that would either ground it or reveal it as a ground. He wants to show a difference at work that is incommensurable with any signifying order. Therefore, he argues that the fantasm has the character of a "matrix" (he speaks of a "figure matrice") rather than a structure, and that in its most "original" formations it points to an absence of origin for the psyche. An "infant figure," I believe he would say, can only be a hallucinatory "figure-image" that would unfold in this "initial non-site" (p. 271). There is quite a bit here that is pertinent for our discussion, in fact—especially his demonstration that the masochistic regression involved in the most originary configuration of the beating scene leads to a "position of *significance*" (which I take to be what he calls "a relation of the subject to the signifier" [p. 345]) that is without any specular redoubling; the subject does not see itself seeing as it does in the two other stages of the scene, which lend themselves to verbalization. The most "primal" scene in this fantasm is not available to linguistic figuration ("I am beaten by the father" is entirely Freud's construction, not something enunciated by the subject). Its phrasing is not available, has never been; indeed, it involves a veritable "desubjectivization" since it is impossible to fix the subject's place in the syntax of the scene—it cannot be located in any of the possible positions (father, child, beating, being beaten). "Desubjectivization" is the term proposed by Laplanche and Pontalis (p. 1868). Lyotard speaks of a subject that is dispersed in "incompossible" points of insertion (thus the space of the scene must itself be understood as multiple, distended). Wouldn't this dis-integration of the subject at the most originary level of the fantasm inflect our earlier discussion of the unfigurable character of the "subject" that suffers the death drive, and hence oblige us to rethink the limits of the "specular" character of the scene? Doesn't it remind us that if we attempt to think together the im-memorial suffering of the death drive and the accession to the day that is "survival" (as the condition of thinking the "communicability" of responsibility), then we must think the exposure as truly open-ended? Lyotard, recognizing the extreme difficulty of this exigency, speaks in his own context of a formal unity that is attributable to the figural matrix; but he also demonstrates clearly that this "form of transgression" (in regard to the order of discourse) is also a transgression of form: the "rhythm" of the fantasm of beating is marked by an arrhythmia.

But let me refer you directly to those pages near the end of *Discours, figure*. To say any more, I would have to take up the psychoanalytic apparatus that Lyotard assumes without significant hesitation. I'm grateful! He did the psychoanalytic work for us by analyzing the "vicissitudes" of the fantasmatic construction (the stages of the fantasm) in relation to those of the multiple drives they articulate. The only thing I would want to do is follow some of the paths he indicated (but didn't take) in the direction of a primary masochism. But he leaves off at precisely the point where the psychoanalytic vocabulary reaches its limit, and I believe that limit is where I want to try to work. That sounds more pretentious than it should, because I only mean to suggest that the questions we've been raising are more philosophical than psychoanalytic (though I would have to say that Lyotard undertakes a *thinking* engagement with psychoanalysis that effectively carries him to the same place; as does Leclaire, in fact, when he says that his aim is to address the question of what it means to speak). Lyotard remarks that he does not want to raise the question of the origin of the "originary fantasm." In this, he follows (and cites) Laplanche and Pontalis, who raise the question but do not pretend to answer it. They note, for example, that Freud's "phylogenetic" speculations point to an attempt to think a structural component in the fantasm that exceeds any empirically determined articulation even as they emphasize, as does Lacan, Freud's search for a grounding in experience, a "real" behind the fantasm. They implicitly acknowledge that the primal fantasm has something of a "quasi-transcendental" character:

> Prior to the subject's history, but nevertheless in history, discourse and symbolic chain, but impregnated with imaginary elements, a structure but organized on the basis of contingent components, the originary fantasm is first of all a fantasm and as such it is marked by certain traits that make it hard to assimilate to a pure transcendental schema, even if it offers to experience its conditions of possibility. (p. 1852)

They also decline—and this is equally striking, I think; it comes in a footnote to the sentence I just cited—to develop the question of the relations between "the level of the oedipal structure and that of originary fantasms," though clearly they understand the fantasm to be the original site of the articulation of desire, its originary *mise en scène*. But as to who organizes this scene, they conclude (and I'm citing the very last sentences of the article): "The psychoanalyst should no longer trust wholly to the resources of his science or even those of myth. It would also be necessary to become a philosopher" (p. 1868).

Let's say a "philosopher-psychoanalyst." In any case, I think I can assert that in discussing the *exigency of the figure* earlier (or, to speak like an analyst: the relation of the subject to the signifier), we were making that step. We were discussing the "logical" ground of the fantasm. Hence my reservation about translating what we have said thus far into psychoanalytic terms. Not that it would be a regression (in a weak sense); it's just that I think we are approaching the *same limit differently* as we attempt to think the limit itself.

One more point: In addressing the second element of their title ("fantasme des origines"), Laplanche and Pontalis note that the originary fantasm is always, for the subject, an articulation of its origins: "Like myth, originary fantasms claim to offer a representation and a 'solution' to what presents itself to the child as a major enigma; they dramatize as moments of emergence, as the origin of a history, what appears to the subject as a reality of a nature such that it demands an explanation, a 'theory'" (p. 1854). I find that "reality" of the origin especially interesting—doesn't it mark that "need" to which we referred earlier? But they also go on to discuss the meaning of the fantasm *for the analyst*. The originary fantasms (the primal scene, the scene of seduction, the scene of castration) "translate, through the mediation of an imaginary scenario that claims to recapture it, the insertion of the most radically instituting symbolic in the real of the body" (p. 1855). The originary scenes, in other words, are about the subject's relation to language and what it brings: the fact of history and filiation, the fact of sexuality. They are about the fact of language itself.

OK. With those abstractions in place, shall I move on to Lacan?

—But your point about the philosophical approach—would that be where we meet an author like Giorgio Agamben? He links the problematic of infancy to a thought of the "being" of language (in fact, it's striking how close his trajectory has passed to your own), and he invokes even the "intuition" of an experience that he links to the fact of infancy. But the problematic, if I understand him, is primarily logical; infancy, in his definition, is the transcendental origin of language and the (non)ground of its historicity in general, the (non)ground of human history, in fact. You're uncomfortable with that reference?

—No, not at all. It's just that I wonder if Agamben doesn't remain in philosophy with his "theory of infancy." Perhaps it's the context and his references to linguistic research; nevertheless, "infancy" seems to remain a kind of deduction. True, it leads him to a thought of the human with which I am pretty much in accord. I like the elegance of what he says about the split between language and speech, or the semantic and semiotic (in Benveniste's sense of the terms). Animals are not denied language, as he puts it; but they do not say "I." Human infancy stands at the site of a discontinuity; it marks the fact of the human entry into language and the necessity of the constitution of a speaking subject. I wonder, for my part, if there are not other discontinuities to be thought with respect to what he calls, after Mallarmé, "la voix sacrée de la terre ingénue" (when he uses the metaphor of the dolphin to express the human emergence from the semantic sea of nature, he is evoking perhaps more than he wishes). But the essential point stands: the historicity of human speech requires a thought of human infancy.

Still, I leave the text uncertain as to what I called earlier "the exigency of the figure." Has Agamben answered it? Etymologies aside, why name this origin "infancy" and not just human finitude? What motivates the figure? Is he following textual evidence (that very indirect evidence adduced by Lyotard, or even that of the texts we are reading—he's certainly aware of them, even if he doesn't cite them), or is he appealing to something else in linking this theme to his larger topic of the possibility of a modern "experience"? He does speak briefly (but in no more than a turn of phrase) of an "intuition." But how are we to think that relation? I don't want to be critical here, and I realize that I've reversed tack with respect to philosophy; it just seems to me that we need to find a way to think together the "general" import of the figure and the singular exigency of its haunting presence, that exigency that makes the figure so strangely motivated. This is partly why the experience of psychoanalysis (at least those forms of psychoanalysis that seek to think relation to a real) remains a crucial reference for us. We have to think the point of crossing between "experience," our experience of that exigency, and the imperatives of thought.

—But wouldn't you be satisfied with the statement that the *infans* marks the *difference* between "memory" and "hallucination"—the difference between them that allows us to raise the question of history or, for that matter, the real (the fact of history, as Bill Haver would say: that there is history). Freud doesn't care, ultimately, about what really happened behind the primal scene. OK, it's a bit more complicated than that; but those who follow him—anyway, those who take up his legacy on this point—are concerned only with the insistence of the question, the "fact" of a relation between the scene and the real. They don't dream of seizing it. The *infans* is there, at that point. I don't see how one can say more. We can attempt to think its necessity and even its structure, as we did with Blanchot, but that's all we have of "evidence" for a general statement. Anything else takes us into the "why" question and, ultimately, theory—a theoretical account that will inevitably offer up the *infans* as the object of its explanation.

—I wonder if Blanchot didn't tell us more. But let me just pick up that phrase of yours: "the *infans* is there." Blanchot would urge us to hear in that phrase the insistence of the *il y a* and point us back to what he means by the "imaginary"; but I think we might also want to go back more directly to Heidegger's *es gibt*. You know that I believe we must rethink the "gift" of this relation from the structure of need and use (*der Brauch*), but the task remains: we must think both the exigency and evidence of the figure from that "experience," from that "giving." I'm sure Agamben would be sympathetic here: his own appeal to experience bears an unmistakable reference to the experience with language Heidegger describes in *On the Way to Language*. Be that as it may, I'm convinced that a topic like this one will oblige us to work toward another thought of "evidence." In every "experience" like the one involving the human relation to language (and isn't that all experience?), the evidence is offered in and through the "giving" that marks the event of language, what Heidegger calls its "essence."

—You're talking about an entire recasting of the question of objectivity. We'll need a bit more than a night for this.

—I don't want to go back to Heidegger now, but I do think there is something insistently "objective" about this topic of ours. As I've put it before, we're dealing with a figure in this *infans*, but a strangely motivated one. I won't try to say more at this point, but I think I can articulate now why this question of "evidence," as I have just phrased it, has led me to leave aside the many discussions devoted to the actual deaths of children—studies of a psychological or sociological character, and then works like Anne Finkbeiner's *After the Death of a Child*, a sensitive and intelligent study in its way. It's not that they are without pertinence. It's just that I fear they actually prohibit access to our problematic, at least initially. Of course, there is always the problem that the force of the testimony they offer (both moral and psychological) makes this speculative construction of the death of the *infans* an uncomfortable affair at times. And the problem is all the more acute for the fact that the mortal exposure we are trying to think is probably *indissociable* from the human relation to mortality and actual death. As you will remember, Blanchot is quite explicit and even severe on this point. So, in fact, we must at some point return to that question of the relation to actual death. But my guiding supposition is that *part* of the force of this relation derives from our "knowledge" of the death of the *infans*, and that we must think the relation to the death of a child from that pre-subjective ground in order to understand how they relate to one another. Again, the relation must eventually be thought, but it all hinges on how the evidence is "given." The exigency to which I'm pointing is a formal one (we must start from that "quasi-transcendental ground" of evidence), and as I've said before, I'm practicing a kind of askesis. But the implications might be profound for our understanding of the human relation to death.

—Will Lacan help with that question of evidence?

—I'm not sure, but I believe that his emphasis on the ethical dimension of his problematic is quite pertinent for us. Shall I turn to the text now?

—Go ahead, I see a lot of pages in front of you.

—I'll try to go quickly; interrupt when you want.

But he would rarely interrupt to object; nothing called for his intervention. Not that the discussion was without interest; he too loved the pleasures of interpretation. But for the interlocutor of the first hesitant steps, the commentary would pass lightly now, like the leaves of a book turned by the wind. And he listened with the echo of other conversations in his ear:

—*Why this drive to comment, to lay things out so? Why not go more directly to the matter?*

—*The matter of my concern is in the words I'm commenting.*

—*I understand. But why lay things out this way, with such passive indirection? Do you imagine these words will go unread without your devotion, that something might be lost?*

—*I suppose so. It's like a responsibility. I'm troubled by the arbitrariness that characterizes the use of texts like this one in so much theoretical discussion. I want to account for the text's provocation, not just affirm it; and I suppose I want to secure something along the way, perhaps nail it down. In any case, an attentive reading always brings out more than one anticipated.*

—*But why do you imagine that more commentary will save anything at all? So what if you've laid out the grounds for a more founded understanding and even discovered a few things, so what? Where does that leave us? When earlier the le-gitimacy of the discussion was the problem, I grasped the need and I could an-swer. Without that question of legitimacy—the discomfort, the hesitancy (the French say "trouble": I love that expression)—I wonder if we have the grounds for a conversation. At least the kind whose promised gift keeps us going.*

—I understand you. I know it's possible to lose oneself in this enterprise (not to speak of others). I also know that precisely that loss is the condition of a kind of event. Thought has always come for me in moments when a kind of submission to the text gives way to sudden attention to a phrase or to an oddity in syntax or grammar. It's a form of askesis, as I said. But the time does come when one must speak to one's concern, however hesitantly. Commentary opens paths, but it also screens; in devotion to the text, one can pass right by the real points of access. In fact, I sometimes feel I'm passing back and forth before the door without recog-nizing it. And then sometimes I recognize it, and instead of stepping through, I comment just a little more, to be sure of my footing, and then I find it has already closed.

—Recognition always comes too late, I think. The thought to which you referred, isn't it only in the step? And doesn't real recognition follow that step? No doubt, it requires preparation. Mary Lydon, a superb reader, remarked to me recently that with a text like Lacan's one must always start anew, no matter how familiar one is with the text, and one must always build up a kind of momentum (like speed on a bike, she said). My experience has been exactly the same. And the character of that preparation varies dramatically from text to text. But still, as Mary knows too, the point comes when one must step beyond commentary. Otherwise, there is no opening.

—Are you asking for another writing altogether? Are you asking for literature?

—Not necessarily; I'm just recalling to you the point from which we began; the interruption in your first steps that invited me.

—I know. I know. I'm just working up momentum. Can you wait?

—Where would I go?

I'll begin then. I think I've already alluded to Lacan's preparation of the dream sequence. Or I meant to—it's crucial to build the context. So: In evok-ing a series of intermediary figures that inhabit the unconscious in its relation to its "cause" (ghosts, sylphs, angels, etc.), Lacan is addressing, he tells us, the "preontological" status (FFC, p. 31/29) of what "waits" or is "in suffering" in that region of the "non-born" that is the gap of the unconscious. He is speaking broadly here—"leaping right in," he says—commenting as much upon Freud's reference to the "indestructible" character of desire and the logical temporality required to think it, as upon the subject of that desire and its objects, as articulated in relation to their traumatic origin. I'll try to explicate some of these relations as we proceed, but here I want to stress just a few general points.

First, in approaching the unconscious or repetition as *fundamental* concepts, Lacan is pushing past the order of the concept as defined by structural linguistics or structural anthropology, and hence beyond the conceptual frontiers of the "human sciences" of that time. The Freudian unconscious, he argues, engages something else, something of the order of what Heidegger tried to think as the "ontico-ontological difference" (he's pretty explicit about this in "The Agency of the Letter"). The point here is not to ground this *fundamental* inquiry in philosophy (and in any case, Lacan's "founding" effort in *The Four Fundamental Concepts* is not a conceptual *grounding*); it is to indicate the level at which Lacan is working when he evokes the "cause" of the unconscious—a *relationality* involving what he terms a "real" that is beyond the order of language, even that dimension of the psyche that is "structured" like a language. The point is a crucial one for grasping the import of Lacan's introductory words in his "Tuché and Automaton" segment and for his subsequent analysis of the dream. It is all too easy, he suggests, to presume that psychoanalysis implicates us in a form of idealism. His own evocations of intermediary figures in the preceding sections toy with this assumption; but those figures (the ghost of Hamlet's father, for example, or the image of the child to follow) point beyond any construction of the imaginary and symbolic orders to which the aphorism "life is a dream" might be applied. The burning child figures in a movement of *signifiance* that engages a reality, *produces* a reality that radically interrupts the economies of the psyche and the social orders that determine them. "No praxis is more oriented than analysis," Lacan declares, "toward what, at the heart of experience, is the knot of the real" (FFC, p. 53). The "knot" in question here, I want to emphasize, is a material relationality that is beyond, or otherwise than, Being ("preontological"), but only as the difference that is its an-archic ground. Nothing less is at stake.

Or so Lacan claims, and the form of the claim—inasmuch as it is an essential part of what makes Lacan's undertaking, after Freud, an ethical one—is crucial here. It is prompted by the evidence offered, "at the origin of analytic experience," by the trauma, specifically by the "insistence" of the trauma and its manner of "recalling itself to us" from the very heart of the primary processes (FFC, p. 55). The question posed to us by trauma is this: if the psychic economy governed by the pleasure principle works essentially to dampen the effects of a traumatic exposure, and if the dream, for example, is in the service of that economy, then why does the dream prompt the resurgence of the trauma in repetition—if not under some figure of itself, at least via some screen that indicates its presence? (Lacan's French, I should note, indicates very precisely that the dream provokes a repetition of the trauma: "Comment le rêve, porteur du désir du sujet, peut-il produire ce qui fait resurgir à répétition le trauma?") It must be that something "quite real" is caught in the system. We may *presume* its presence, Lacan insists; we require it as necessary (it is *"exigible"* [FFC, p. 55/55]) in order that psychic development not be reducible to a mere dream. "We," Freud and company, we who follow Freud in the fever of our research (FFC, p. 54/54), working in the wake of his desire, demand that *there must be* the presence of such a reality. And to this demand, Lacan asserts, indeed answer those radical points in the real he calls encounters (FFC, p. 55/56), points that oblige us to conceive of reality as "set under," or "suffering" in abeyance.

> Reality is in abeyance there, a there that awaits. And the *Zwang*, the constraint, that Freud defines by *Wiederholung*, governs the very diversions of the primary process.
>
> The primary process—which is nothing other than what I have tried to define for you in my last few lectures in the form of the unconscious—must, once again, be apprehended in its experience of rupture, between perception and consciousness, in that non-temporal locus, I said, that forces us to posit what Freud calls, in homage to Fechner, *die Idee einer anderer Lokalität*, the idea of another locality, another space, another scene, *the between perception and consciousness.* (FFC, p. 55/56)

In the tension between Lacan's exigency (part of the essential legacy of Freud), and the constraint (*Zwang*) that governs the relation between a reality in waiting and the movements of the primary processes in their "experience of rupture," there issues the *obligation* to pose the idea of another scene. We must, *once again*, seize the unconscious in its interruptive presence—once again because it never offers itself to conceptual grasp except in a praxis that must constantly be renewed (and this is not a "seizing"); but "once again" also in the sense of *after Freud*, whose manner of proceeding defined what Lacan names somewhat enigmatically here the "ethical status" of its being (FFC, p. 34/33). What exactly does he mean by "ethical," you'll ask. Well, I don't have any clearer answer than last time. To address this question adequately, we would have to take up the entire question of the relation between psychoanalysis, philosophy, and science, as Lacan sets these terms to work here, in his *Four Fundamental Concepts*, and throughout his writings. We would have to address the meaning of the word "praxis," and consider how the "cause" of the unconscious relates to what he terms the "Thing" in the seminar devoted specifically to ethics. We would have to pause to consider his "I don't search, I find" (FFC, p. 12/7) in relation to Freud's own feverish search for a real behind the fantasm. Through all of this, however, we would not find Lacan denying to psychoanalysis an object or minimizing the reality of the unconscious. We would find instead an emphasis on the manner in which that reality consti- tutes itself—*"se fait"*—*within a transferential structure*, which is where the problematic of repetition is properly engaged. The praxis of psychoanalysis cannot be thought outside the structure of transference, just as the founda- tions of that praxis cannot be attained without attending to the desire of the one who inaugurated it. Lacan is fully aware of the *performative* character of his inquiry—he is posing the foundations. But he is doing so *after Freud*, and specifically from the limit marked by Freud's need to shore up the name of the father with the "myth" of the Oedipus complex ("Certainly, at my age now, and in my epoch, I am in a position to introduce into the domain of the cause the law of the signifier, at the site where the gap is produced. Nevertheless, if we want to understand what is involved in psychoanalysis, we must go back and bring forth the concept of the unconscious from that time in which Freud proceeded to construct it, since we can only bring it to completion by carry- ing it to its limits" [FFC, p. 26/23]). The unconscious, once again, must be thought from that limit marked (and transgressed) by Freud's desire.

—So the thought is ethical both in its assumption of Freud's transgressive movements, and in its relation to those movements. The thought is ethical in that it assumes, writes, its legacy in a praxis without foundations that is as much answerable as it is adventurous.

—Yes. And to that we must add that the "legacy" in question is of a quasi- transcendental order that engages the grounds of good and evil, beyond good and evil. Lacan makes this clear when he introduces the dream of the burning child. In fact, Lacan's first significant mention of the dream occurs immediately after his remarks on the ethical status of the unconscious; he situates Freud's attention to the dream precisely there. I'll cite the whole passage because Lacan's remarks will prove crucial to an interpretation of his reading of the dream.

> Freud shows that he is very well aware of the fragility of the fabric of the unconscious where this register is concerned ["passion," "truth," "the ethical"?—any of these referents are possible] when he opens the last chapter of *The Interpretation of Dreams* with the dream which, of all those that are analyzed in the book, holds a place of its own—a dream suspended around the most anguishing mystery, that which links a father to the corpse of his son close by, his dead son. As he succumbs to sleep, the father sees rise up before him the image of his son, who says to him, *Father, don't you see I'm burning?* He is burning for real, in the next room.
>
>   What is the point of supporting the theory according to which the dream is an image of desire with an example in which, in a sort of flamboyant reflection, it is precisely a reality which, virtually copied, seems to wrench the dreamer from his sleep? Why, if not to evoke for us a mystery that is nothing other than the world of the beyond, and some secret or other shared by the father and that child who comes to him to say—*Father don't you see I'm burning?* What is he burning with, if not what we see emerging at other points designated by the Freudian topology?—namely, the weight of the sins of the father, borne by the ghost in the myth of Hamlet, which Freud couples with the myth of Oedipus. The father, the Name-of-the-father, sustains the structure of desire along with that of the law—but the inheritance of the father is the one designated to us by Kierkegaard, his sin.
>
>   Where does Hamlet's ghost arise from—if not from the place from which he declares to us that he was in the full flower of his sins when he was surprised, cut down. And far from providing Hamlet with the prohibitions of the law that would allow his desire to survive, it is a matter at every moment of a profound placing into doubt of this too-ideal father. (FFC, p. 35/34–35)

Let me hold off commenting these lines, since we should first turn to the dream itself. But I want to add that when Lacan himself takes up the dream, he does so after another reference to Freud's passionate, almost anguished effort to reach "the first encounter, the real that we can assert to lie behind the fantasy." Freud himself is under a kind of compulsion when he seeks the truth of the first encounter and engages the problematic of sexual trauma:

> We can feel throughout this analysis that this real carries the subject with it and almost forces it, directing the research to such a point that we can today ask

ourselves after all whether this fever, this presence, this desire of Freud's is not what conditioned in his patient the belated accident of his psychosis. (FFC, p. 54/54)

I need hardly emphasize further how precarious this term "ethical" is in Lacan's reference to Freud's research (and presumably his own). Clearly the ethics of psychoanalysis are at stake in the uncompromising character of Freud's endeavor—he does not fail his desire, even before the limit (which he helps lay down) of the oedipal law. The unconscious takes on its "ethical" character in that almost oedipal approach to the very limit of desire. Lacan's return to the limits of psychoanalytic theory as governed by Freud's desire is in turn "ethical" by the fact that it does not shy in following Freud, and even assumes that relation as the condition of its research. So there is a legacy involved, as I mentioned earlier. But we must also understand that the "legacy" is not just a symbolic inheritance. It is a relation to the other. And here we meet the sense of the term "ethical" proposed by Cathy Caruth, who takes her inspiration from Levinas when she argues that the dream of the burning child concerns an ethical dilemma at the heart of consciousness itself insofar as the latter has its traumatic "origin" in its relation to the death of others. Here is how Caruth puts it:

> Ultimately, then, the story of father and child is, for Lacan, the story of an impossible responsibility of consciousness in its own originating relation to others, and specifically to the deaths of others. As an awakening, the ethical relation to the real is the revelation of this impossible demand at the heart of human consciousness. (*Unclaimed Experience*, p. 104)

We will need to take up the dream to measure the force of these words, and our task, as I see it, will be to draw out this force by exploring a bit further what the death of a child is.

—So your approach now concerns the question of the relation to *autrui* somewhat more precisely than before. Blanchot did not separate the question of the *infans* from that of the relation to *autrui* in his remarks on responsibility; but he also left it undefined. You want to address that question directly now?

—Precisely. Lacan introduces the dream in the second section of his "Tuché and Automaton" lecture, after his reference to the necessity of posing the idea of another scene between perception and consciousness, and after illustrating just how easy it is to "seize" this scene in everyday life. In his own recent experience, for example (this is the first of two personal asides in this segment—

indeed, personal experience frames the analysis of this dream with strangely anonymous sources in Freud's text), he has found himself dreaming *in awakening* after a knock at the door and before gaining consciousness. Awakening, as he defines it here, is a "gap" that prompts the resurgence of consciousness ("What is there that motivates the emergence of the represented reality" [pp. 56–57]) and within which the subject of desire presents itself in the strange temporality of its *significance*. We won't know what Lacan was dreaming as he was "knocked," as the English say, but we may presume what he is/was at that moment. Recognizing that someone has called upon him:

> I must question myself as to what I am at that moment—at that instant so immediately before and so separated in which I began to dream under the effect of this knock that is, apparently, what awakens me. I am, as far as I know, before I should awake [*avant que je ne me reveille*]—this "ne," called expletive [or pleonastic], and already noted in one of my writings, is the very mode of presence of this *I am* before awakening. It is not at all expletive, it is rather the expression of my infolding, each time that it must manifest itself. The language, the French language defines it well through its usage. "Will you finish before he arrives?" [*Aurez-vous fini avant qu'il n'arrive?*] (FFC, p. 56/56)

Lacan can't resist musing with his audience about the possible content of his dream with this little illustration of the function of the pleonastic *ne*. But he has also swiftly defined what he will later name the double meaning, the "double service" of awakening (FFC, p. 59/60) by suggesting that it is the vanishing appearance of the subject of desire in the logical time of *significance* that spurs to consciousness. What awakens the subject to representation, it seems, is the awakening (and passing) of the subject of the unconscious. What awakens, to use another vocabulary, is the subject's exposure *en différance*. This is sketchy, but it prepares us to recognize the complexity and ambiguity of the scene Lacan reads in Freud; it prepares us to recognize how Lacan will alter the dream's axis of reference, and will do so from the first words:

> You will remember that unfortunate father who went to lie down in the room next to the one in which his dead child lay—leaving the child in the care, the text tells us, of another old man—and who is struck, awoken by something. By what? It is not only the reality, the shock, the *knocking* of a noise made to recall him to the real; rather, this translates, and precisely in his dream, the quasi-identity of what is happening, the very reality of an overturned candle setting light to the bed in which his child lies.
>
> This is something that seems hardly suited to confirm Freud's thesis in the *Traumdeutung*—that the dream is the realization of a desire. (FFC, p. 56/57)

We may be struck here by two things, starting with the fact that Lacan has shifted the emphasis from visual to auditory phenomena. Whereas Freud stresses the dreamer's awareness of the light in the other room, Lacan introduces a *knocking*: "the knocking of a noise made to recall [the dreamer] to the real." Is he picking up Freud's own attention to auditory phenomena where the primal scene is concerned? (A motif, I would note, that goes way back, at least to the speculations on the origin of language offered by Herder.) His later references to noise (FFC, p. 57/58) and "a little noise" (FFC, p. 59/60) indicate that he links this knocking to the sound of the falling candle (which would indeed be a little noise). But the paragraph I have just cited makes it clear that the knocking has another source; the forced character of its syntax disarticulates the "knocking" from the sound in the other room and reduces this latter to a "quasi-identity" translated by "the reality, the shock, the knocking" of the noise in the dream. What awakens is thus a "reality" in the dream, or a reality passing *through* the dream that is of a quite different order from that of the perception that appears to trigger its advent and which "also," in its quasi-identity, draws the sleeper to his encounter.

I won't pause to consider the impact of this account of the dream on Freud's two theories: that the dream realizes a desire, and that a dream serves to protect sleep. Caruth does this well in her essay on the dream. Instead I'll proceed directly to Lacan's argument that the knocking that awakens lies *in* the words addressed to the father by the child, words that Lacan will offer in their original German with accompanying translations in order to preserve something of the force of their *significance*. What is it that wakes the sleeper?

> Is it not, *in* the dream, another reality?—the reality that Freud describes thus— *Dass das Kind an seinem Bette steht*, that the child is near his bed, *ihn am Arme fasst*, takes him by the arm and whispers to him reproachfully, *und ihm vorwurfsvoll zuraunt: Vater siehst du denn nicht*, Father, don't you see, *dass ich verbrenne*, that I'm burning? Is there not more reality in this message than in the noise by which the father also identifies the strange reality of what is happening in the room next door? Does there not pass through these words the missed reality that caused the death of the child? Does Freud himself not tell us that one must recognize in this phrase what perpetuates for the father these words forever separated from the dead child that would perhaps have been said to him, Freud supposes, by reason of the fever?—But who knows, perhaps these words perpetuate the father's remorse that the one he placed near the bed of his son to watch over it, the grey-haired one, will perhaps not be up to fulfilling his task, *die Besorgnis dass der greise Wächter seiner Aufgabe nicht gewachsen sein dürfte*, he will not be, perhaps, up to his task. Indeed—he's gone to sleep. (FFC, p. 57/58)

Lacan will isolate the child's sentence in a most powerful fashion in the course of his account, preparing thereby his subsequent distinction between the imagery of the dream and the invocation through the child's voice, a "splitting" of the dream (Lacan speaks of a *schize* [FFC, p. 68/70]) that allows him to identify the different registers of its signifying process and thereby honor the division of the subject that occurs at the site of the encounter the dream commemorates (FFC, p. 51/51). I will return to this point, but here I want to attend simply to Lacan's manner of stressing the way the reality that awakens *inhabits* the words. It is not the dream that awakens exactly—it is something in the dream conveyed by the dreamed child's words; something in the words, beyond the words, that Lacan names a "reality": "Does there not pass through these words the missed reality that caused the death of the child?"

The last sentence echoes so much in the context of this seminar that we are clearly enjoined to ask what Lacan means by "cause," what he means by "missed reality," and even what he means by "death." Is Lacan referring to the empirical death of the child, or perhaps to another death, even inseparable from the latter? Clearly the "missed reality," the cause of the death that is spoken in the child's words involves something more than physiological or even psychological determinations, something more than what any medical science, including psychology, could adduce in an etiology of the fever. (When Lacan introduces his notion of "cause" in the second chapter, he takes up precisely such a notion of determination, noting that Freud is not interested in a possible causal relation between the unconscious and neurosis, where "cause" is understood in terms of some law of determination: "On that point, Freud quite willingly makes the Pilatian gesture of washing his hands. One day or other, they'll find something, humoral determinants, whatever—it's all the same to him. For the unconscious shows us the gap whereby neurosis accords with a real, a real that may well, for its part, not be determined" [FFC, p. 25/22].) And why does this reality so engage the father's desire? Something in the child's sentence, Lacan tells us, *perpetuates*, for the father, these words *forever separated* from the dead child who said them, presumably at the time of his fever. They are perpetuated, undoubtedly, by something more than the father's guilt at having missed something in the condition that caused the actual death, and perhaps even something more than the poignancy of the address itself. For the words seem to touch an "indestructible" (cf. FFC, p. 33/32) in the father's desire. But who knows, Lacan adds, perhaps they perpetuate the father's remorse for having placed beside the child an older man (the dreamer's father, or a figure thereof?) who will not be up to the task. If they are an expression of guilt of sorts, they may derive some of their force from an anticipation of the older man's failure. For the dreaming father too may have known (or is now knowing with the dream's revelation, *après coup*) a paternal failure to see, he too may be burning in a knowledge of abandonment, have known or be knowing a kind of death.

However we read this sequence, it seems clear that Lacan's emphasis on the manner in which the dream isolates the child's words and *perpetuates* them (the etymology of this word suggests a going toward or a seeking, by means of or through) is meant to remind us that however compelling the child's invocation, the dream must be read from the basis of an analysis of a dream's place in the primary processes—it must be understood in relation to the father's desire. But this is not to say that we are dealing simply with wish fulfillment. The confirmation of Freud's theory of desire will in fact shake (or prove to have shaken, like a traumatic blow) the edifice of *The Interpretation of Dreams*. As Lacan puts it in a kind of provisional conclusion to the section of the lecture we are reading, Freud knows his own awakening before the encounter commemorated in the dream:

> If Freud, amazed, sees the theory of desire confirmed, it is indeed a sign that the dream is not just a fantasy fulfilling a wish.
>
> For it is not that he maintains for himself, in the dream, that the child is still living. But the dead child taking his father by the arm, an atrocious vision, designates a beyond that makes itself heard in the dream. Desire presents itself there for the loss imaged at the cruelest point of the object. (FFC, p. 58/59)

The dream, in other words, is a presentation of desire in its relation to what Lacan calls elsewhere an "unconditioned" or an "absolute" (these are his terms for the "cause" in "The Signification of the Phallus") by which "the power of pure loss" surges only to withdraw in and by the subject's relation to the object-cause of its desire. I will have to return to this last "object," the *object (a)* (whose place in the dream is abundantly recognized by Ellie Ragland-Sullivan), and perhaps defer a full account of the process of *signifiance* that occurs with the manifestation of desire. But I want to underscore with these few words Lacan's fundamental point that the dream of the burning child engages what Freud came to call the death drive, a "desire for loss."

Are you getting tired? You're not saying anything.

—No, go on. I'm savoring the pleasures of the passage, that's all. And I'm remembering other discussions. The pages pass quickly, I find.

—You mean you've lost the desire to interrupt? Well, I'll go on. I think that if we are to get at Lacan's work with this text, we have to lay things out a bit. The question of *autrui*, for example: we need to lay out the structure of that dream.

—No problem. As I said, I'm enjoying myself. But I sense too that we'll need to leave the horizon of this commentary if we are to respond to what brought you to this text.

—I know. To what I've said thus far, then, I need to add that even with such a designation of the final order of reality engaged by the dream, we have actually said little. And we should not leave behind the paragraph by which Lacan carries us to this conclusion, for it refocuses our attention on the site of the encounter commemorated in the dream and re-anchors this encounter in the confrontation with the child.

> This phrase, said in regard to the fever—does it not evoke for you what I called in one of my last addresses the cause of the fever? The action of preventing what is happening in the neighboring room, however pressing it might be by all appearances—is it perhaps not also, perhaps, felt as being in any case, now, too late—in relation to what is at stake, in relation to the psychic reality that manifests itself in the uttered sentence? Is not the dream which is pursued essentially, if I may say so, an homage to the missed reality—the reality that can only constitute itself by repeating itself indefinitely, in an indefinitely never attained awakening? What encounter can there be henceforth with this being forever inert—even when it is devoured by flames—if not that encounter that occurs precisely at the moment when the flame, by accident, as though by chance, catches him? Where is the reality in this accident? If not that something is repeated, something finally more fatal, *by means* of reality, a reality where the one who was charged with watching over the body, still remains asleep, even when the father reemerges after having awakened. (FFC, p. 57/58)

The "atrocious vision" of the dreamed child, as we have seen, is a figure of the father's desire that points beyond itself—toward a "beyond" that resonates in the child's sentence. What awakens, in this structure of *signifiance*, is initially quite "separate" from the child in Lacan's account. And yet when Lacan reiterates the structure of reference in the dream (the structure of the dream's production in relation to the outside reality by means of which it is accomplished), he makes it clear that the missed encounter and the missed reality "honored" there involve the child's actual (and past) presence in an essential way. Once again, we have a crossing of the "transcendental" and "reality"—an instantiation of "ontico-ontological difference" at a material site. Lacan insists upon this point. But he also introduces a singular paradox. The question that has brought us to this paragraph concerns the "other" reality that awakens the dreamer (this point of focus will be reiterated by Lacan near the end of the section), and Lacan has now firmly situated that reality in the address of the child. Yet he also tells us in the passage we are reading that the dreamer *pursues* the dream in order to sustain the encounter. There is a pressing need to act in relation to the terrible accident that has befallen the child's corpse—the dreamer appears to know, at some level (he is "sensing"), that he needs to act. But in relation to the matter of the child's words, the dreamer senses that action will be, once again, too late; and however pressing the reality in the other room, there is a more pressing need (the compulsion of the *Wiederholungszwang*, we may presume) to honor the "psychic" reality the dreamer encounters in the child's words. There is a crucial knowledge forming about "lateness" here, but Lacan's phrasing and intonation also point to the importance of another kind of knowledge. He makes it clear that the dreamer remains at the site of the child's address in order to approach a reality that can *be* now only in repetition: "ne peut plus se faire qu'à se répéter indéfiniment, en un indéfiniment jamais atteint réveil." In an awakening, indefinitely never attained. The dreamer pursues the dream in order to reside in "the phenomenon, the distance, the very gap that constitutes awakening," the "logical" time/space of repetition that opens between the initial perception, the "little bit of reality" that starts the sleeper, and the return to consciousness in the anguished response to the empirical accident. Thus the question recurs: what accounts for the passage between dreaming and consciousness—what prompts the awakening? No doubt the encounter can only occur via the intrusion of the reality in the other room, and for a subject that is already responding to that reality. Thus, we might say that "awakening," the movement of repetition wherein the dreaming subject produces a reality *for itself* via the address of the child, unfolds within another awakening. But even if we hold aside the question raised by this "itself"—the question of the splitting of the subject (is it one subject who speaks via the child, receives the address, and responds to the reality in the other room; there must be some communication between these instances if the dreamer is "sensing"—this is the whole point of the ontico-ontological crossing—but what is it?)—we must ask: what awakens the one who receives the address? Or what prompts the act? Lacan makes it clear that the dreaming subject has every reason to remain at the site of that "indefinitely never attained awakening," every reason to sustain the encounter and defer action, even if that encounter presupposes some relation to what is happening in the other room. So what impels the dreamer to leave the dream?

Cathy Caruth's suggestion is that the dreamer awakens *in response* to the child's words and *in order* to respond to them. She describes, movingly, a "paradoxical attempt *to respond, in awakening, to a call that can only be heard within sleep*" (p. 99). Needless to say, this description of the father's awakening diverges considerably from what we have seen thus far in Lacan's account. But Lacan has also told us little about the dreaming subject's passage to consciousness, so it seems worthwhile to entertain Caruth's argument. Her thesis is that the awakening may be read in two ways. She describes, first, a failure on the father's part to see the burning to which the child points in the dream. This failure is inevitable: the father, as father (one who wishes to see the child alive) cannot face the child's testimony of its agony and thus turns from the dream, in his attempt to respond, only to awaken to a repetition of his previous failure. To respond to the child's appeal is, in this case, to miss it, again.

A second way of reading the response shifts the meaning of what it is to awaken *as a father*. In this case, the father is enjoined to confront the child's actual death by the child himself (the one who died unwitnessed). The child commands him, in his spectral return, to leave the dream—the wish for the child's survival—and survive after him by telling the child's story (a phrase Caruth presumably takes from Lacan's reference to "commemoration" and the larger context of her meditation on what it means to witness). To awaken in this case, Caruth argues, is to receive a relation to the child's dying and to "perform" that relation, to "say" what the death of a child is:

> The only way truly to hear is now by listening not as a living father listens to a living child, but as the one who receives the very gap between the other's death and his own life, the one who, in awakening, does not see but enacts the impact of the very difference between death and life. . . . The father's response to the address is not a knowing, that is, but an awakening, an awakening that, like the performance of a speaking, carries with it and transmits the child's otherness, the father's encounter with the otherness of the dead child. (*Unclaimed Experience*, p. 106)

The father does not awaken to his being as father, we might say; rather, the awakening is the contraction of the bond (to the child in its death). The father receives the relation in awakening—an awakening, Lacan would add, to the scene that includes the older man's failure.

Now, this powerful description of the event is prepared by a rather forceful appropriation of Lacan's text. On a different occasion, I'd want to consider the way Caruth construes portions of Lacan's reading (her interpretation of the term "encounter," for example). And I have to say that I'm made a little nervous by her way of introducing the notion of performance, for it seems to redouble the "action" of awakening in a manner that departs from Lacan's account. The latter point is not simply a matter of textual fidelity (it's hardly clear, in any case, what "fidelity" means in the context of a reading of Lacan), for this reference to a performance seems to prepare the promise of a kind of ethical *knowledge*—a possible translation of the ethical injunction lying in the child's words into an Ethics. Isn't that what emerges in the subsequent section of her essay when she says the following: "The implications of such a transmission will only be fully grasped, I think, when we come to understand how, through the act of survival, the repeated failure to have seen in time—in itself a pure repetition compulsion, a repeated nightmare—can be transformed into the imperative of a speaking that awakens others" (p. 108)? I don't want to phrase my objection too strongly, for I too am seeking another relation to the event; and I should acknowledge that Caruth proceeds to temper her statement ("for now, however . . . ") by pointing quite appropriately to the way Lacan's text sets out to transmit the awakening in its own way. Perhaps I should merely note a query in relation to the word "transformation" ("the repeated failure . . . can be *transformed*"). I have the same relation to it as I do to references in some of the Lacanian literature to an eventual "subjectivization" of the cause. No doubt, something of that order is Lacan's ambition. But what kind of assumption is implied there, what agency, what subjectivity? I want merely to question the idea that the opening of the ethical relation could be appropriated. I doubt Caruth is making that step, but the "active" dimensions of the word "transformation" merit attention.

But enough resistance. At the heart of her argument is a crucial point: namely that much of the force of Lacan's account (particularly his way of isolating the arresting words: "Father, don't you see I'm burning?") derives from his way of exploring what the dream presents of "an ethical relation to the real." Caruth recognizes in the "otherness" encountered by the father and transmitted in the response of his awakening the presence of an address, of an ethical imperative that she links to the address of *autrui* as thought by Emmanuel Levinas. The dreamer's awakening is traumatic, she argues, inasmuch as it displays "the necessity and impossibility of responding to another's death," an *originary* responsibility for consciousness:

> The accidental in trauma is also a revelation of a basic, ethical dilemma at the heart of consciousness itself insofar as it is essentially related to death, and particularly to the death of others. Ultimately, then, the story of father and child is, for Lacan, the story of an impossibility of consciousness in its own originating relation to others, and specifically to the deaths of others. As an awakening, the ethical relation to the real is the revelation of this impossible demand at the heart of human consciousness. (p. 104)

I need hardly rehearse why I would agree, in part, with these important words, following Levinas, of course, but also authors such as Bataille, Blanchot, Lacan (with his meditation on the transference), and even—perhaps first of all— Heidegger, who answered this ethical imperative by stating, and failing to honor, the *philosophical* obligation to think the *Dasein* from *Mitsein*. A great deal rests upon what is meant by death, of course. Whereas Bataille would be inclined, I believe, to stress the actual or "potential" death (as Caruth frequently writes) of the other (consider his "Nietzschean Chronicle," for example), Blanchot refers, for his part, to a more primordial exposure inseparable from the vulnerability of the mortal being. Heidegger did the same, and it is such a structure (considerably radicalized) that prompts Lacan to speak of an existence "between two deaths." But rather than return to this material, I want to add that we must also recognize the singular complication arising from the fact that the dream is a product of the father's desire. It is the father's dream, to put it simply (though perhaps too common-sensically: to whom do dreams belong?), and the traumatic address, whatever its source, proceeds from "father" to "father," from the father *as father* to the dreaming subject. Even if we acknowledge this point by suggesting that the address of the other exceeds any articulation and could only be brought to speech in a "traumatic awakening" like the one Caruth describes so well, we must deal with the fact of the father's desire. This was the original question, after all (Freud's and Lacan's): Why does the dreamer produce the trauma in repetition? Caruth's answer, I presume, is that the impossible ethical dilemma at the heart of consciousness requires repetition, and that the performance of speaking enacts a survival that can become the ground of an ethical stance. Lacan's answer may not ultimately be so different—that is, once we introduce the question of transference and think the possibility of action and the assumption of desire from that ground. But in relation to the dream sequence, his answer, as we have seen, is more immediate: in the dream, desire presents itself for the loss, imaged at the cruelest point of the object.

Does this contradict the claim that the trauma has something to do with the ethical demand to which Caruth refers? The answer hinges, obviously, on what Lacan means by "loss." It certainly seems improbable that he is referring to the actual or potential death of the child—this would give the death drive a sinister turn that in fact turns quite short of Lacan's understanding of this notion. No, the vision—or rather, the address: the "cruelest point of the object" lies in the voice—is atrocious, but it designates, as he says, a *beyond* that makes itself heard in the dream, and the father's desire concerns this "beyond." There is no way of establishing, *de jure*, that this beyond is actually brought to the dreamer in some way by the child, that the relation to the other is in fact fundamental for this dream and ultimately for the father's awakening *as* father. There is no irreducible evidence that the father is not producing an image of *himself* via the figure of his child and the words spoken during the child's past fever—in fact, this is probably *also* the case. But the suggestion that we have to do with the "after"-fact of an address that brings relation to a beyond is compelling—both "intuitively," as the Anglo-American philosophers would say (and let us recognize the evidence of the force of this address for a host of commentators—have any other three pages from Lacan drawn this much attention?) and perhaps even "logically," in the sense to which I alluded above ("la présence est pour nous supposé exigible"). I would put it this way (and you'll recognize what is now a very old question for me): is it possible for the father—or any subject—to honor a relation to the *infans*, whose passing is the ground of his own speech and life, except in the (past) presence of an other, and thus in response? Can the father have access to the "beyond" that is designated in the dream without being, at the same time, a *witness* (or without the intercession of a "witness"—the place of the analyst, for example)? To translate these considerations into a conclusion: must there perhaps . . .

—"Must there perhaps"? Is that supposition?

—Must there perhaps (yes, perhaps the most fundamental one) be a witness to the child's address for it to come to speech (and could this be part of what Lacan means when he says that "only the father as father—that is to say, no conscious being" can say what the death of a child is)? And does the father perhaps also need the address of the child to say his "own" burning—to present his desire? The address may also be the condition of the father's relation to his "own" experience of conflagration, which is the real object of this dream. Following this argument, we would say that *there is*, indeed, an address of the other that communicates the "otherness" of the dead child. But the words bearing this address—actually spoken by the child at some point or fantasized by the father—open access to and at the same time represent ("as a representative for representation") another "original" relation that involves the father's own "primal scene." The "accident," the catastrophic or traumatic event for the dreaming subject, lies in this access; the address exposes the father to another experience of loss, and *this* exposure awakens. The circumstances of this awakening are "accidental" to be sure, but they are the condition for the repetition in question.

Can I go a bit further? The sequence, if we project it narratively, would be roughly as follows. The father has undergone a sustained suffering that cannot but wear away resistance. In the intensity of the scene (a long vigil before and after the death, the near proximity of the corpse), an inevitable sense of responsibility or even guilt concerning the child's death exposes the father to another guilt that Lacan evoked in his first allusion to the dream in speaking of the sins of the father—his inevitable failure to fulfill a symbolic role required of him by the child at the moment of a conflagration that is comparable to what Blanchot describes as the death of the *infans* (I will return to this shortly). Perhaps the intensity of the father's suffering is enough to give him access to the child's evocation of this *other* death in words that may have spoken only of a fever but for the father, at least, have come to express knowledge of the imminence of death. Perhaps the father also requires the sense of remorse he feels from the basis of his knowledge of the older man's potential failure, a knowledge that exposes him to memory of his own experiences of abandonment. There is in fact no way of determining "cause" and "effect" here—no way of telling whether the father cedes, in his suffering, to an address from the other he has not been able to hear until now, and then, *in this exposure*, and in the specific circumstances, effects a kind of relay to his own immemorial suffering, or whether the incident in the other room opens a relation to this primal suffering that then allows him to use the child's words in their full resonance to perpetuate the encounter (could he hear the child's words except from his own suffering?). Cause and effect may, in fact, be entirely beside the point at the level of experience we are considering here—an entirely different logic may be required (one resembling the "circular" logic of the hermeneutic circle in Heidegger's *Being and Time*, where being-toward-death is the condition of what Heidegger terms "birth," and vice versa). Let us simply note for the time being Lacan's insistence that the repetition can *only* occur by means of the reality in the other room, that the encounter occurs *between* dreaming and awakening, between the older man who is still dreaming and the one who dreamed in order not to awaken. Thus, it seems possible to assert, following Lacan, that the (chiasmic?) crossing of generational lines of responsibility, in the exceptional circumstances of the accidental fall of the candle, makes the capacity to hear the child's address in its ultimate import (the indication of a death that is the non-ground of ethical relation) a path of access to the father's own being *en souffrance*. But again, we may be forcing what is a kind of simultaneous exposure into an inadequate narrative logic. Perhaps we must think the passage of awakening as, also, a kind of communication between exposure to the address of the child and exposure to the "primal scene" (?) of the dreamer—in which case, the ethical relation exposed by the child's words would be a kind of communication of that originary experience (perhaps this is what Lacan means by a shared secret, "un secret partagé"—which could also mean "divided"—between father and child [FFC, p. 35]). It is clear, in any case, that the dreamer uses the words of the child to proceed to this "unique" encounter, which can only be undergone in a dream and only be commemorated in the repeated act of a rite (psychoanalysis, for example?). The child's words, in the force of their *signifiance*, give access to what cannot be otherwise faced; the dreamer takes this access and uses it for the presentation of desire, but also uses it, however atrocious it is, as a screen or limit. Hence the strange temporality—a movement that is at once perpetuation and awakening, approach and withdrawal. The dream is a path of access that the Orphic dreamer can only travel so far. At the limit of desire an awakening must occur, if it has not already occurred by reason of the unbearable conflict between a desire following the path of the death drive and a subjectivity that is already responding to the events in the other room.

—So how, exactly, do you understand the secret shared between father and child? What is that "other" guilt to which you referred?

—Let me approach this in a formulaic way. As regards the relation to the other in this scene, I would put it, schematically, as follows: The voice speaks in and by way of the relation to *autrui*, which is to say in and beyond the subject and in the singular anonymity of the *infans*. It is not an other being who speaks in this scene; it is the other "inside." We need to introduce here the relation of father and child (the law), but I believe we could say, initially, that the address comes in the relation of father and child as a relation between the father (who is dreaming in the proximity of one who may well represent a father) and what Lacan calls the Other. The awakening derives from the father's encounter with another dying (remember that Lacan speaks of being between *two* deaths), an encounter with the default of the signifying order for which he should, in principle, stand in support. When Lacan says that the child is burning with the weight of the sins of the father, he is saying, I believe, that he is burning in exposure to the irremediable, the inexpiable, of an unwarranted existence.

I am tempted to return here to Bacon—all those references to Aeschylus—in order to approach the primordial guilt evoked here (and in order to avoid Christian determinations of the child's passion). But I'll stay a bit with the formulas and attempt to follow the hints Lacan offers in his references to Hamlet. They point back to his seminars of 1958–59, where he speaks of the trauma suffered by the desiring subject who confronts in the Other a signifying default (S(Ⱥ) is the formula)—"the lack of a signifier," as Pontalis puts it in his summary of the seminar, "to reveal the being that the signifier has nevertheless raised as a question." Before this lack (to be, as Lacan defines it: *manque à être*), the subject is without recourse, *hilflos*, as Freud put it. Pontalis continues: "It is in this *Hilflosigkeit* that we translate as distress that Freud finds the essential experience of the trauma. . . . The essence of desire, in our view, is to organize the metonymic flight of being called for by language" (p. 265). Of course, Lacan introduces into this trauma a constitutive sexual dimension, so that knowledge of default is also knowledge of a heritage of desire: the sins of the father, and of the mother—hence a dimension of the guilt known by the child (I'll come back to this as we turn to the figure of Antigone, whose experience Lacan designates as "more radical" in this regard than Hamlet's). But if the pain known by the child involves an irreducible history of desire, a family *atè*, so to speak, it also involves the pain of history "itself." What is at stake in the child's distress is an experience (before experience) of the opening of history, an experience of the "fact" of history. It knows the material conditions of any memorialized history: what the subject must *forget* in order to emerge in its desire. In his seminar on the ethics of psychoanalysis, Lacan tells us that the subject, at its phenomenal birth, *is* this forgetting:

> A subject originally represents nothing more than the following fact: he can forget. Strike out that "he"; the subject is literally at his beginning the elision of a signifier as such, the missing signifier in the chain. (EP, p. 264/224)

I've skipped ahead with this citation, but it will help us approach Lacan's reference to Hamlet and the motif of not knowing. For what is initially crucial in that reference is Lacan's argument that what distinguishes the ghost's message is that it confronts the son with the father's express knowledge of his own perdition and of the maternal crime. Once he receives that message, Lacan argues, he knows quite a bit more than he wants to in order to honor the father's name. He knows, *from the father* (who knows best—the unconscious one, that is), a lack in the Other sufficient to threaten his very capacity to desire. As Jane Gallop notes, following strong hints from Lacan and Pontalis that she quite demonstratively forgets, the situation is the opposite of the one illustrated by a dream analyzed by Freud in an essay from 1911, "Formulations Concerning Two Principles of Psychic Functioning." A patient who has recently suffered the death of his father dreams repeatedly that his father returns to him and speaks in an ordinary manner, *without knowing he is dead.* Freud interpolates the hidden text of the subject's desire by rewriting the dream text roughly as follows: "he wished that his father were dead and his father did not know that he wished it." One could well read the interpolated wish simply along the lines of the usual oedipal scenario, but Lacan emphasizes the defensive character of the unconscious wish itself. The son had suffered with the father a pain, as Pontalis puts it, "close to that pain of existence where nothing more inhabits him than existence itself, and everything, in the excess of suffering, tends to abolish that final, indelible term that is the desire to live." The subject approaches the point of assuming what appears as an absolute of pain, but defends himself from that confrontation through the scenario of wishing for the father's death. The repressed aggressive desire thus protects the very possibility of desire by sustaining an ignorance. The subject projects ignorance upon the other and claims a knowledge for himself. Within this structure, the "he is dead" offers no danger—no danger, that is, of exposing another death. By interposing the image of "oedipal" rivalry between himself and the final term of his existence (which he has approached in the proximity of the father's agony), he retains a support for his desire and finds the passageway by which he can escape being directly engulfed. He triumphs in knowing that the father does not know, but his triumph is a shield. Freud, as Lacan emphasizes repeatedly, has similar recourse to the oedipal scenario itself (recourse to *theory* if you will—but here theory is properly a myth) in order to avoid the "absolute master" which is not simply death in the sense of a passing away, but the possible death of desire itself in exposure to the "truth" of this myth—not that the father or God are dead, to borrow a phrase from *The Four Fundamental Concepts*, but that the father is unconscious—that the father has *fundamentally* abandoned us. That is the meaning of the default in the desire of the Other.

—Do I remember something about Shakespeare and a dead child? But I'm also thinking about another son whose fate more urgently demands our attention. Have you suggested that the child who suffers the sins of the father and burns, perhaps, with a pain even more terrible—the conflagration of the origin, let us say—is voicing abandonment? "Father, don't you see I'm burning?"—is that the equivalent of "Father, why have you abandoned me?" Is he burning in an equivalent of the Passion?

—I believe this is Lacan's view. But there is also more here than abandonment, if I may say so. There is also a kind of "pure desire" (Bernard Bass's term) for precisely what desire defends itself against in the dreams we have considered thus far and in the image of the crucifixion erected by Christianity. This pure desire is a desire for death, which Lacan reads not as a desire for a return to inanimate being, but as a desire for nothing, as the human relation to the *lack to be* which is the ground of relation to the signifying order. To this latter desire, he couples (though I still find this coupling enigmatic) a will to *jouissance* that exceeds what desire can sustain and does so via the interposing screen (preserving desire from the conflagration that threatens) of the subject's relation to what Lacan calls the object a, the object cause of desire—an image, precisely, of what the subject seeks to rejoin, namely its own nihilation. The object a, by which desire presents itself here in relation to its cause (the "absolute condition," as Lacan puts it in "The Signification of the Phallus"), is not the apparition of the child, as we have seen, but rather its *voice*—the dream is traversed, Lacan says, by a *schize* "that is to be situated between what refers the subject in the machinery of the dream, the image of the child who approaches, his look filled with reproach, and on the other hand, what causes the subject and in which it falls, invocation, voice of the child, solicitation of the look—*Father, don't you see . . .* " (FFC, p. 68/70). The "infant figure" thus stands at the near side of the limit marked by the object a, that limit where the "will to *jouissance*" is mediated.

—As you speak, I think less of the crucified Christ than of Antigone (unless the figure of the Crucifixion is at that first level of which he speaks, where the image "refers" the subject). Doesn't Lacan read the figure of Antigone's

visible desire, that *himeros*, as such an object-cause of desire? And as I remember, he even insists upon referring to her as a child, or a "kid," *la gosse*
(despite the fact that she has shared the final destiny of her father, wandering
around for god knows how many years with that stubborn old man, attending
the unthinkable, final passage—she knows about other deaths, that child: "I
come as dear friend to my dear father, / to you, my mother, and my brother
too. / All three of you have known my hand in death").

—Indeed. Lacan, by the way, does not fail to follow a long tradition in recognizing in her a precursor figure of the Christ. She knows her own version of
the Passion, which Lacan persists in phrasing in a Christological form.
("Father, why have you abandoned me?" is said in the play literally, he declares, when—as far as I can tell, anyway—her plaint concerns in fact the absence of any *friend*: "With no friend's mourning . . . unfriended now I go."
Philia is the crucial term here, as I tried to argue recently—I'll have to pass
you that paper.) The crucial point is that the *himeros enarges* to which you
have referred—what emerges from the eyes and upon the eyes as she is seen in
her shining beauty: the separating object a, in other words—figures in the
moment of the passion. The emergence of her beauty marks a limit point for
desire, the limit of the desiring subject's relation to its death. Let me cite Lacan
here. The *himeros* is "that visible desire that comes forth [*se dégage*] from the
eyelids of the admirable young girl" (EP, p. 327/281). It marks "a certain relation to the central field, but also what prohibits us from seeing its true nature,
what blinds us [*nous éblouit*] and separates us from its true function." In other
words, the beautiful, in its *éclat*, is a barrier that halts or confounds desire (this
is a powerful reading of the traditional function of the beautiful) even as it
points beyond:

> The true barrier that stops the subject before the unnameable field of radical
> desire inasmuch as it is the field of absolute destruction, of destruction beyond
> putrefaction, is properly speaking the aesthetic phenomenon inasmuch as it is
> identifiable with the experience of the beautiful—the beautiful in its beaming
> brilliance, that beautiful of which it is said that it is the splendor of the true.
> (EP, p. 256/216)

It points beyond, but in its confounding, limiting function, this *éclat* of the
beautiful functions in precisely the way the Crucifixion figures in the Passion.
("Anamorphic" because this image of the young girl's radiance unfolds in and
through the movement of the play, Lacan argues, and is thus analogous, in its

appearance, to that phallic anamorphic figure—a figure of the Crucifixion again—that Lacan brings to the seminar in one of those wonderful show-and-tell moments.) As for the Passion itself, as Lacan reads it, it is about the death of God, as we considered it earlier. I'll cite again at some length to recover that context.

> That's the problematic from which we begin [he has just evoked the Freudian response to the myth of the death of God]. The sign unfolds there that I proposed to you in the graph under the form s($\cancel{A}$). Situated, as you know, in the upper left section, it offers itself as the final response to the guarantee demanded from the Other concerning the meaning of that Law articulated in the depths of the unconscious. If there is nothing more than lack, the Other defaults, and the signifier is that of his death.
>
> It is as a function of that position, itself dependent on the paradox of the Law, that there is proposed the paradox of *jouissance* that we are now trying to articulate.
>
> Let me observe that only Christianity gives its full content, represented by the drama of the Passion, to the natural character of that truth we have called the death of God. Indeed, with a naturalness beside which the approaches to it represented by the bloody combats of the gladiators simply pale.

—Gladiators?

—I'm not sure, but I'm thinking of what Bataille and Leiris make of the bull-fight, or Bacon, for that matter—aren't those also commemorative rites, where the rite has to do with the human relation to the signifier? Let me continue.

> What is proposed to us by Christianity is a drama that incarnates literally [literally again!] that death of God. It is also Christianity that links that death to what happened to the Law; namely, that without destroying that Law, we are told, but in substituting itself for it, in summarizing it, in taking it up again in the very movement that abolishes it—thus offering the first weighty historical example of the German notion of *Aufhebung* . . . —the only commandment is henceforth "Thou shalt love thy neighbor as thyself." (EP, p. 227/193)

—Let's forget the gladiators. . . . This theme of the death of God: do you remember Blanchot's reiterated citation of that phrase, "Whoever sees God dies"? *The Madness of the Day* stages that scene, but so does the "primal" one, I suspect (the phrase comes back late in *The Writing of the Disaster*, I believe). That phrase, I think I understand now, is actually Blanchot's meditation on that same theme. How strange a path in the proximity of Levinas . . .

And then that theme of the neighbor. Is that *Aufhebung* of the Law also a sublation of the relation to the other that Lacan offers to us briefly near the beginning of the seminar on ethics under that name he takes from Freud's *Project*: the *Nebenmensch*? And might it have something to do with Antigone's *philia*?

—You haven't left me much to say. Let me begin by completing the point about the Crucifixion. If the Christian representation of the Passion flirts with a confrontation with the default of the Other, it nonetheless shields us (and you notice, Lacan consistently says "us" in speaking of Christianity) from the confrontation with what lies behind the image of the Crucifixion. The exposed figure of the Christ is like the Sadian object (which has its own *éclat*, its own beauty): a *stase* of suffering "that affirms that what is cannot return into the nothing from which it has come":

> This is the limit that Christianity has erected in the place of all the other gods, under the form of that exemplary image drawing secretly toward it all the threads of our desire.

What remains at a crucifixion, in this reading, is a barrier. The sublimating apotheosis preserves something of that "human" that is implied in the notion of the *ex nihilo*. But in elevating this "human thing" on the cross, it denies the residue to which Antigone testifies. And this is where we must take the full meaning of the figuration of Antigone's desire. True, her image, placed as it is at the limit of the human relation to its finitude, confounds our sight ("the function of the beautiful being precisely to indicate the place of man's relation to his own death, and to indicate it to us only in a blinding flash" [EP, p. 342/295]; "*Himeros enarges*, there is the central mirage, which both indicates the place of desire in so far as it is desire for nothing, the relation of man to his lacking to be, and prevents one from seeing it" [p. 345/298]). In this, it functions exactly as does the phrase from the dream of the burning child: what appears in Antigone's eyes is like what sounds in the child's voice. In each case, we are dealing with the object a. But this blinding figuration at the limit of desire also engages a beyond—it bespeaks what Lacan terms a "radical desire" (ultimately for what he calls the Thing). Lacan says it when he evokes the conflagration induced by the child's sentence: "The phrase is itself a firebrand—on its own, it brings fire where it falls—and one cannot see what burns, for the flame blinds us to the fact that the fire carries to the *Unterlegt*, to the *Untertragen*, to the real" (EP, p. 58/59). It blinds us, but there is also exposure. If we didn't know this last conflagration, there would be no need to wake up.

Here I am approaching the limits of what I want to say (not to speak of my understanding). But I want to emphasize that there is something "beyond" the desire for death as Lacan figures it in his *Ethics*. He says something like this himself in relation to the notion of *jouissance*:

> What is beyond is not only the relation to the second death, that is to say to man inasmuch as language demands of him that he account for this, that he is not. There is also the libido, namely what in fleeting instants carries us beyond that confrontation and makes us forget it. And Freud was the first to articulate boldly and powerfully that the sole moment of *jouissance* known by man is at the very place where fantasms are produced, which represent for us the same barrier as regards access to that *jouissance*, the barrier where everything is forgotten."
> (EP, p. 345/298)

Now, it is not ultimately clear to me that *jouissance*, as Lacan describes it in this text, is ultimately separable from the relation to the "second death" (though perhaps I'm resisting something—am I the only one who finds *jouissance* to be a rather opaque signifier in this text?). Isn't that what makes the relation to the *jouissance* of the neighbor so terrible, what made Freud recoil at the Christian injunction to love thy neighbor? But it seems clear that "radical desire," as a relation to the nihilation the subject, must assume as its own in the engagement with the signifier, the relation of which the chorus speaks in *Oedipus at Colonus* with the phrase "*me phunai*" (words Lacan assigns to Oedipus, and which I am tempted to translate in view of Lacan's linking of the *me* to the pleonastic *ne* as: "not to be, even"), engages more than the *nihil* that opens with this signifier. Let's take Antigone rather than Oedipus. The anamorphic figuration of desire that appears at the moment of her passion screens an extremity of affliction that is comparable to that of the burning child. But Antigone's desire reaches beyond the *atè* that is a kind of affliction in the family line (an affliction extending beyond the irreducible conflict between the brothers, back to its source in the father's curse and from there to that origin that is the mother's desire, a "criminal" desire and an impasse "more radical" than Hamlet's, "marking the origin of tragedy and humanism"). It is a desire for a death with which she has always claimed intimacy, but also, and inextricably, a relation to the other, to which she appeals in the name of friendship or love. In the act of this *philia*, as we see in her transgression of Kreon's law, she serves an irreducible that is the being of her brother, a "being" that cannot even bear the predicate "criminal." Lacan, as you know, claims that her choice is to assume the crime: "Antigone chooses to be purely and simply the guardian of the criminal being as such." But if I have understood his earlier remarks on the *ex nihilo*, we must phrase things differently. Polyneices may be labeled "criminal" only in the economy of good and evil; to be sure, he *is* nowhere else (in this sense, perhaps, his being, any being, is irreducibly "criminal," irreducibly "evil"—but aren't we back then to a Christian formulation?). But this relation to the signifier is not without a remainder, which Antigone honors in the form of Polyneice's corpse. Antigone honors the real of the relation between the human being and the signifier.

One must not hypostatize this real—it cannot be thought apart from what Lacan calls "the presence of language." But it also cannot be reduced to the *nihil* that is structurally implied by that presence. Beyond the subject's return to its own nihilation (beyond the death drive in certain of its figurations in this text), there is at stake the recovery of a relationality that involves minimally, yes, the return to the *Nebenmensch* as it figures furtively in Lacan's discussion. But where Lacan takes *neben* in the direction of *der Nächste*, the neighbor, and thus into a proximity of veritable indifference, I would want to try to think a different usage (*jouir de* is also "enjoy the use of"). I'm going fast, I know, and I think that Lacan envisions other configurations of the relation marked by *neben.* There is the place of the analyst, for example (consider the brief remarks on the gift of a "désir averti" [an "alerted desire"] near the end of the volume [EP, p. 348/301]; they should be read together with what he says about the presence of an alterity in *The Four Fundamental Concepts*). But a large portion of the seminar on ethics is given over to the figure of the neighbor, who marks the site of an unbearable *jouissance*, a "radical evil" for a psyche under the governance of the pleasure principle. The latter *jouissance*, as Lacan develops it, is inseparable from an aggressivity turned against the self by a superego left unbound by the default we have considered in the symbolic law; thus Lacan speaks of a "*jouissance* of transgression," calling upon Sade via Blanchot's meditation on Sade's "transgression of all human limits," his approach to "a center of incandescence or an absolute zero" (EP, p. 236/200–201). We find here all of the extremity of affliction we tried to understand in regard to Lacan's reference to "the cruelest point of the object," something very close to Nietzsche's "Dionysian" (about which Lacan has his own words of caution, though I refer to the Dionysian that Nietzsche conceived via the path of cruelty). But the place of the neighbor's *jouissance* is also marked in other references to the sexual act that do not necessarily conform to "the [Sadean] idea of a technique oriented toward a sexual *jouissance* that is not sublimated" (EP, p. 234/199). We are told that in the space of the neighbor ("not with the fellow self whom we so easily turn into our reflection . . . but this neighbor who is closest to us, the neighbor whom we sometimes take in our arms" [EP, p. 232/197]) a *jouissance* is possible that "enables one human being to be for another in the place that is both living and dead of the Thing" (EP, p. 348/300). I may be mistaken in doing so, but I take that to be the place opened originally by the *Nebenmensch*.

—And why is that a space of indifference?

—Again, I've been going fast, but Lacan claims that the presence of "fundamental evil" ("méchanceté foncière" [EP, p. 219/86]) in the neighbor is indistinguishable from "that heart within me which is that of my *jouissance*" (p. 219/186). He is the *same* (p. 233/198): "To love him, to love him as myself, is necessarily to move at the same time toward some cruelty. His or mine?, you will object. But haven't I explained to you that nothing tells us that they are distinct? It seems rather that it is the same cruelty, on condition that those limits that oblige me to posit myself opposite the other as my fellow are overcome" (p. 233/198). It's just after those words that Lacan takes his distance from the Dionysian evoked in the "psychologism" of Freud's "current disciples."

—Forgive me, but I'm beginning to find this motif of cruelty a bit stifling.

—Well, that's my point. I think he's turning a bit short with this play on the "same" of the "interior or emptiness" met in the relation of *jouissance* (EP, p. 233/198)—short of what he himself offers. Of course there are other relations of love than the ones he has evoked in this seminar (including the courtly); think of his later remark to the effect that only love allows *jouissance* to condescend to desire. But to stay with the context we have sketched here, I would argue that it is also another love that carries Antigone into a more generous usage (Sade's is "generous" as we learn in "Kant with Sade," but still . . .)—not a relation with "the same," but a relation without relation with one who is near.

Again, I'll have to pass you my text before you leave tonight. But to summarize, I would say that what is *also* at stake in the thought of a "radical desire" is the opening of another form of relationality, a material relation that is not with some brute nature or even an unmediated "body," however fragmented (the place of language is irreducible), but rather the originary exposure to the *Nebenmensch* who is close, im-mediately proximate, in the manner of that human that suffers the signifier. This is part of the real that is at stake, *se fait* in every act of "real intelligence," any usage that engages the (missed) encounter with the other.

A pause opened. More an interruption than a pause: as though a conclusion had announced itself unexpectedly, like an unwelcome visitor.

—Have we reached the common ground of the scenes we've been reading?

—Have we found what brought us here, you mean? I can't forget your earlier anxiety around that question.

Well, nothing common, in any case, and certainly no ground. Perhaps we've in fact reached the site of a proximity—from a theoretical point of view at least. It would be the proximity of *neben,* or *close.* But as to whether we've managed to occupy that proximity. . . . Let me just say that I wonder whether we've reached even our point of departure. A moment ago, I thought we had something. But the statements have dissipated, as statements always do. I'm sure it's all correct. There may even have been some profound moments. But really, have we made a step of any kind? Even the farthest reaches of theoretical discourse feel sometimes like a very familiar track.

I wondered if it was now my turn to recall him to his "suppositions," his responsibilities, the engagements he had undertaken. Not in regard to me, but to the conversation, the promise of the conversation. It seemed to me he was denying something already well advanced.

I was finding my way to this thought when he interrupted my words. Not words yet, but the first expressions of discomfort.

—Forgive me, I'm always ready to abjure everything as soon as I sense the lightness of the concept. Language without exigency, "theory."

—When we started, you doubted your capacity to sustain a discourse on our topic; now you are cursing discourse.

But we both knew that a "discourse" had never been the aim. We both knew that he had faltered and I had entered (clumsy supplement!) at the point of a need, an exigency—the exigency of another relation to our so-called "topic." In all honesty, I couldn't really claim we had progressed. But from the very first introduction of Leclaire's phrase—was it a phrase?—I had sensed a pull in the directions we were taking, a light pressure. And the need to find the path was still impelling the conversation.

—I'd like to back up. I wonder if there really is such a proximity between the texts we've been reading. Or let me put it differently, because we've seen clearly enough that there are points of proximity. There's no denying that they offer at least comparable figures of a limit-experience with language. More than "comparable," in fact; there is a force in those meditations on the death of a child that almost requires we entertain the question of their relation. Of course, Lacan and Blanchot offer the scenes we've been reading against backdrops of considerably different understandings of difference. Even if we bracket the place of the phallus in Lacan and open the "absolute condition" as he describes it in "The Signification of the Phallus," we still have the problematic of the *il y a* in Blanchot. But from a distance, we could say with some justice that these differences are not the crucial point; we could emphasize that each of the texts we are reading honors the place of a real, that each inscribes at that site relation to an other. And we could add, still in the mode of the long view, that Lacan's meditation on the dream of the burning child answers fairly precisely to Blanchot's words on the exigency of the figure, and that Blanchot's own writing answers to the exigencies of the fundamental reflection sought by Lacan. I mean "answers" in the strong sense; the space of the infant figure stretches between the dream and the supposition, on the hither side of representation. Each figuration bears the marks of saying.

None of this would be wrong, and there is a great deal yet to be developed from these bases. But I'm wondering whether the proximity we've supposed and explored hasn't blinded us in some respects. Or maybe it's the pathos inevitably stirred by these scenes; maybe each one blinds us in the manner of the phrase from the dream of the burning child. Not so much to the extremity that lies beyond as to the manner in which they are assumed in each case. Blanchot himself may be a little culpable here inasmuch as he frames his récit with his reflections on the phrase from Leclaire. He couldn't avoid it, it seems. But how can we avoid reading that text in a tragic key, much as Lacan does with Freud's child? Yet, there is nothing intrinsically tragic about Blanchot's scene, even if it's clear from the larger context of *The Writing of the Disaster* that it holds terrible dimensions. The one remaining affect of the scene (its "interminable feature") is joy. The child knows his own *jouissance.* And where does Blanchot go with that feature of the scene? We know where Lacan goes, at least in the seminar on ethics that has allowed us to pursue the themes of abandon and default at the level of the symbolic; he goes toward the sovereign understanding of the Oedipus at Colonus, toward the *me phunai.* But does Blanchot follow such a line? And is there not perhaps a fundamental difference here? Isn't the question of "another relation" played out in that trajectory?

Think about it. We said very little about the theme of *jouissance* in Blanchot's récit, "the ravaging joy to which he can bear witness only through tears, an endless stream of tears." We noted without further consideration the words of the commentators who speak of "joy and ravishment" at accession to a "power to die" ("un pouvoir mourir"). But I think you would agree that Blanchot cannot be writing here about a triumphal assumption of the negative, even if there is an undeniable relation to the negative. No, in the space of the "secret," where that "endless stream" has flowed, the child knows the birth of another day. Or let me put it this way: in its birth, the child knows a different relation to the day than that of a reflexive, negating consciousness. I cannot help but think that *this* accession to the day is of a fundamentally different nature from anything described in the modern metaphysics of subjectivity or from anything psychoanalysis has given us thus far in its notion of the subject. I don't know how far I can go with this, but I believe I can approach it via that "yes" that Blanchot describes in *The Madness of the Day.*

—That "yes" you once called "ethical"?

—Exactly. Do you remember the narrator's description of his joy in the opening paragraphs of that text? Having known a death (or deaths) not unlike that evoked in the primal scene (though more "final" in character—they evoke more a final judgment and an apocalypse, though these fires of a day gone mad do follow another scene of strange, perhaps transgressive, joy involving a mother and child). . . .

—Your hero is also an Oedipus of sorts—his doctors wait at the "crossroads" after the incident of blinding.

—Absolutely. But his experience has transformed his relation to the negative. Having known that death, the narrator accedes to a happiness that he claims to find almost only in women, "beautiful creatures" who do not struggle against death. His own expression of the yes comes in a stunning inversion of a Cartesian affirmation: "I am not blind, I see the world—what extraordinary happiness! I see it, this day outside which there is nothing. Who could take that from me? And when the day fades, I will fade with it—a thought, a certainty that enraptures me" (*The Madness of the Day*, p. 6). The relation to the day as an inalienable but also unappropriable gift takes the form of an affirmation that includes something like a reflection, for death is assumed as a "willed" evanescence: "Ce jour s'effaçant, je m'effacerai avec lui." He doesn't say simply that he will fade with the day, in dependence on the day, as some kind of condition of his being. He says that with the effacement of the day—I need to translate "cognatively" to bring this out—he too will efface himself. His ecstatic joy lies in that thought, that certainty, and his certainty is a reflection, a transcending reflection that is a yes to death, a yes to the day and a yes to death. There is the *pouvoir mourir*. Barely a reflection (the day too *s'efface*— *je m'efface* is of the same grammatical construction), and "certain" by reason of an inevitability, the assumption of mortality is nevertheless a form of freedom. The metaphysics of subjectivity, in some of its forms at least, envisions a kind of suicide as the highest act, or a tragic affirmation that takes fatal destiny upon itself (think of Schelling and his tenth letter on *Dogmatism and Criticism*). This affirmation is only at the slightest remove from those (dialectical) turns, and yet it differs infinitely by reason of its in-finite assumption of the mortal gift of the day.

Lacan too finds the exigency of another relation in the transcendence of that "not to be, even." But I find something decidedly masculine and limited in that beautiful stance he goes so far as to name "the true subsistence of the human being." For it limits itself to the assumption of nihilation that marks the slight presence of the subject in relation to the order of language, the subject's transcendence.

—I'm not sure that's fair. There's quite a bit more to say on the topic of *jouissance* in Lacan, quite a bit more than you added yourself. There is also the *humour* he evokes in the opening pages of *The Four Fundamental Concepts*— that way of assuming the place of the fallen object that has nothing to do with irony, tragic or otherwise. And then the references to comedy at the end of the seminar on ethics or in the seminar on transference. All of that should be pursued.

—Of course. There is no reason to set things up exclusively and choose sides. But it does seem to me that in the seminar on ethics the modality of the "ethical" assumption remains tragic. And such an assumption denies the "yes" to which I referred.

—It's true that in the seminar on ethics the "tears" remain those of the petrified Niobe who figures the death drive. (Bernard Bass stresses in a compelling way the whiteness of the snow, though the play also points to its melting.) But even in Blanchot the eyes dry. Listen to the last words of those commentators on "survival":

The ever-suspended question: having died of this "ability-to-die" that gives him joy and ravages him, did he survive—or rather, what does 'to survive' mean then, if not to live by acquiescence to the refusal, in the drying of emotion, withdrawn from self-interest, dis-interested, extenuated to the point of calm, expecting nothing.—Consequently, waiting and watching, because suddenly wakened and, knowing this full well henceforth, never wakeful enough. (WD, p. 179/116)

—Yes. But it seems to me that the wait to which they refer partakes of the infinite of patience and passivity that belongs to responsibility. True, it seems an *askesis* of another modality than the joyful acceptance described in *The Madness of the Day*; but it proceeds from a yes. And we could well turn at this point to Blanchot's *Death Sentence*, which describes a transmutation of that patience into another yes of relation. But I don't want to launch into another textual analysis; the hour is too late. My point has been to remind us of the character of the engagements invited by the scenes we have been reading. I don't need to read Blanchot against Lacan—I can't claim to have gone far enough with either of them. But I do think that the "yes" of responsibility I have tried to draw from Blanchot's text has a decisive—no, not a decisive, a *generous*—place for our effort to engage what is at stake in the question of the death of the *infans*. And I wonder, in fact, if we couldn't rethink the problematic of childhood from that yes. Our first step, perhaps, would be to return to the "an-archic yes" Levinas himself finds at the heart of responsibility.

—You are recalling to me suddenly Elisabeth Weber's memorial words on Levinas in Washington. You remember that she drew from *Otherwise Than Being* to consider the work of the "Group for the Psychoanalytic Study of the Effects of the Holocaust on the Second Generation," reading their analysis of disruptions in the capacity for "metaphorization" in children of holocaust survivors in relation to Levinas's notions of persecution and responsibility.

—I remember that when I heard that address, I thought immediately of our problematic. Weber's thesis, as I understand it, was that the children in question suffer the legacy of their parents' terrible experience at the level of what Levinas terms the "transcendence of language," the very ground of relation to the other. It's not a legacy, perhaps; it's rather a failure in legacy that the children can know only as exclusion. They are excluded from a secret of sorts, exiled from their parents' past, no less than the parents themselves who frequently cannot "symbolize" the extremity of persecution they have suffered. The forms of repetition to which they have recourse—the analysts speak of a pre-conscious "concretization," a bodily "trans-position"—suggest that these attempts to *gain relation* to their parents' experience carry them back to the grounds of persecution itself, to the very transcendence of language. They return to the site of the "yes" of responsibility, suffering deaths that occurred, as Weber puts it, before their birth.

Of course, with this turn in the motifs of exposure and persecution we hover on the edge of both pathos and pathology; we would need to follow Weber's full analysis to keep from going over. But I came away from this reflection with a renewed sense of the importance of the question of legacy for any reflection on language and childhood (we saw it already, of course, in Leclaire and in Lacan's meditation on the family *atè*), and I am struck by the sheer force of this association of childhood and the an-archic yes of responsibility. As Jacques Derrida has told us in his "Nombre de Oui," and as he has demonstrated at least since the time of "Pas," the quasi-transcendental structure of an originary "yes" takes multiple forms. But perhaps the infancy that has haunted us is indeed a singular figure of the yes. The example provided by Elisabeth Weber reminds us that the yes of infancy is not necessarily a light one. But it opens to the gift of the day—at least there where it is affirmed, again (and it must be if there is to be speech). Childhood opens the space of that affirmation. We see it even beneath the rain of infantile objections, all those "nos."

—But wouldn't that early engagement—that early gift, that early death—require an entirely different thought of exigency and need, not to speak of "lack"?

—The "yes" is a response—originary, but not the "origin." What is required is another thought of relation. But I dare say we've made a start.

"Humor"? His smile indicated we'd reached an end this time. At least for this night. When I moved to the door, he went to his desk for the pages on Antigone. *He could never bear to see me leave without a text—he called it "the least he could do as a host." I suspected he was obliging me to return. But I think also that he didn't know how to trust the exigency of the conversation itself, or at least his own capacity to engage it. That vulnerability sufficed as an invitation, could never suffice.*

Appendix: Antigone's Friendship

> "The basis of communication" is not necessarily speech, or even the
> silence that is its ground and its punctuation; rather, it is exposure to
> death, no longer the death of myself, but the death of *autrui*, whose
> living and closest presence is already the eternal and unbearable
> absence that is diminished by the work of no mourning. And it is in life
> itself that the absence of *autrui* must be encountered; it is with this
> absence—its startling presence, always under the prior menace of
> disappearance—that friendship is played out and at each moment is
> lost, a relation without relation, or without other relation than the
> incommensurable (for which there is no place for asking whether one
> must be *sincere* or not, truthful or not, faithful or not, since it represents
> in advance the absence of bonds or the infinite of abandon). Such is,
> such would be the friendship that discovers the unknown that we are
> ourselves, and the encounter of our own solitude which we cannot be
> alone to experience.
>
> —Maurice Blanchot, *The Unavowable Community*

She acts in friendship, or love: *philia*. She can articulate only obscurely the
laws that guide her actions (however absolutely she appeals to those laws),
and she will even allow, in brief moments of doubt near the end of the famous
kommos, that her acts may not receive divine sanction. Ultimately, she doesn't
know the laws upon which she acts. But she claims firmly and consistently that
she acts in *philia* and even for *philia*. What is the meaning of this claim?

Lacking the requisite philological skills, and even the appropriate critical
support, I propose to approach the question modestly—that is to say, step by
step, and in complete reliance on the efforts of the established translators.[1]
Thus, my remarks will do no more than approach what this question holds for
a well-founded critical analysis of the play. But my hope is that I will at least
touch the horizon of the question of friendship as it has come to occupy recent
philosophical discussions addressed to ethics and to the question of the grounds

of politicality and sociality; for it is from that horizon that I have been drawn to address the topic in the play. With that aim, I'll try to engage, in the latter part of my paper, the reading of *Antigone* proposed by Lacan in his seminar on ethics, a reading that leaves largely untouched the question of *philia*, but which has shaped in an important way recent approaches to the question of ethics.

Step by step, I said. I'll pause over five stations for this question—five sites where the relation of *philia* is thematized. There are others; the bonds of *philia* traverse the play in such a way as to form a dense network (and are not always explicitly named). When Antigone, Ismene, or even Kreon refer to "my own" in the sense of kindred, evoke a "sharing," or speak of another as "dear," as in the very first line of the play, they are evoking relations covered in some way by the term *philia*, relations which involve someone who is *philos*. But I will limit myself to the major explicit references to *philia*, which appear, as I have said, in five sites. Five times, I would say, the meaning of the term is implicitly defined or is the object of a struggle.

The first of these lies in the initial exchanges between Ismene and Antigone, exchanges that literally turn around the meaning of *philia*. The exchanges begin and end with references to aspects of the notion, and pivot around a central statement of engagement on Antigone's part. The first instance comes when Antigone asks her sister, from within that dual form that Steiner evokes so well in his commentary,[2] and after a powerful evocation of the extreme of destitution they have reached as the last survivors of the accursed line of Oedipus, what she knows of the fate of "our friends." She is referring here to their brothers, and most specifically to the one who is treated as an enemy and who lies unburied (the reference to Kreon's proclamation makes that reference apparent). But since Ismene is still not aware of the edict against her brother, she misses the reference, presuming that "ours" means "those of our city." Already we have spanned some of the meanings of the term. For *philos*, as Benveniste explains in his famous article on the term,[3] can be used either for close kindred or fellow countrymen (the guard will later use the term in this latter sense to refer to Antigone [l. 438]). Antigone, however, immediately draws the line of reference that was implied by her earlier evocation of the afflictions that have unfolded from the family's fate by laying out the terms of the edict and raising the question as to whether Ismene will act nobly in accordance with her line. Her question is chilling: Will Ismene be able to assume the family affliction, or the "woeful fate," that *atè* of her family?

Ismene, for her part, can barely conceive of the act her sister invites her to share. As we see in lines 49–60, she recoils from the immediacy of the bond to which her sister has called her. We read her distance in her way of juxtaposing her appeal to civic authority and the force of the men in power with a highly formalized account of the terrible deaths of her parents and brother—Oedipus has to be counted twice here—and a repeated insistence on the *auto* of self-destruction that she would face with a sister who will later be termed "autonomos." She seems to sense what is at stake, but cannot conceive it; when she twice refers to the "impracticable" (*tamekana*) in the subsequent exchange, she is referring to the impossible not in a Bataillan sense, if I may say so, but rather in a practical one. Ismene cannot occupy the same space with her sister; she has no relation to that extraordinary vocative with which Antigone opens the play from the night of destitution that will form the ground of her act. Antigone hears the distance instantly. She is treated as harsh in many commentaries, and she certainly is. But the fact is that she recognizes between her and her sister an absolute *differend* from which she proceeds to speak, denying to her sister that being *with* (the preposition is *meta*) that marks the mode of relation she seeks.

> I wouldn't urge it. And if now you wished
> to act, you wouldn't please me as a partner.
> Be what you want to [!]; but that man shall I
> bury. For me, the doer, death is best.

And then the crucial words defining her act:

> Friend shall I lie with him, yes friend with friend
> when I have dared the crime of piety.
> φίλη μετ᾿ αὐτοῦ κείσομαι, φίλου μέτα,
> ὅσια πανυυργήσασ᾿ . . . (ll. 69–74)

Lloyd-Jones gives: "I am his own and I shall lie with him who is my own." (l. 68). The *meta* sounds twice to mark Antigone's desire. Is her passion sexually determined? It is difficult to avoid recognizing the evocation of incestuous desire, even if we recall the way Antigone voices, in her *kommos*, a similar hope of joining in friendship those who have died before her and for whom she has cared with her hands. The line is also a dark reminder that the one who speaks is the daughter and sister of Oedipus, and that she is speaking of Oedipus's son and brother. But it is not altogether clear that the evocation of incest here has any greater weight for our determination of Antigone's evocations of *philia* than does the later reference to Antigone as one who cries "like

a bitter bird which sees the nest / bare where the young birds lay" (ll. 424–25).[4]
To make my point far too summarily, I would propose provisionally, and by
hypothesis, that *philia*, as we are dealing with it here, does communicate with
desire; but the desire in question is essentially different from the *eros* that motivates Haemon (at least as the Chorus describes it). It is a passion of another
order—it is tinged with something like the desire Blanchot evokes in his meditation on Orpheus and Eurydice and Tristan and Isolde.[5]

But to stay within the principal terms of the exchange with Ismene, we note
that *philia*, as Antigone names it here, is first a *fidelity* (she says that she will
not betray her brother) to one she names her own—fidelity unto death. And it
is a *public act*. Repeatedly she emphasizes that the performance of the rites of
burial must be undertaken openly. They must be announced, exposed. When
Ismene urges her to keep the deed secret, she responds that she will hate her
sister even more if Ismene does not denounce her. We might read these declarations, following Ismene, as an instance of Antigone's "hot-heartedness" and
as a statement of her commitment. But I believe we should also recognize that
Antigone is saying that Ismene's behavior will be *more* hateful—that is, *less*
loving—if she fails to honor the glory, the appearance of Antigone's deed.
Does the *philia* in whose name she acts, have, therefore, some essentially public character? There is little philological evidence for such a usage, so we
should perhaps reserve the question of the relation between the essential
openness of the act (the *testimonial* character of *philia*, the witnessing involved
in it) and the glory attached to it. But however we evaluate Antigone's claim to
an audience or her refusal to honor the restrictions imposed by an oppressive
political force, it is clear that her act requires exposure and thereby raises for
us the pertinence of the question of friendship or love, as we are exploring it
here, for reflection on the political or ethical relation.

There is one last appearance of the notion of *philia* in the exchange we are
considering. It comes, as I indicated earlier, in Ismene's last words. To
Antigone's menace of hatred, thrice repeated, Ismene responds:

> Go, since you want to. But know this: you go
> Senseless indeed, but loved by those who love you.
> ἀλλ᾽ εἰ δοκεῖ σοι, στεῖχε· τοῦτο δ᾽ ἴσθ᾽, ὅτι
> ἄνους μὲν ἔρχῃ, τοῖς φίλοις δ᾽ ὀρθῶς φίλη. (ll. 98–99)

Antigone has declared that she is going to an honorable death. Ismene, separating now from her sister, perhaps definitively, speaks of *philia* in the sense of

the term that Michael Naas has documented in Homer.[6] *Philia*, as he demonstrates in his analysis of the instantiations of the term in the vocative, names proximity at the moment of loss. But Ismene does not know the meaning of "proximity" as Antigone has evoked it in referring to her refusal to be kept from being *with* her own (l. 48). She is already at an infinite distance from her sister when she gives voice to the separation.

The second textual station to which I have referred comes in the opening declaration of Kreon and in the exchanges that follow between him and Antigone. Kreon opens the forthcoming debate with a categorical determination of friendship as following upon a relation to the state:

> And he who counts another greater friend
> ["more dear," gives Lloyd Jones:
> καὶ μείζον᾽ ὅςτις ἀντὶ τῆς αὐτοῦ πάτρας
> φίον νομίζει,]
> than his own native land, I put him nowhere. . . .
> Nor could I count the enemy of the land
> friend to myself, not I who know so well
> that she it is who saves us, sailing straight,
> and only so can we have friends at all. (ll. 182–90)

For Kreon, prospering *political* relations are the condition of friendship, and the political relation comes first. Moreover, there is an exclusive relation between political enmity and friendship. That latter claim is the one that will lie at the center of the subsequent debate between Kreon and Antigone. Your brother, Kreon says, will not bear to receive the same honors as one who was his enemy. But Antigone, evoking the laws of the dead ("Hades demands these laws" [l. 519]), claims the right to a different usage. (I am "translating" line 521 as does Hölderlin, and Heidegger after him: "Who knows what usage is holy below?") Kreon responds with an absolute application of his earlier exclusive logic:

> Never the enemy, even in death, a friend.
> οὔτοι ποθ᾽ οὐχρός, οὐδ᾽ ὅταν θάνῃ, φίλος. (l. 522)

At which point we hear the line that has exposed the play to Christianization more than any other (though there are others):

> I cannot share in hatred, but in love.
> οὔτοι συνέχθειν, ἀλλὰ συμφιλεῖν ἔφυν. (l. 523)

Does she mean "by birth"? I believe that the "sharing" that Elizabeth Wyckoff observes is perhaps a bit closer to the *originary* or "natural" relation that Antigone is claiming.[7] For, after all, she has already denied love (*philia*) to her sister, and she will do so dramatically in the lines immediately to follow. If it is possible for her to exclude Ismene in almost the same breath as these words, then it would seem (though heaven knows this girl is not above contradicting herself) that the *partage*, the "sharing with" she evokes is of another, perhaps more "originary" character than the familial bond. The *philia* Antigone evokes is not *simply* a relation dictated by kinship (and perhaps not even essentially so determined). It may in fact be hard for her, even impossible, to dissociate the relation from the blood tie (she speaks principally in these terms, as we might expect; let us think again of her initial assumption of the fate of her line, let us think of her history—the care she has devoted, with her hands, to those closest to her). But when she says that she shares naturally in friendship or love rather than enmity, she is saying that *philia* is the more original, that it is a "closer" relation than enmity and must prevail. Past affliction and usage (usage as regards the dead, the laws of Hades) has made this relation to death the one she immediately favors.

You may hear that I am using Heidegger's interpretation of the Heraclitean *philia* to help define this sharing or inclination on Antigone's part. *Philia*, Heidegger tells us (explicating the term *philosophia* and reading the words attributed to Heraclitus as fragment 123: "physis kruptestai philei"), is "to bestow favor."[8] Antigone "favors" or inclines in this originary sense. She chooses death; she offers herself originally to the death of the other. From the ground of the family *atè*, from an extreme of destitution and affliction, she knows death intimately ("my life died long ago," she will say shortly [l. 559]) and inclines to death. She shares absolutely (that is, without reciprocity) in a relation to death—originally, or before any other relation. Ismene does *not* share that relation; even when she accepts death, she does not offer herself *to* death in the same manner (as will become clearer in a moment). So Antigone does not favor her sister's desperate attempt to join her. The dead brother, on the other hand, lies exposed in the most extreme abandon. Antigone inclines to death and turns from her sister.

> *Kreon*: Then go down there, if you must love, and love
> the dead.
> κάτω νυν ἐλθοῦσ', εἰ φιλητέον, φίλει
> κείνους·.... (ll. 524–25)

A bitter Sophoclean irony, since he pronounces in scorn and utter incomprehension something that touches on the very nature of her desire. Antigone inclines "by nature" to the mortal essence of the one who is close. Lacan will assert that she incarnates the death drive.

The distinction I have tried to draw between the postures of Antigone and Ismene appears dramatically in the third textual station to which I have referred. It follows immediately the lines we have just considered. Ismene is led out of the palace and attempts, in desperation, to join her sister in her guilt, her suffering, and her death. She desperately seeks her companionship.

> *Ismene*: I did the deed, if she agrees I did.
> I am accessory and share the blame.
>
> *Antigone*: Justice will not allow this. You did not
> wish for a part, nor did I give you one.
>
> *Ismene*: You are in trouble, and I'm not ashamed
> to sail beside you into suffering.
>
> *Antigone*: Death and the dead, they know whose act it was.
> I cannot love a friend whose love is words.
> ὦν τοὔργον Ἄιδης χοἰ κάτω ξυνίστορες·
> λόγοις δ᾽ ἐγὼ φιλοῦσαν οὐ στέργω φίλην.
>
> *Ismene*: Sister I pray, don't fence me out from honor,
> from death with you, and honor done the dead.
>
> *Antigone*: Don't die along with me, nor make your own
> that which you did not do. My death's enough.
>
> *Ismene*: And what desire for life will be mine if you leave me?
>
> *Antigone*: Ask Kreon. He's your kinsman and your care. (ll. 536–49)

I'll stop there—it is a terrible exchange. How can Antigone refuse what is, in effect, right now, a mortal act on the part of her sister? Antigone says that she cannot tolerate a loved one whose love (*philia*) is only in words. But Ismene's words, right now, are an act. She asks to be allowed to join her sister in her guilt and thereby exposes herself to the penalty of death. Is this not an act of friendship? How do we understand Antigone's refusal to share in love at this point?

Antigone responds initially, of course, in relation to their past exchange and the recent events, and she speaks now from an absolute sense of what is just for the dead. Here, in the midst of her *agon* with Kreon, she claims to know the justice proper to Hades and the character of the honor due to one who has acted as she has. She knows what deserves honor (and love) and what does not. Friendship or love, *philia*, Antigone reminds us, *is an act*, an act of testimony, and it is *not just* to claim to share it, even in solidarity, if one has not done the deed at the moment it is called for. But once again: Ismene is *now* carrying out what we might presume to be an act of *philia*. Why does Antigone refuse her gesture?

I have already suggested what I take to be the answer: namely, that Antigone is holding absolutely to a different sense of relation from the one that now motivates Ismene. Ismene wants the company of her sister, even if this means death. *Life is not worth living otherwise.* But Antigone is answering to an entirely different relation between life and death, and she is necessarily alone.[9] Let me try to put it this way: Antigone is indifferent to the offer of companionship, even hostile to it if that companionship means denial of the form of action she has embraced. Perhaps she could still acknowledge an act of love or friendship from her sister; she will in fact lament its absence in the *kommos* to follow. But friendship, for Antigone, is not "companionship"; in friendship, she tends to the mortal essence of the other, and friendship could only be the sharing of such an inclination. It is a companionship without companionship (a "community without community," to speak like Blanchot). For it is addressed to something in the other that does not allow an intimacy of any kind—an intimacy between individuals, that is. When Ismene commits herself to death, she does it from life and in the name of life ("And what desire for life will be mine if you leave me?" [l. 548]). Antigone chooses death in the name of death. That is why her act is *to deinotaton*, "strangest of all," as Heidegger defines it with the words of the Chorus.[10] Antigone is *to deinotaton* because she serves death out of a position of absolute extremity. She acts from a place of destitution or ruin, from an "outside" she proclaims as already claimed by death, already gripped by the usage of the dead. To grasp the enormity of her act, and to see the solitude she claims, justly, one must take the measure of the place from which she speaks, which is a place of affliction, of ruinous fate; and one must understand the direction of her action—namely the other's death. Lacan's meditation on the familial *atè*, and his suggestions, to which I will return, concerning the usage to which she appeals in relation to the dead (both of which are deeply informed by Heidegger's meditation on the human *Dasein* as *to deinotaton*), give us some sense of this measure. Antigone stands at the limit of the "world" or the "day." Claiming this ground from the very outset of the play, she already stands apart. When she then acts upon this claim in the name of friendship, she stands in solitude or in an absolute relation, because she is giving herself over to the other's death. It is perhaps conceivable that this relation could be shared (Antigone conceived of such a thing at the outset of the play; Ismene could not), but the common act would have no common ground. To share the act would be to share a relation without relation. Antigone is absolute in her commitment to this friendship, and thus she stands absolutely alone— not as an individual, in a modern sense, but as one who is without relation to the sphere of living relations.

I am not sure how to phrase this statement about Antigone's radical solitude in any more precise terms. But I believe that this theme of solitude is brought forth by the last textual site I want to consider, the last station of Antigone's "passion." I quote now from line 878:

> Unwept, no wedding-song, unfriended, now I go
> the road laid down for me.
> No longer shall I see the holy light of the sun.
> No friend to bewail my fate.
> ἄκλαυτος, ἄφιλος, ἀνυμέναι
> ος <ἀ> ταλαίφρων ἄγομαι
> τὰν ἑτοίμαν ὁδόν.

Aklautos, aphilos—unwept, unfriended. In the midst, first, of general lamentation (the Chorus initially breaks into a stream of tears), and then in an admiration of her glory that embodies the public approval Haemon claimed to have heard, admiration that reflects a presence that is almost comparable to that of a divine being, Antigone claims to have been abandoned. She emerges, in her interaction with the Chorus, with a presence that is both touchingly human and awesome (Lacan's emphasis on the emergent splendor of Antigone is deeply founded). But she is solitary, standing in only the most tenuous relation to the voices with whom she speaks. The "unwept, unfriended" is a sign of that distance, as is her manner of taking the Chorus's words for mockery at one moment. When she compares herself to Niobe, that distance is marked at its most extreme point. This is where she assumes her "most supreme trait" ("der höchste Zug," Hölderlin declared), her proper figure.[11] Lacan will say that this is where she gives a *figure* to the death drive.

But her sense of separation also has a more subjective cast that should perhaps be termed "abandonment." And this is where the lamentation regarding the lack of friendship reaches most deeply.

I go without a friend, struck down by fate
live to the hollow chambers of the dead.
ἀλλ᾽ ὧδ᾽ ἐρῆμος πρὸς φίλων ἡ δύσμορος
ζῶσ᾽ ἐς θανόντων ἔρχομαι κατασκαφάς· (ll. 920–21)

These recall lines 848–50, where she also speaks of being unwept by friends
and of entering the realm of the dead as a stranger: "never at home with the
living nor with the dead." She then follows with an expression of doubt concerning the divine usage to which she earlier appealed:

What divine justice have I disobeyed?
Why, in my misery, look to the gods for help?

Does she doubt even that her parents and brother will receive her in friendship? In lines shortly before the ones I have just quoted, she indicates that she
doesn't *know*, but that she is confident, or she hopes, that her loved ones will
receive her with love by virtue of her acts of care.

Still when I get there I may hope to find
I come as a dear friend to my dear father
to you, my mother, and my brother too.
All three of you have known my hand in death.
ἐλθοῦσα μέντοι κάρτ᾽ ἐν ἐλπίσιν τρέφω
φίλη μὲν ἥξειν πατρί, προσφιλὴς δὲ σοί,
μῆτερ, φίλη δὲ σοί, κασίγνητον κάρα·
ἐπεὶ θανόντας αὐτόχειρ ὑμᾶς ἐγώ. (ll. 897–900)

Ismene is once again excluded: Antigone calls herself the last of the line and
looks forward to meeting only those she has tended. She then gives an explanation that many have considered simply unworthy of Sophocles. For my part
(and without the requisite philological expertise, once again), it seems supremely worthy. For Antigone has touched a point in her acts that is beyond
articulation. In her doubt, it is entirely fitting that she should produce an explanation that is incommensurate with the grounds of the act of *philia* we
have considered thus far. If anything, her reasoning underscores the fact that
she does not know—and appropriately so—the exact grounds of her act. The
usage she has followed has an unwritten basis. If Antigone shares in love, not
hate, it is not according to logical distinctions like the ones she produces.

Lacan, however, finds a compelling logic in these words, and to approach
the question of usage I have just alluded to, I would like to follow his account
and then attempt some final words on friendship.

To make this turn, I should note once again that in his seminar on the ethics of psychoanalysis, Lacan draws heavily on the notion of usage that Heidegger develops initially in the mid-1930s and throughout his later work—in the essays on language, but also in texts like "The Anaximander Fragment," "The Question of Technology," or the essay on *Gelassenheit*.[12] The fact is, we find it everywhere in the later Heidegger, because it is the term with which he thinks the articulation of *Ereignis*, language, and humankind. Usage, *der Brauch*, is the disjunctive jointure of that articulation, a jointure achieved in a reciprocal play wherein humankind is said to be used for truth and required for the event of truth inasmuch as this event cannot occur except by way of a human usage that is something like its finite ground. That reciprocal play is the ground of both *poiesis* and *praxis*. *An Introduction to Metaphysics* already develops this notion at some length in the very discussion of *Antigone*.[13] But I would also point forward to the discussions in *On the Way to Language*, where Heidegger makes a step that Lacan will follow in his seminar on ethics. He asserts there that when the essence of humankind is engaged in and by the relationality I have described, this usage marks a limit that is a relation between the human, in the materiality that is proper to it, and language. A difference is marked, in other words, wherein the human is delimited as such. Lacan's formulation of this *logical* exigency leads him to speak of "the human that suffers the signifier." His reading of *Antigone* turns upon his argument that Antigone bears witness to that dimension of the human when she undertakes the criminal act of observing burial rites for her brother. He understands Antigone's act, in other words, to be an act of fidelity to the human, to the presence of the human. A presence, he adds, that has a singular claim (in this case, as in every case).

One could designate other focal points in his argument: his compelling reading of Antigone's "splendor," for example, and the "sublimating" character of that apparition. But Lacan also makes it clear that he understands the "anamorphic" character of the image or figure of Antigone to emerge from the ground of what I have tried to describe as her solitude, from the limit that is constituted by her assumption of the familial *atè* in the mortal act of serving her brother. The key place he accords to Antigone's words of justification late in her *kommos* speaks to this dimension of his interpretation. With a certain triumph *vis-à-vis* the entire history of the play's critical reception, he claims that Antigone's words make perfect sense.

His argument, to reiterate, has a logical basis. The institution of the signifier, he asserts, introduces into the totality of being a void or, more precisely, a relation, from which the signifying network unfolds. The human use of language, he asserts, is *ex nihilo*; it proceeds from the relation it opens between an emptiness—a *nihil* that defines the "real" place of the human—and the signifier as such.[14] That site, that relation between the human and the signifier that language cannot (but) say whenever it speaks "truly" or "originally," is the limit where Antigone takes her stand. Her act effectively marks this site; she is witness (*martyr*) to the irreducible claim of her brother's being—a claim constituted by nothing more than the presence of a corpse, the nothing of a corpse. This non-thing that has fallen from all legal protection and is falling even from every social relation still holds an absolute claim by virtue of the fact that it marks *what remains* of a being that has borne a name within the social order; the remainder of an existence that is irreducible to symbolic determination, though this fact of existence is given only by the presence of language. Antigone is *autonomos* in her act; she is testifying, justly, to the extra-legal grounds of the law. Her service does not take a form that would be recognized by Hegel. She bears witness, rather, to a dying that is the (non)ground of all speech and human life, all communication, as Blanchot puts it in the passage I quoted as an epigraph.

I am suggesting, in sum, that Antigone's act of *philia* must be understood as an act of witness or responsibility in relation to the claim of the other. But does such an act require the grounds offered by Antigone? Lacan implicitly claims that it does, that in speaking of the "unsubstitutable" character of her brother, and of the absoluteness of the claim represented by this bond, she testifies to the *singular* presence of the other. Now, I concur fully with the necessity of thinking this singularity of the claim. But if we follow Lacan's own argument concerning the place of the human in "the field of the Thing," might we not also have to acknowledge that this presence is essentially anonymous and thus irreducible to any determination by the order of the symbolic? By the name, we could say, but also *before the name*. Couldn't Antigone, by Lacan's own logic, have made a comparable argument for any other she chose to bury—couldn't she have alleged the singular claim of any other—of anyone, at least, of whom she could say *philos*? The latter is a company of those who are "close," to be sure, but it is certainly not restricted to those who are no longer "substitutable." Doesn't the unique, "substitutable" other also partake of the honor due to all the dead by usage?

It goes without saying that there are powerful determining conditions for Antigone's act, conditions that are historically defined, however partial her motives. Such conditions vary historically, to be sure, and they will be instantiated in an always singular fashion—singular for precisely the fact that the grounds of *philia* ultimately exceed historical or symbolic determination. So I would not want to deny the pressures of that determination; we see them clearly enough in the legacy that Antigone assumes, and in the dense structures of custom from which her act emerges. The usage of *philia* is inseparable from the latter forms of "social usage." But it is also, in its event, excessive in relation to those bonds—it escapes its reasons in its always singular occurrences. It is on this basis, I think, that it is possible to find in Antigone's evocation of *philia* (in her words and her acts) a link with a more modern experience of "unavowable community." This is why Antigone's prodigious act of friendship accrues political and ethical meaning as it subverts the instituted claims of every ethics and politics.

ANONYMOUS

FIGURES

Part Three

An Art of the Possible: A Dialogue with Salvatore Puglia

Some time ago, two years perhaps, Puglia sent me the reproduction of an old photograph shadowed with an X-ray image. It showed a man in a chair in a severe, upright posture, a demonstrative posture of some kind (was this originally for medical purposes?). He had affixed two red lines from corner to corner, effectively crossing out the image. On a little scrap of paper, he added his regards and noted that he was involved in a new project that should take about six months; his aim, he said, was to destroy the photographic image. As I prepared for our dialogue, I wondered about the fate of that project.

s.p. I've come to the conclusion that the battle to bring the photographic image into question is doomed to failure.

c.f. But after all your interventions in the medium of painting, all the work you've done with overlays of graphic images of every kind, and then the constant disruptions of the image with writing and archival materials (and this from the very beginning), why all the drama? And why does it center around photography? I presume it has to do with questions of historical legacy and testimony, with what I take to be—for you—a historical or even ethical task. But photography also seems to *torment* you in some ways. Bataille (the reference is relevant, I think) evokes in one of his titles a hatred for poetry. Yours, I think, is a hatred for photography.

s.p. A long time ago, I saw the images of torture in Bataille's *The Tears of Eros*. From that moment on, my relation with photography was terminated. I asked myself whether all photography after this image was not its equivalent and thus comparable to an act of torture. For several reasons: because it has an affinity with a surgical operation, and then by reason of its role as a passive witness before atrocity. There is a cruelty in the act of photographing a hu-

147

man being. Whenever the figure is reduced to a sign—a sign with meaning, a schema, a diagram (we see this most dramatically in clinical photography)—there is such an act of torture. I say to myself that in order to attack this, one must in one's own turn torture the image. So it became a matter of traversing, piercing, transpiercing the image as the only possible way of subverting photographic violence, the only way of escaping photographic totalitarianism, the unassailable presence of photographic reproduction.

C.F. To liberate what?

S.P. The possible. The possible of a world, which I can only think in the plural. Not another possible world, in other words, but the multiplicity of the possible. So, for example, the image can be doubled with shadow. One can more than double: one can multiply and thereby suggest that escape of the image from itself. The superimposition of texts had the same function—distancing the image from itself.

C.F. You know that I find in the multiplication of the image a powerful form of reduction. First there is a kind of suspension—I think of a purgatory or a captivity of some kind; some of your figures remind me of mute ghosts (a strange twist on the clinical capture). But in the multiplication of the image there is also a reduction of the image to a zero-degree of representation, which liberates it. The image loses its meaning (as defined in any scientific, medical, historiographic, or monumental form). It bears a history, to be sure, a mark of history, but it seems to mark more the fact of history itself than any given history. That's where I see the liberating potential.

S.P. Yes, that's the other possibility. And it may be that the shadow is the most visible and legible thing. I don't mean to introduce a mystic discourse on the shadow as real essence. That's not necessary. But the projection obtained might be the "originary" image, or rather the image in a state of purity, a kind of graphics or signature, or a monogram, as Kracauer says in his famous essay of 1929. One mustn't forget the infinite possibilities in the Greek *graphein*.

But again, it's not a matter of the shadow being more real than the object. The shadow just accompanies us. Either one is there or one is not there. When one is dead, one no longer makes a shadow on the earth. Perhaps it's just that simple. One can see the shadow as our ambassador, as our public relations manager. For Peter Schlemil, it was the only thing that made him acceptable to us. For my part, I tell myself that in order to reopen communication one must restore the shadow, and with it the possible.

Salvatore Puglia, *Ashbox*, 1987. Canvas. Photograph courtesy of the artist.

Salvatore Puglia, *Uber die Schädelnerven*, 1993. Iron, glass, acetate, x-rays.
Photograph courtesy of the artist.

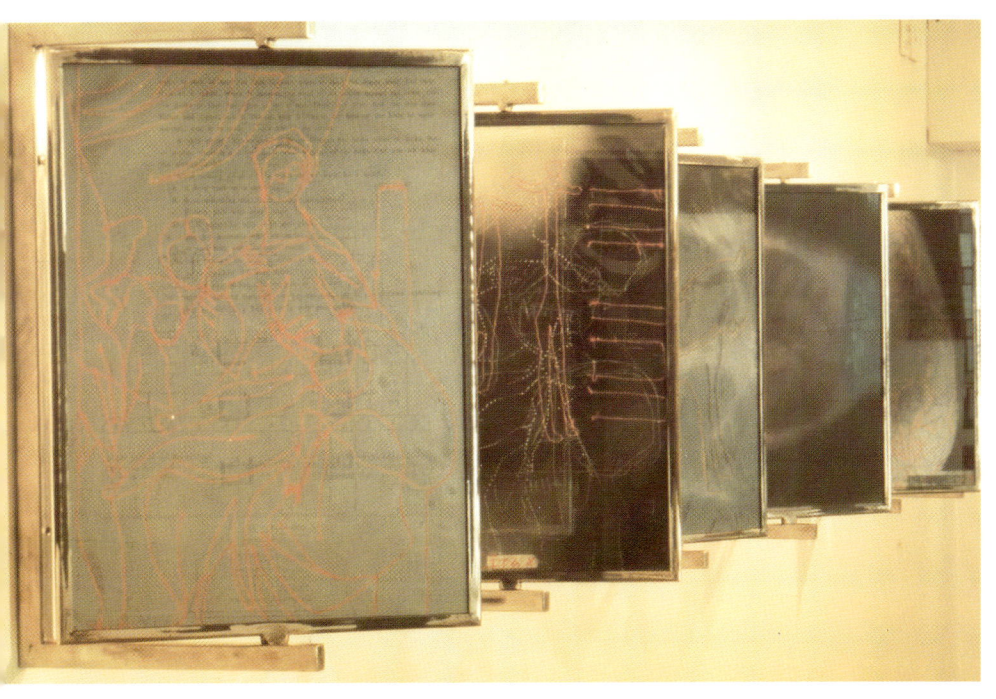

Salvatore Puglia, *Figure humaine*, 1994. Iron, glass, acetate, thread, x-rays.
Photograph courtesy of the artist.

Salvatore Puglia, *Ninna, Nanna*, 1995. Gelatin, pigment, iron, acetate, glass. Photograph courtesy of the artist.

Salvatore Puglia, *Les âmes du purgatoire*, 1994. Iron, glass, acetate. Photograph courtesy of the artist.

Salvatore Puglia, *Essai sur l'origine des langues,* 1995. Resin, plexiglass, iron, zinc.
Photograph courtesy of the artist.

Salvatore Puglia, *Still Lives*, 1996. Polyester, resin, iron. Photograph courtesy
of the artist.

Salvatore Puglia, *Stèles mobiles*, 1992. Wood, lead, wax. Photograph courtesy of the artist.

As for history and testimony, the answer is complicated because, as you know, I gave up the discipline of history. I stopped wanting to *demonstrate* something about the past, to seek meaning, when the only meaning something has is that it existed, that it should have been possible. I'd had enough of that mindless positivism that consists in saying: "Look: that's how it was—I'm going to show you and tell you how it was."

c.f. But why photography, exactly? Is it that our historical imaginary is structured by the photographic image today? Or are you combating the overwhelming presence, the omnipresence, of reproduced images?

s.p. On the one hand, there is that omnipresence. But from the very beginning I was disarticulating the elements of representation. Even when it was a matter of paintings. There were always reduced elements; phrases that were extrapolated, transcribed, translated into other languages, sometimes portions of words or letters, sometimes tiny pieces of torn archival material where only a few words were visible. There was always a dispersion, a spatial explosion, and isolated floating elements that were unified only by a kind of context, for example, color. (The working protocol was one of exploring and bringing forth pigments that had been tossed on and then worked with a sponge, so that the support structure and its elements would emerge, slightly hidden.) Then I started treating the image and writing in the same way.

But in concentrating on the question of the past in a more direct fashion, it became necessary to take on the question of the photographic image itself. Because it's true that there is an identification, a kind of superposition of our historical memory and the image. It's possible that we've passed from historiography to iconohistoriography, that our memory depends much more on the image than on written transmission. And there we have photography and all its variations. Like I said the first day, while needing to use the photograph, it was crucial not to accept the *dictat* that is the given, saturated image . . . never to accept it as adequate presentation or as a beautiful object. In this sense, photographic technique does not interest me.

c.f. Your relation to history has evolved, hasn't it? Your work is more and more focused on the question of history.

s.p. I think the temporalization has been a choice. At the outset, the painting tended to escape temporality.

c.f. I presume you're speaking of a kind of historicity rather than the temporal factor introduced into the work itself (which I know is important to you).

s.p. Yes, "temporality" in the sense of dating. It's been a way of getting past the rather vague discourse on a supposed origin, an originary state placed in the fog of a common heritage or a common history. The aim is rather to approach individuals who have lived and have left us a real legacy . . . and thus to bring together a bit more the questions of legacy and witnessing. And then, perhaps, a small ideological question: escaping testimony to oneself. Painterly work tended more, I think, in the direction of a witnessing to one's own existence. In the turn to more explicitly historical materials, it was a matter of approaching a responsibility (not purposefully, but as an afterthought): responsibility not only for oneself, but as a saying. In this sense, photography is like a bridge. A means to use. It shouldn't be central. It should be a medium for a passage.

c.f. I've been struck by the way your movement away from painting has also distanced you from those strong efforts you made to evoke your Neapolitan background. I confess that nothing was more beautiful for me than those colors and materials. I started to see them everywhere. But you left behind the need to mark that relation. I no longer see the reference to Italy.

s.p. On the contrary! It's coming back slowly. I'll show you. . . . Color, the graphic concept, that writing in space that emerged, like . . . an anamnesis. There too antiquity was involved, and the idea of a legacy, of everything that remained in a fragmentary state. The act of leaving, of taking my distance from Italy, allowed me to attend to it. Whereas, when I was too close. . . . What interests me now is the incapacity of people to interrogate what they have done, what they were in the past, the Italian past. When I see people of the generation of my parents . . . how they continue to be incapable of self-criticism. The very fact that they did certain things, more or less by choice, prevents them from having a critical perspective. It prevents them, fundamentally, from changing. That fidelity to what has been, as though the capacity to say that one was perhaps mistaken at a certain moment in one's life represented a mortal danger. It's the shock, I think—what scares them is quite simply experience itself, which they know as a kind of shock. I'm trying to think about that. For example, I did some work with a small image of my father taken when he was four or five years old. They dressed him in a fascist uniform, like all the children at the time, and took a picture of him making a fascist salute. I took that single photo and reproduced it in all sorts of ways, using the negative and overlaying various writings and materials, then an overlay of shadow with colors varying between a very soft pink and a very hard brown, thinking that an image like

Figure 5 Boy in fascist uniform.

that could not but present something disquieting, even something horrible. Because it's a tender image that nonetheless anticipates everything to come. An image, and a way of working with it too, that plays between the poles of the horrible and the seductive. So, I presented it with considerable trepidation. I held an exhibition in Rome. My father, presented in large format, dozens and dozens of times on a wall. Of course, he came to the exhibition. I feared his reaction tremendously. He might consider himself an object of ridicule and get angry. Well, it turned out he was delighted, extremely happy. Why? Because he was *there*. As he had been in the past. He hadn't grasped the questioning at all! He was represented, so it was good. The rest was buried. You understand? The image is good. We lived, we did that. It was good because we did it. We remember; therefore we were. Therefore it's good. (*Laughter*) So in this sense, once again, the battle with photography was lost.

c.f.   There are several fronts there, no? There is a battle with the seductions of the image—its saturated presence, its character as "given," as you sometimes put it (by which I understand its capacity to "absorb" reference or seduce one into seeing its relation to the referent as immediate), and then there is its aesthetic side. On the other hand, there is the (no doubt related) question of the image and its relation to memory.

s.p.   Yes; the stance at the outset is anti-aesthetic, even if one might feel great empathy with a particular object. But I tend to resist enthusiasm, which serves those involved in imitation. I believe that this procedure of transforming documents, which approaches a painterly handling, is one that uses the instruments of an aesthetics of taste but must end by being anti-aesthetic. But however disquieting or ambiguous the images, however much I multiply them, it's difficult to avoid the thing being taken at the end as an aesthetic experience. Even images that are there to trouble the conscience, even images like that can be perceived as beautiful or seductive. One can always go wrong. And there is always the danger of going too far, or transforming the photograph to the point of denaturing it and leaving, well, a mere image—as you can see, there's no winning. All one can do is take on the photographic images, haunted as one always is by their power of seduction and substitution, and in all the disgust one feels for their hegemony. Just as (I owe this to Rodolphe Burger, who attributes it to Plato) one can only do politics while being disgusted by politics. But one must do politics.

As for the question of memory, part of my need to torture the image comes from my rage against the need to attach mourning to a sole representation, as to a photo on a tomb. That one should need to fix or capture memory in this manner, renouncing or abdicating a more inner, more unconscious, and perhaps truer memory. Instead, one hangs on to a more episodic, punctual memory. At the same time, I recognize the vital need for such a thing. It's always ambiguous. Yesterday, we read in Klarsfeld's book [*Puglia and I had visited the Centre de Documentation Historique, a museum and library devoted to Holocaust studies, to consult Serge Klarsfeld's volume on deported French children; the letter to which Puglia refers was displayed in an exhibition sponsored by the Centre*] the letter from a young deported girl who in the most extreme danger and affliction wrote to her family: "I want photos—it's more important than bread." One can only respect such a thing. One must respect it. But at the same time, I feel a great rage against the incapacity to live in a visual void. To need always the handrail of the image. The incapacity to live without handrails. So a frontal assault is inevitable. Or to say at least that the image can express something else, or several things. Give it shadow, cut through it. . . .

Also, on this question of memory, I have the impression that [historical] consciousness is something that takes us beyond the question of memory. There is a kind of Scylla and Charybdis here: those two poles of memory treated by the great Soviet psychiatrist Lurija. In the first, an individual is condemned to recall every instant, every experience, and cannot rid himself or herself of that obsession. I believe that corresponds to a modern condition. We stand in passive fascination before the images of our history, however horrific. And then there is the related phenomenon we discussed a while ago: memory is good in itself. Once again: we remember, therefore it's good. All expression, all lived experience is good. I suppose this is a common thing; but in terms of historical reflection, I think it is part of the post-modern mentality. In any case, I believe that the watchword "Remember, remember" does not suffice. It's only a first stage, and it can even prohibit passage to another kind of memorized experience. In this respect, I adhere to the position of Claude Lanzmann, who has taken a distance from Spielberg's obsession with the restitution of what is lost. Lanzmann puts it this way, as I remember: "What counts is informing. In the literal sense: giving a form. Where is the form? One adds stories upon stories. Only works of art can transmit."

Then there is the other pole, where we have an individual whose memory is scattered, fragmented, dispersed. This was the case with an officer of the Soviet army who had lost his memory after the explosion of a shell and could only recover it (though he never really recovered it) after an uninterrupted work of writing. He would write the past events, little by little, even if he forgot what he had written two lines before. Through writing, he recovered his memory piecemeal. It worked like a leopard skin. There are very beautiful sentences in which he recounts how he awoke from his state of forgetting after three days; he began to remember Lenin, the spring, the Soviet Union, the fact that he had a sister and a mother.

Whereas in the other case the individual suffers from an inability to forget images. Every episode is linked to something visual. I like to try to move between these two poles.

C.F. One can certainly see the second in your laborious transcriptions. You've told me how painful it can be to engrave on glass for long hours. But clearly, in moving between those two poles, you are also seeking to move *beyond* them. You spoke of a "memorized experience." On other occasions, you've spoken of a *thought*.

S.P. Of course. But it is a matter of something more than intention. And that's another question I've given a great deal of thought to recently. You raised the question of address in our first discussions. Well, if it is a matter of presenting a photographic image (which, as long as it is photography, involves the presentation of some content—something that was there at a given time; that's inescapable) the address always locks us into the necessity of a statement, an intended meaning [*vouloir-dire*] that situates itself finally in the field of *good* intentions, a veritable scourge in our time. I'm not against intended meaning per se; but it must be forgotten along the way. It has to be forgotten *en route*, so that at the other end there is something that stands on its own, something that belongs to the intervening execution but that is already beyond it. If one remains under the imperative of a statement, there is a kind of contamination—the work will be caught up in that malady that is a problem for so many artists: by which I mean the inability to forget intention, an unrelenting good will. As for my own concerns as an artist, I'm not there to express myself. I've always seen my work as a process of interpretation. . . .

C.F. At dinner last night, we discussed the suffocating pressures of the culture industry in Paris. Ariane [Chottin] maintained that there had perhaps never been less freedom of expression than in recent years. Every word, every gesture, seems to suffer a specular capture in the space of representation. No claim can be made in the public space—however authentic—that escapes the play of mirrors and lights. Each gesture only augments the general effect of capture and evacuation, the general emptying of the act. At that point, I tried to develop some of my thoughts on a different pragmatics of thought and art, a pragmatics that would not answer to a determinate means/end relation defined by a structure of representation and cultural value, and that would involve a different structure of intellectual relations (a pragmatics whose "object" would be the *pragma* of existence—something very close to what you called the possible, or "possibles," of a world). I even got into a discussion of *Antigone* to evoke the ethico-political dimensions of a *public claim* that would unsettle the symbolic order itself in the name of an exigency of an ethico-political order. I don't want to launch into that now, but it seems to me that what you have said about a praxis directed to the possible may correspond to what I was trying to evoke. I'm very struck by your dual sense of an ethico-political imperative of a historical order, and your willingness to risk an undertaking without any defined telos—a praxis without the guide of any representation of its goal. And I'm all the more struck by the fact that this is in the very uncertain realm of art, with all its *material* obscurities.

s.p. We should come back to that: the choice of engaging matter (with its own properties, always to be discovered) in a dialectic with an idea. A kind of alchemy. And we need to define better that to which one responds while this process is underway. In any case, I think what one finds, when one loses oneself underway, is a time that is not linear but, in a sense, immanent and spatial. And in losing finality and the intention to pass along a message, one finds oneself again as witness to one's time. One becomes oneself a *stèle*.

c.f. I'd almost prefer to pause and let those words stand without comment. But I'm struck by that word "alchemy."

s.p. Perhaps the word is "metamorphosis." I think of it as a kind of metamorphosis. Let me try to approach it this way. Things only become real—in art, I mean—when a foreign gaze meets them. They are addressed to others, so there must be exchange and transmission, there must be communication. But at the same time, if they are caught up in meaning, if they are too close to the essential topic, too close to a denunciation, say, they will lose their force, their *striking* force, which derives from an address to the emotions. The initial pathos must be transformed, coldly, that is, without remaining in that enthusiasm, so that one can propose at the other end an impact that is also emotional, and which would touch the consciousness (even though something of the point of departure would be lost). In that sense it is a political undertaking. The least effective and least rigorous is the desire for a political art, an art of denunciation. For it becomes *kitsch*. What is kitsch but a displacement in scale, a pure citation?—that is, a citation of one's own way of having seen some history. Statements are not enough. Someone who has chosen to use the weapons of art must use them properly; they are weapons of metamorphosis. One should consider oneself an agent of metamorphosis.

c.f. How do you understand that impact on emotion and consciousness? You've also spoken on occasion of a kind of vitality.

s.p. Well, it's true that the impact in question involves the cords of sensibility, something on the order of sensation. Bacon says something like this. But it seems to me that they are not far from consciousness. The artist's own procedure of transformation involves a thought that is unconscious, but which also involves a reflection that leads to what I understand as a *visualized thought* (not a "visual thought"—that's a little different). The result should be something on the order of a little shock, an electro-shock that precedes consciousness by just the tiniest temporal fraction. But again, one mustn't confuse aesthetic extremism (which, according to the Jacobin Adorno, is the only justification of the work of art) with the moral extremism that manifests itself in the choice of subjects that are difficult to look at. Nothing is more boring, off-putting, and useless than this moral extremism, since it comes down to being a citation of one's own audacity. They are like works that name their object very precisely and thus illustrate it. Like sex: you show a man performing fellatio. Or death: you show a cadaver at the morgue. No, it can't be a matter of simply showing strong images. In fact, such things can be very reassuring. We know it exists: someone has taken on the job of going down to the morgue; or someone thinks they show us sexuality by showing the sexual act. It's very reassuring; someone is there to do it in our place. But it's only illustration. It adds nothing. Or yes, it adds something—it fills a lack in our imaginary. But it doesn't open anything. It fills. Whereas the type of shock I'm talking about is not of the order of the visible, though . . . how can one put it exactly? . . . it's still a form.

But still, it must be something that is unexpected. Because one must . . . that is, it's right to pose the question of originality. It's right to ask where one is situated. Where one situates oneself in relation to the epoch, in relation to what others are doing. To seek one's place, to seek to say what the others are not saying. One can demand the unexpected of oneself and propose it to others. One starts with an idea and one goes toward an encounter with materials. That's where the unexpected must occur. In that sense, it's not really a question of a project, but rather a state of ambiguity.

C.F. To return to what you said about metamorphosis as a political procedure, I was thinking about your words yesterday on Rodolphe Burger's political intervention with "Egal Zéro" [*a compact disk commenting on the recent political crisis in France at the time of the elections and directed principally at the rise of racist ideology and governmental complicity*]. You said you thought it was an important sign of something that is happening now that such an artist, who has used the most diverse materials in his music, should pass to a more directly political mode, without sacrificing anything of the artistic side.

S.P. Yes, I think it's something good. It's the result of a state of urgency. There are moments when one must express oneself in a certain way because there is a state of urgency. There is nothing worse than lacking battles to fight, even on the aesthetic plane. But if I were called on to make a painting on the same subject at this point, I don't think I could do it. . . . There is the whole voluntarist side of the thing, which I want to avoid. In the place of will, I want there to be a necessity. A thing is valid or becomes valid when the one who did it could not do otherwise. It is not a matter of courage or will, it is a matter of necessity. A matter, in that sense, of placing oneself in such a position and of choosing that activity in order to live by it. There must be a necessity, not just an inclination . . . an effort at imagining being something. One has to go at it to see if it's true. Once one is involved, one stays because it is necessary. One couldn't do otherwise. In the case of Rodolphe, the same necessity . . . he couldn't not do that.

C.F. You've introduced a topic I wanted to take up—your choice of a form of life, if I can put it that way. I don't want to make this personal, but I admire tremendously your fidelity to your work, your way of constantly engaging—through very long hours—that undefined movement of transformation we've discussed (by which I mean your willful loss of willed direction) and your way of doing it always in relation to a context of working friendships, that is to say, a "company" of people who pursue comparable projects along singular paths, an an-archic constellation. The difficult immigration to Paris and the constant travel belong to this commitment, it seems to me. Given your limited resources, I can't but be amazed at your endurance, your inventiveness, your stubbornness. I'm stressing your itinerant side here, but there's also another side, which is visible in this atelier. That is to say, I see you very much as a kind of artisan working with modest means—like the foreign artisans working behind the blinds of what appear to be closed shops in this *quartier* (who are unable to work openly for want of the proper papers). There is a relation to your materials and your site in this, but there is also a class identification of sorts, and a socio-political choice. You lack, however, the social structure that would support an artisan's activity.

s.p. Yes, it's a more paradoxical position. On the one hand, an artist like myself stands on the margins of society. On the other, I depend on the most privileged sectors. One is not truly independent in such a situation—one depends on people for whom one's work is a luxury.

c.f. But it seems to me that the people who are moved to buy your work are in most cases individuals for whom it is not really a luxury, or at least not a superfluous one. Some would even describe your work as a vital need. At least I would—for me, it's a matter of keeping reminders nearby.

s.p. That's important, that one sense in the other who recognizes your work and helps support you a sacrifice of some kind, even a little bit of suffering in the choice, because that's the return for your own sacrifice, what you put into it. There is nothing more debilitating, nothing empties you more than when you sell something at a high price, even too high a price, to someone for whom it really doesn't matter. This can even be true of a merchant. I remember an episode once in Morocco where I had to buy several pairs of sandals from a shoemaker. We spent several hours haggling, each of us developing our arguments. At the end, when we finally agreed on a price we were so moved that we fell into each other's arms. Yes, an artisan . . .

c.f. And there is the political choice. At the Centre de Documentation, I felt recalled once again to my own political choices. And most of all, I remembered the importance of politics—the existence of the political, if you will. (I believe that experience has to be undergone constantly and repeatedly—it is furtive by nature.) "Never to forget"—that also means never to forget the political. Not just because the horrors we saw must not be allowed to repeat themselves (and that's the big question in Paris these days, isn't it: "Is it happening again?"), but rather because they *are* repeating themselves, today. Or not *repeating* themselves exactly ("Is it happening again?" is really the wrong question), but assuming always new configurations. It hit me again very strongly. As though all the little preoccupations, the little fantasms, everything programmed by the technocratic structures of this society of consumption (including important dimensions of my professional life) suddenly fell away. This is banal, I know. But it seems to me that your choices as an artist and your relation to history, above all, have something to do with such an experience. And I feel as though I can understand the fidelity in relation to that experience—your capacity to carry on despite the material challenges and the pressures of a culture that does not exactly encourage such a path.

s.p. Absolutely. It involves a kind of reconciliation with oneself. It's another kind of engagement. And I was fortunate to find it . . . an ethical engagement that takes the form of producing visual objects designed to touch the vitality of the other. In touching the consciousness of the other, it should also touch and renew their vitality. In that sense, it's a political engagement. That's the aim of the work of art . . . in that sense, yes. And I hope it goes beyond the appeal that the past not be allowed to return.

c.f. But the endurance is not an easy thing. And I find it all the more arresting in that it is coupled with a certain lightness. There is a constant *insouciance* in your artistic gestures that radicalizes your marginal position. Perhaps it's simply your perverse side, but I think something else may be at stake.

s.p. It's that one can't do otherwise. Once one's in it, one doesn't ask too many questions. You have to go see. You follow your idea, chase after it in order to see what will come of it. No questions. One is carried along by . . . it demands each time. . . .

c.f. Let me try to reformulate this. There is a tremendous self-effacement in your work. You leave a few traces of your person, but always lightly. You do things in such a way that someone might well take notice (in the official art world, for example); but there's an equal chance that you won't be noticed. You play at this movement, which consists in presenting and effacing. Even your exhibitions are marked sometimes by lightness. What's at stake there? I don't know if I'm touching on something you will recognize. Perhaps it's just an identification on my part, since I sometimes withdraw to such a point that people can't grasp what I'm doing (or worse: they take the withdrawal as a mystifying tactic). I don't want to insist on similarities, I'm just trying to bring out something I think I see.

S.P. Well, there is an aspect of flight. And then an aspect of self-loss, a self-loss that is at the same time a seeking of oneself elsewhere. Which is sometimes so strong it takes over and makes one forget to promote oneself as someone living today.

C.F. Indeed. But there's also a miming of that movement in your work. I note that sometimes you present your objects in such a way that they might well not be seen. For example, those little blocks of transparent resin containing photographs of unidentifiable objects you found in the street. You leave them around like things in the street. Or you bring them out like little cards, laying them out quickly to see if there is a response (hardly letting one form) and then gathering them up. You offer them lightly, and the offer itself can go by almost unnoticed amidst other distractions. There is a kind of mimesis in that gesture, a miming of your object.

S.P. Of course. Neither authority nor demand. I don't know if it's the right thing to do—just barely to pose what's been made rather than announcing ostentatiously its presence.

C.F. But there are other ways of thinking about it. You could seek a dialectic with other artists and critics by seeking response in a more concerted way.

S.P. It's not that I'm avoiding such a dialectic. I even think of myself sometimes as existing essentially in a network of exchange, a communitary tissue of sorts. Each time someone looks at my work and *says* something my route takes a turn—either along the lines of what has been suggested to me, or against them. So my trajectory is shaped by these encounters. But the "art world" is another matter. The problem there, since the outset, is that my point of departure in the world of written materials continues to be very present and visible. Which means that the things I do continue to have their feet in disparate domains. That unsettles many people in any given milieu. So, without achieving an eminent quality in any domain, they touch on several at a time, say the visual and the conceptual. Even from a formal point of view, these are not really paintings, not really photography, not really sculpture—but a little bit of each. That unsettles tremendously; above all in the milieu of art. When galleries have come to look, it's been clear that they were troubled by the changes in format: by the fact that it starts off from a pictorial basis, with colors on a canvas, then passes to a kind of collage with an overlay of writing. Then photography, and the photography is framed by lead because there is also radiography (among other reasons). And then the radiography becomes so transparent that the object detaches from the wall to produce a shadow. And then it detaches from the wall again to stand up in the midst of a space, and there is an additional superposition of colored images. Afterwards, that image becomes absolutely linear, suspended like a shroud. Even if I or someone close to me can find a unifying discourse for all of this, someone who is to represent the work hardly knows what it is he or she is representing. Because there's no signature. So there are very clear reasons for this position of marginality. Which is not to say that it's something I want to claim; there's nothing to defend in the limitations it brings. Work doesn't go on if one can't pay the rent. But the fact is, I've taken a different route from the one to which I think you've alluded. I live in and by that network of encounters. That's what I "represent" in my capacity as artisan, if you will: that community. But it's clear that this is a type of choice that presupposes a kind of sobriety and dogged persistence in everyday work; it presupposes a consciousness in relation to certain things. It's important not to have too noisy a relation to what one does. A practice that is not too humble, but sober.

c.f. Sober; but there's also that humorous side.

s.p. Is it a kind of auto-commiseration?

c.f. Self-irony, you mean? I don't think so.

s.p. Sure: "Look how they put me in a jar, like a fish in a jar." It's the irony of the *pitre châtié.*

c.f. Not at all. In any case, it's not the essential. Let's take the recent work with resin, since you've just alluded to it. I presume you were referring to those stands holding the resin pieces containing photographic imprints or even things like fish skins; they stand about like museum signs, a *signalétique,* you call them. I find them enormously parodic.

s.p. The question I'm working through there has to do with containment and a kind of signaling.

c.f. It strikes me as a form of allegory. But go ahead.

s.p. Well, just like the mortuary mask (so admired by Döblin in his famous preface to Sander's volume on photography), the resin is supposed to conserve the appearance, the visible form of something that was living. It's close to taxidermy, that desperate attempt on the part of scientists to conserve the form of the appearance *a futura memoria*, for a future memory of something that is no longer. I redoubled this procedure by inscribing photography into it, and by enclosing the photograph in resin, or by taking the image *with* the resin. So I'm thinking about taxidermy there, "naturalized" animals that are placed in a "living" position. It's the question of the museum, of the impossibility of a museum of natural history, of living things. There is an expression in Naples: they speak of the "third death" of a fish. The fish dies three times. The first is when he is caught; the second is when he is consumed (this is the beautiful death where he is prepared and eaten). The last does not belong to his "biography," and is actually the second. In the market, they attach a string to the tail and to the head, drawing it in such a way that the fish appears to be jumping. Then they encase the fish in ice and remove the string. That's how he's presented, in that simulacrum of life. They bend him so that he is presented and sold as though he were living. It's as though he were a statue of himself, not something to eat. That's what I'm doing with the resin, more or less—a parody of what the taxidermists do in a museum. It's a matter of representing the third death of the animal. You notice, by the way, that there is no writing this time. There are two superimposed images of animals. I'm certain that there is an unconscious relation to what you discuss in your text on Bacon regarding the animal, at the limit of language.

c.f. Are you seeking something archaic in that process?

s.p. No, at least not in the sense of a search for an origin. What's interesting, as Deleuze says, is neither the beginning nor the end. It's the middle, where we are and where things come about. No, it's something like an *ecce animale*. Look what they did with him. Look.

c.f. So there is a great protest, but in the form of an extreme parody.

s.p. Yes, parody; obviously there's parody of the whole relation to memory housed in the museum, and of certain aspects of the scientific undertaking.

c.f. But there's also a more fundamental humor. There is always humor in your art. The mobile *stèles*, for example. One has to laugh.

s.p. Yes, they take away even the right to mourning, or they oblige one to carry it with one, instead of leaving it on a column designed for that purpose. And now I'm a mortician for fish. You know that you must be careful in the market in Naples. Since the sign of freshness in fish is red gills, there are vendors who go so far as to add a little red paint to them.

C.F. I suspect you're taking my words in the direction of self-irony again. There is that side of your work, of course, and sometimes you push it pretty far. But that's not the essential in what I'm trying to get at. I think that it's rather the arrival of ideas that makes you laugh. In following the ideas, you laugh. It's not irony. It's humor in relation to what comes, in relation to the fact that ideas arrive and continue to arrive with each additional step. Self-irony can be a lapse in relation to the work. I don't mean to be presumptuous, but I think that what I am pointing at is very different.

S.P. No . . . my hesitation is just that I hadn't thought of that element. Perhaps the idea is born in a movement of humor, but. . . . It's curious because I have always thought that humor was ultimately the incapacity to take a distance from oneself. But I think you have something there. It's true that when you look at the wrapped-up works of art [*Puglia has been collecting photos of monuments and works of art wrapped for protection during the Second World War*], you want to laugh a little.

C.F. It's not about staying with oneself at all—that's the whole difference between humor and irony, at least as the French language gives it to us. In irony, there is always self-relation, even in an abyssal movement of self-negation; in humor it's more a movement of liberation in relation to the self.

S.P. And discovery of the other, is that what you mean?

C.F. Yes, humor is a movement of exposition, of being exposed and assuming exposure.

S.P. In any case, whether it be humor or . . . there is an aspect, how shall I say, of . . . let us say an aspect of tenderness. Because it seems to me that humor presupposes a form of *attendrissement*, and thus a pathos (if we think the latter in relation to being moved or touched and not as a sentimentality). Like the old man who is respectable but already senile. Like the fish in a ridiculous position. Like wrapped-up monuments, or the tiger that has been opened up in an anatomy experiment. I always sense, there, subjects that have been stolen from themselves, violated, or alienated from themselves. In fact, I pursue this "third death," this transformation of something dead or forgotten into a simulacrum of something living, indeed all of this work in relation to legacy, almost reluctantly. I experience almost a regret over the fact that this alchemy, this sea change, can be done. And there is no doubt that there is a ludicrous side to the process, at least in the works on the museum, natural history, or the museum that is our life. But one can also say that what has been forgotten or left aside (hence the necessity of archival work and flea markets) can also resuscitate, prompt anew a vitality in those who look. There is, despite everything, an appeal to the fact that there is a *possible*. It is not just a mourning; it is an affirmation. It's true that it starts from a respect—the kind of respect one has for a grandfather, old and a little bit out of it. Respect and proximity. So one speaks of what is lost, and the fact of naming is a first articulation along the path of a saving—though one can never truly save. But there is that option offered by saying or naming, sometimes by showing. Showing can be a bit like a silent discourse in its effect. One shows what could be.

c.f. So Derrida was perhaps on the mark in writing about what he called your attempt to save the phenomenon.

But I'm reminded now of the response you've given me regarding the motif of crucifixion. That you feel closer to the Pietà, even though you have turned more than once to the crucifixion with an image that is clearly pagan.

s.p. It's a magnificent invention, that god who allowed himself. . . . But the vertical figure is too direct. It's hard to do anything with that vertical, face-to-face confrontation. I prefer the supine figure. And I think I'm closer to the Stabat Mater, closer to the survivor, the one who has lost someone. Because at the heart of it, there is the idea of surviving to bear witness. Not being religious, I don't see in that image a resurrection to come. In the Pietà I see what remains.

Anonymous Figures

The exhibition greets us with a row of anonymous faces and speaks of memory. For whom are these faces recorded? The question would press if we knew nothing of the artist, for these figures *require* something of us. But if we happen to know something of Salvatore Puglia's attitudes regarding the social bases of his practice and his commitment to community (reflected already in the role friendship has played in his itinerary as an artist), then we may well take this question, in all its ethical and political reach, as the question of the exhibition. It is a question about the conditions for participation in the acts of memory presented here; or, more simply, a question about the conditions for engaging these works. To what mode of aesthetic/social relation do these works invite us? Who can engage them and "who" might leave them? These should be the first questions for an introduction, in any case, for the images invite caution; the traditional approach to the aesthetic object and the traditional notion of the exhibition may occlude their most fundamental dimensions—it may be that a manual of usage is required here, not the copy suited for a catalogue or for a critical essay.

Puglia has described his project in this exhibition as one of memory.[1] An abstraction proper to memory as it has been conceived since antiquity (an abstraction that is irreducibly graphic) will provide the grounds for a practice of recollection that engages what the Greeks understood of the relation between memory and thought, even while questioning these grounds of intelligibility, or pointing beyond them. (And let us follow Puglia in underscoring the word "thought"—for it is a matter always of "a possible world" beyond any "specific instance" that might find its meaning there.) Is this foregrounding and super-imposition of the forms of inscription Aristotle described in his account of memory[2] still in fact a form of anamnesis? There is, to be sure, reproduction here, and re-collection of a kind: the *legein* of careful transcription and spatial

Figure 6 Salvatore Puglia, *Uber die Schädelnerven* (detail). Photograph courtesy of the artist.

articulation. But it is a recollection of schemas, images, text, and traces that never gathers contextual or historical meaning. These abstracts of anamnesis seem assembled by no more than the passive synthesis of a haunted psyche vainly interpreting the inscriptions it has suffered and unable to resist a crowding of associations without contextual or analogical justification. They remain signs (or text) and present themselves as such. But they form no historical record and give no coherent image of the past. The human figures that appear here remain anonymous, suspended in the notation, documentation, or graphic analysis (the reproduction of outline or the internal exposition by x-ray) that overlays them or forms their background. They remain souls in a kind of graphic purgatory—a purgatory nowhere better illustrated than in *Uber die Schädelnerven*, where the figure, hovering between type and individual (the images are from clinical studies of the nineteenth century), barely more than a sign and yet almost a portrait, seems imprisoned in an apparatus that multiplies its form by exposing it to a shadowplay that redoubles the absence. These souls are refugees of the historiographic/ethnographic/scientific imaginary, with no escape from the image.

But the fact that these figures *almost* emerge from their sign-character as icons of themselves should not be lost here. It is true that Puglia is subverting the specular satisfactions of historiography and refusing any humanistic pathos, as he critically transcribes some of the acts of disappropriation to which photography has lent itself in this age of mechanical reproduction. Further, his practice of abstraction and juxtaposition fragments the grounds of historical identification and prohibits any construction of these figures as representatives of a group, a class, or even humankind ("Man") in general— no ideology or "disciplinary" determination has a hold here. Yet the figures that appear in works like *Uber die Schädelnerven* nevertheless lend themselves to a form of recognition. They do so, paradoxically, by virtue of their very anonymity and the work of "abstraction" that produces it. A segment from Puglia's own fragmented series of remarks on *Uber die Schädelnerven* will help us approach what is involved here:

> To the pathos of intact memory we will oppose a will to save the unsaved, the unidentifiable.
>
> "Looking at things from the proper level, however, everything in police affairs is a matter of identification" (Alphonse Bertillon, *Identification anthropométrique, instruction signalétique*, 1893).
>
> The obsession with identity and identification transforms individuals into cases, types, emblems. We are going to restore to faces their veils.

Figure 7   Salvatore Puglia, *Uber die Schädelnerven* (detail). Photograph courtesy of the artist.

> The uncanny should occur more in the sudden familiarity of the unknown than in the surprises of the familiar. Before the composite image, I experience the revelation of finding myself in the place of the described man. This authorizes me to look at his portrait, which is my own.
>
> It is a question of taking the head of the image and twisting its neck.[3]

Each of these statements tells us something about Puglia's endeavors, as does the parataxis at work in their juxtaposition. But let us concentrate on the penultimate statement. A sudden experience of identification in the face of an anonymous figure (unknown, but also eminently recognizable in its "abstraction": the "composite figure" is a pure product of reproducibility) is contrasted here with a more familiar experience of *Unheimlichkeit*. Reclaiming an experience of substitutability at the level of the *type* ("sudden" because its ever-present possibility is normally veiled—the image itself is complicitous here), Puglia posits as a kind of imperative for his art the production of a recognition of the anonymous, an uncanny substitution wherein the viewers may be surprised to discover that they are *not* this image, or may realize that they too could occupy this place.

How does Puglia seek such an event? In *Uber die Schädelnerven* and related

Figure 8 Salvatore Puglia, *Uber die Schädelnerven* (detail). Photograph courtesy of the artist.

works, it is through an aesthetic process that does not negate but rather suspends the abstraction proper to all photographic documentation of the human form,[4] an abstraction particularly apparent in the photograph of the clinical case or sociological type. Puglia takes his point of departure from precisely the reproducibility of the human form given by photography and exploited by what Bataille termed the "intellectual voracity" of modern science. He foregrounds this reproducibility, and "backgrounds" with the generalization of internal structure enabled by the x-ray. Occasionally a kind of analysis of abstraction by hand and eye (as in Puglia's *La figure humaine*) seems Puglia's primary concern. But in every case, the citation or "staging" of the reproduced image in a complex play of framing, the remarking of its abstraction by the x-ray (offering also a rich play of light and shadow), and then the work of inscription and textual overlay, together render the graphic image a sign—a sign with no meaning beyond the vague temporal marker it bears. The effect resists conceptual capture; we are confronting art. But in the estrangement produced by this becoming-sign of the human image, its becoming-*figure*, we have a kind of offering of intelligibility without signification. A figure emerges from the veil of inscription and the play of light and shadow that might recall Hölderlin's famous line from "Mnemosyne": "A sign we are, without meaning."

We are a sign because we trace signs, Heidegger said, evoking with his reading of this line in *What Is Called Thinking?* a work of the hand that would draw out the human essence and allow it to emerge in its fundamentally historical character in the time of *Technik*. We cannot assume, of course, that Puglia would follow Heidegger in the latter's understanding of the human essence, despite their shared reference to the Greek legacy. This is not to presume any clear determination of what Heidegger meant when he referred to "the human" (the question remains still to be developed); but it is almost certain that Heidegger could never have turned in Puglia's manner to the dispossessed and the "inappropriable" for an understanding of what might exceed the grasp of modern humanism and its increasingly "inhuman" incarnations in the realm of *Technik*. We would have to acknowledge, too, that Puglia's poietic practice, his "pragmatics" (where the *pragma* is the possible of a world) diverges considerably from anything envisaged by Heidegger in his meditations on art. It seems possible to affirm, nevertheless, that the transformation to which Puglia subjects the graphic image carries us toward that becoming-sign of the human, which Heidegger grasped as the trace of the "usage" by which something like history is possible—that "use" of the human for the ad-

vent of a historial destiny that Heidegger understood as the only possible basis for a passage beyond the contemporary order of *Technik*.[5] If we could
glimpse that usage as such, Heidegger suggested, we would enter the dangerous ambiguity of *Technik* and find the tension, the freeing "counter-draught"
by which the beginnings of movement might be engaged. *Technik* is Janus-
faced, he declared: in the very disappropriation of the human we find the
trace of another history.

But to find this trace (concentrated, we may surmise, in the extreme void,
the extreme enigma of the sign without meaning), it would be necessary,
Heidegger hinted, to push *Technik* to its limits. What might such an enterprise
look like? This is hardly the place to explore the few clues offered by Heidegger.
Nor can I pause to review the varying successes of contemporary hyper-
modernism. For this occasion, let it suffice for me to suggest that Puglia has in
fact answered Heidegger's imperative by confronting the technicity of the photographic image (in what I termed earlier the "reproducibility" of the human
form) in such a way as to ex-pose a dimension of the technical grounds of human presentation in the modern era. What is produced in his use of the image
is precisely "a sign without meaning," a figure that offers to historical or conceptual identification little more than the historicity of its very presentation, of
the *form* of presentation by which the portrayed individuals show themselves
as the "subjects" of a certain stage of photography.[6] Beyond this capture (only
roughly datable), they offer only their abandonment, an irrecoverable pastness
that conveys the mere fact of history—a "fact," however, that could never strike
us as it does were it not for an opaque insistence, a haunting address that bespeaks, despite everything, the human. This is indeed "little more," but it makes
the "sign without meaning" anything but abstract. For while Puglia suspends
our capacity to interpret the human figures (no attribute, no class mark, nor
even a "pathological" trait allows us to fix these individuals such as to declare
what or who they represent), he also renders to them a singular density, producing an effect that evokes what Giorgio Agamben has termed the "whatever"
of a singularity for the age of technical reproduction. The "substitutability" of
these figures might well recall to us Agamben's elusive references to a relationality he names a "coming community."[7]

So do we find an affirmation of community, after all, some sort of positive
invitation or some ethical appeal? There is, as I noted at the outset, an address
in the figures of *Uber die Schädelnerven*. But what *requires* in their mute presence is not some intelligible claim (they appeal to no justice or recognition),

nor even some basis for empathy, a common human substance that would extend beyond the reach of the marks of history they bear. They offer *nothing* for identification; we (we?) stand before them without relation, or without other relation, as Blanchot would say, than the "incommensurable." But this incommensurable (what resists the common measure of representation) is nevertheless *there*—ex-scribed in the very muteness or silence, the absence of those vulnerable presences that is given to us in and through Puglia's exhausting labor of ex-scription. "Ex-scribed": I return to this neologism in light of the thematized "X-scription" that appears in *Les âmes du purgatoire* and in view of the manner in which Puglia both suspends and redoubles the trait in such a way as to bring forward its material presence and remark thereby what is lost in the abstracting work of representation or language in general.[8] Puglia's photo-graphics abstract, to be sure, but in the incessant work of overlay, condensation, juxtaposition, and reflection by which the human image *becomes figure*, in the multifold re-marking of the reproducible trait by which Puglia redoubles its presence, there emerges the trace of an alterity that is nothing other than the singularity of the (human) being abandoned to representation. The "communitary" ground of this work, its ethical engagement, lies in its manner of remarking this abandoned presence.

But I do not think we can evoke this "ethical" dimension of the work without noting that the exigency it communicates is inseparable from a disquieting reminder of the death that is embodied in the becoming-sign of the human. Puglia's *Les larmes d'Eros* is gently insistent in this respect. It recalls to us Puglia's highly ambivalent relation to representation of the human figure, especially photographic—his inability to dissociate all such representation from a form of torture.[9] The "please, please don't," appearing in proximity to works like *Uber die Schädelnerven*, does not just transcribe the image's attempt to hold us at its surface, its request that we not touch and thereby violate the illusion it maintains (a prohibition Puglia constantly ignores). Rather, it is the recitation of a vain hesitation proper to language's very act of transgression, and thus a reminder of the death it brings in its murderous abstraction. Puglia is always testifying to the body of this death.[10] Of course, there is no warrant, no legitimation for this testimony (as Puglia tells us by taking Celan's title *Aschenglorie* as one of his own, reminding us thereby that "there is no witness for the witness"). But this is an essential part of what makes this testimony ethical. It is also what makes it genuinely historical; there would be no "history" if there were no such testimony—there would only be abstraction. The

Figure 9 Salvatore Puglia, *Les larmes d'Eros* (detail). Photograph courtesy of the artist.

Figure 10 Salvatore Puglia, *Les larmes d'Eros*, 1994. Iron, zinc, acetate, glass, hair. Photograph courtesy of the artist.

sign without meaning is not abstract; its empty opacity is a trace of the historical being that is lost to it. In re-marking this trace, Puglia calls us to the *real* grounds of community as given by language.

And memory? Meditating on observances of *Kristalnacht* and on displays of the AIDS Quilt, Bill Haver has argued that the recitation of proper names in these ceremonies is a recitation of *anonyms* that lends not to identification (in sympathy or empathy) but to a knowledge of community based on the substitutability of "whatever" singularity. Of course, these instances of *mourning the stranger* involve other and more immediate (though not unrelated) experiences of our finitude. And we must not forget that Puglia's exhibition is offered as art and is partially *about* the representation of the anonymous. But are we not called to a comparable relationality by his gestures of commemorating "the unsaved, the unidentified"? If we glimpse what Puglia has exposed of the conditions of recognition, we will grasp the ethics of this gesture and know what these acts of anamnesis offer and require in their unforgettable presence.

REFERENCE

MATTER

Notes

ABBREVIATIONS

EH   Nietzsche, *Ecce Homo*
EP   Lacan, *The Ethics of Psychoanalysis*
FFC Lacan, *The Four Fundamental Concepts of Psychoanalysis*
GM   Nietzsche, *The Genealogy of Morals*
WD   Blanchot, *The Writing of the Disaster*

Where double page numbers appear, the first number refers to the French translation, the second to the English edition.

INTRODUCTION

1. I could not pretend to say where such innocence was lost in relation to this project, for this is knowledge that must perpetually be reacquired. But I would note that the work in this volume was written in the wake of an effort to work through a notion of *usage* that makes it possible to speak in a consequent manner of the limits of language and the disrupted relationality that must be thought there. This notion of relationality, which is the basis of my references to a "pragmatics," is developed in *Language and Relation: . . . that there is language*, and extended in the texts gathered here.

2. Blanchot, *The Writing of the Disaster*, p. 72.

3. Lacan, *The Four Fundamental Concepts of Psychoanalysis*, p. 59.

4. Levi, *Survival in Auschwitz*, p. 63.

5. There is the *common* character of the dream first of all, a trait that the dream of the burning child shares inasmuch as it is reported to Freud by a patient who claims to have reproduced elements of it after hearing it discussed in a lecture; then there is the structure of the dream's formation in relation to its circumstances.

6. An instance of the testimony to which I refer comes in Robert Anthelme's

L'espèce humaine, a book to which Maurice Blanchot devotes several invaluable pages of dialogue in *The Infinite Conversation*, pp. 130–35. Blanchot meditates on the "reserve of speech" that each prisoner knows in affliction and from which each seeks delivery, joyously, at liberation. This reserved speech, he says, is the speech of *autrui*: "a speech unheard, inexpressible, nevertheless unceasing, silently affirming that where all relation is lacking there yet subsists, there already begins, the human relation in its primacy" (p. 135). But this speech, as Anthelme tells us, could not find expression at the time of liberation: "It was impossible. We had hardly begun to speak and we were choking." Immediately after citing these words, Blanchot asks: "Why this wrenching? Why this pain always present, and not only here in this extreme movement but already, as I believe it is, in the most simple act of speaking?" (p. 135). Infancy, as I will suggest, is a dimension of the opening of human relation ("human relation in its primacy"), an opening *of language* that cannot be brought to speech and yet attends every speech event like the trace of a primal scene.

7. I should note here that I am not the first to address the texts I will read in this volume, or even the topic of infancy itself. For the latter, I had before me the lead of Jean-François Lyotard's *Lectures d'enfance*, and a contribution by Giorgio Agamben (*Infancy and History*). My approach to Lacan's text was also shaped by the many critical commentaries addressed to the pages on the dream of the burning child, foremost among which is Cathy Caruth's discussion in *Unclaimed Experience*. (I also want to mention another scholar from Yale University, Luc Kinsch, whose doctoral work on Mallarmé's poem "A Tomb for Anatole" drew my attention back to this fascinating text.) I can only hope that my reading complements their own; it is not meant as a more definitive analysis. Indeed, if the meditation I have undertaken were read as a bid for critical hegemony, the essential would be lost (the "essential" relating to something Shoshana Felman has attempted to think under the name of witnessing).

A PREFACE ON CRUELTY

1. Nietzsche, *On the Genealogy of Morals and Ecce Homo*, p. 217. Henceforth, I will use the abbreviations EH and GM to refer by section to the individual texts in this edition.

2. A phrase I use especially in light of David Halperin's treatment of this topic in *Saint Foucault: Towards a Gay Hagiography*, a book that brings home to us the very material character of cultural invention (not to speak of the severe challenges involved). If I have anything to add in this context to Halperin's evocation of Foucault's "usage" of the self, it concerns the structure of reflexivity to which he alludes and the "ontological" dimension of this usage. I would like to take a notion of the

"use" of the self beyond any model of linguistic constructivism or any pragmatics that does not engage that *pragma* that is the concern of "being in the world."

3. I refer here to the influential reading of Nietzsche proposed by Alexander Nehemas in *Nietzsche: Life as Literature*, and statements such as the following: "To be what one is, we now see, is to be engaged in a constantly continuing and continually broadening process of appropriation of one's experiences and actions, of enlarging the capacity for assuming responsibility for oneself which Nietzsche calls "freedom" (p. 191). Elsewhere Nehemas speaks of "that relegation that transforms melancholy and misery, passion, pain and effort into experience and knowledge, into the material of the future" (p. 162). For Nehemas, the latter is material for an essentially aesthetic construction equivalent to a Proustian artifact. Nehemas tends to avoid the motif of cruelty (cf. p. 192), and when he must face it, he produces a rather scant discussion that immediately veers toward the specter of "physical cruelty of the worst sort" (p. 218). Needless to say, his reading of *The Genealogy of Morals* suffers accordingly (see p. 206, where he fails to recognize how the philosopher as "sovereign subject" differs from the "barbarous noble").

As for Rorty, his famous distaste for cruelty has a delightful resonance here, even if he is concerned with something quite other than a form of self-relation (but then one could hardly count on Rorty to pause over the form of self-relation I am treating here). I have discussed the persistence of the metaphysics of subjectivity in Rorty's pragmatism in "Community and the Limits of Theory" in *Community at Loose Ends*.

4. Nietzsche, *The Gay Science*, §290.

5. It should also go almost without saying that a number of counter-citations can be proffered against the general line I am taking here. I am following a logic implicit in Nietzsche's reflections on the finitude of the will, and attending to Nietzsche's thought of difference (which I take to be a version of *ontological* difference) over against pragmatic versions of Nietzschean perspectivism and will to power that avoid any real questioning of the subject. Needless to say, there is a strong strain of metaphysical thinking in Nietzsche's text (Heidegger demonstrated this powerfully); he lent himself easily to what Lacoue-Labarthe has named a "national aestheticism," or to softer, humanist versions of self-cultivation.

6. I would note here, however, that the lightning wielded by the sovereign subject (cf. Nietzsche's words in *Ecce Homo*, "I speak no longer with words but with lightning bolts" [p. 281]) is not the same as the lightning of the violent acts of the "blond beasts" that Nietzsche describes in the first and second essays of *The Genealogy of Morals*. And it is not the same thing as the lightning character of the deeds described in the very important §13 of the first essay, where Nietzsche explains how the man of ressentiment interprets the act of the strong by dividing the

doer from the deed and positing a "good" subject who would be capable of not acting. Nietzsche's sovereign subject comes at the end of a long history in which the will has temporalized itself, so to speak, and acquired a memory. Nietzsche may well explain in *Ecce Homo* that the sovereign creator *has no choice* in the act of creation, and is one with his deed, thus attributing to the creator the immediacy of thought and deed that Nietzsche ascribes to the strong noble type. But this act of creation is of a different, more complex structure than that of the deed of the blond beast.

7. For a discussion of the Nietzschean concept of honesty, see Jean-Luc Nancy, "*Notre probité*," pp. 61–86.

8. "Speculative," or *interpretive* inasmuch as it is devoted to the pre-history of the will that could write such a history: the will that is endowed with a memory and the capacity to promise. Werner Hamacher develops this point quite powerfully in "The Promise of Interpretation: Reflections on the Hermeneutic Imperative in Kant and Nietzsche," in *Premises*, pp. 81–143.

9. It could be worthwhile to explore Nietzsche's argument that the origin of all social relations lies in exchange, in the relation of creditor and debtor, and to explore more fully from this ground the rather un-sovereign pleasure that the creditor (or thinker!) takes in pain. See, for example, §8, where Nietzsche describes the relations between buyer and seller, creditor and debtor, as "the oldest and most primitive personal relationships," the first site of encounter between individuals and the origin of all social relations. The preoccupation with exchange at these early stages of humanity constitutes "thinking *as such*," Nietzsche declares. He then adds that the relations founded in buying and selling are "older even than the beginnings of any kind of social forms of organization and alliances: it was rather out of the most rudimentary form of personal legal rights that the budding sense of exchange, contract, guilt, right, obligation, settlement, first *transferred* itself to the coarsest and most elementary social complexes" (GM, p. 70).

10. To address this question properly, we would have to take up the entire question of spectacle as it figures throughout the *Genealogy*. Does the spectacle that justifies existence, or at least makes it interesting, not serve to distract a will that is otherwise exposed to a senseless suffering and its own "basic fact" (p. 97)? Can spectacle, in this perspective, belong to a Dionysian affirmation? Hasn't such a will already fallen from the tragic (or not yet attained it)? But the spectacle offered by life (its old trick to justify its evil [p. 68]) or by the philosophers (to entertain their gods [p. 69]) differs from the one offered by the birth of bad conscience, or rather the *interest* afforded by such a spectacle differs from that of the former instances. For the birth of bad conscience holds an engaging promise (p. 85).

11. Here we meet a question I touched upon at the start: does a developed so-

cial complex—a complex of sovereign subjects—recover in some way this "natural poiesis," which produces a highly articulated but organic social structure? Many of Nietzsche's political declarations seem to point in this direction—and this is the Nietzsche who lent himself to the mythopoieic ambitions of German fascism. I think we will see, however, that the concept of sovereignty points to a different conception of the grounds of social relation: the "sovereign" pathos of distance does not lend itself to *one* political space or offer a ground for such a space.

12. In "The Promise of Interpretation," Hamacher links nicely the first and second essays of the *Genealogy* by suggesting that the will of moral (and supramoral) humanity is the will *of interpretation*: an interpretation that is made possible by grammar (the first essay) and carried out in language (as we see with the motif of branding in this passage). The will (at least the will of human history) exists only as its own explication. It is not the *subject* of interpretation; rather, interpretation belongs to its structure. I will add in what follows that the cruel turn that is proper to the will (part of its structure, but also such as to undo any self-possession) carries the will to the limits of language.

13. Cf. GM, pp. 36–37. Deleuze offers a very precise and strong account of *ressentiment* in relation to the active and reactive structures of the will in *Nietzsche and Philosophy*.

14. In describing Zarathustra, Nietzsche declares, "In every word he contradicts, this most Yes-saying of all spirits; in him all opposites are blended into a new unity" (EH, p. 305). This would be an example of the kind of counter-citation I referred to above. But we might also recall Nietzsche's reference in the *Genealogy* to "those well-constituted, joyful mortals who are far from regarding their unstable equilibrium between 'animal and angel' as necessarily an argument against existence" (p. 99). The character of the unity in question remains difficult to grasp, but it is clear that the Yes and the No are not dialectically related and that no mediation gathers this unity. The peculiar form of the will's drive toward its own limit (which I will describe shortly) is not subsumable in an economy.

15. Is *Selbsttierquälerei* the condition of this literature (a necessary, prior exploration), or is the literature itself the cruel practice in question? Nietzsche's first words in this passage might suggest the latter: it is because he is practicing this cruelty in his work that he cannot endure it.

16. It is in these terms that I read Nietzsche's description of "what Zarathustra wants": "This type of man that he conceives conceives reality *as it is*, being strong enough to do so; this type is not estranged or removed from reality but is reality itself and exemplifies all that is terrible and questionable in it—*only in that way can man attain greatness*" (GM, p. 331).

17. *The Writing of the Disaster*, p. 72.

18. See the translation of this essay in *Visions of Excess*, pp. 202–12.

19. The phrase is from the title of his book: *The Body of This Death: Historicity and Sociality in the Time of AIDS*.

WHAT REMAINS AT A CRUCIFIXION

1. Starting with the first *Crucifixions* of 1933 and the *Three Studies for Figures at the Base of a Crucifixion* of 1944 (Bacon's real "beginning," he suggests), and then continuing up to at least 1988 with the second version of the *Triptych* of 1944.

2. Needless to say, our reading of the motif need not be a function of Bacon's declared intentions—even his intention to disrupt the structure of "reading." I will not pursue here the extraordinary historical density of the motif in its Christian and pre-Christian forms, though I will turn to Lacan's description of its place in Christian thought later in this volume in order to evoke something of its resonance.

3. Sylvester, *The Brutality of Fact: Interviews with Francis Bacon*, p. 23. Subsequent references in the text.

4. I will be developing in this essay a notion of exposure that also informs, I believe, a rich reading of Pasolini proposed by Michael Hardt (as yet unpublished).

5. Deleuze, *Francis Bacon: Logique de la sensation*, chapters 6–8, esp. p. 41.

6. *Francis Bacon*, p. 41 (my translation).

7. I am not certain that one can generalize as I have, but see the opening words of "The Jesuve": "I have acquired over what happens to me a power that overwhelms me . . . " (*Visions of Excess*, p. 73).

8. Bacon uses the term "image" rather freely to name what he is attempting to render. It is what is given in appearance ("the appearance that you see at any moment, because so-called appearance is only riveted for one moment as that appearance" [p. 118]), what is offered by the "slight remove from fact" that is achieved by the photograph ("Through the photographic image I find myself beginning to wander into the image and unlock what I think of as its reality more than I can by looking at it" [p. 30]) or via an imagination that seems entirely unbound by reference and offers images like "slides" that fall in one after another (p. 21). The remove from reference is nowhere better evoked than in his explanation of the inspiration he took from a photograph of grass so trampled and torn that it took on the shape of grass (p. 162).

As regards portraits, Bacon notes that his recording involves memory in an essential fashion:

—(DS) You prefer to be alone?
—Totally alone. With their memory.

—Is that because the memory is more interesting or because the presence is disturbing?

—What I want to do is to distort the thing far beyond the appearance, but in the distortion to bring it back to a recording of the appearance.

—Are you saying that painting is almost a way of bringing somebody back, that the process of painting is almost like the process of recalling?

—I am saying it. And I think that the methods by which this is done are so artificial that the model before you, in my case, inhibits the artificiality by which this thing can be brought back. (p. 40)

9. I refer here to Bataille's marvelous little text, "The Language of Flowers" (*Visions of Excess*, pp. 10–14).

10. On this point I must disagree with Deleuze if I understand his argument correctly. Deleuze asserts that Bacon paints *heads* (the head of a "body without organs"), not visages. I would concur that he often paints in the portrait the body's *suffering* of forces, but one also finds in his human figures a compelling gaze. I would take as one particularly strong example Bacon's preferred portrait of Michel Leiris (the portraits of 1976 and 1978 are reproduced in *Sylvester*, pp. 146–47).

11. Deleuze, *Francis Bacon*, p. 10.

12. I draw the term "exscription" from Nancy's essay on Bataille ("L'Excrit," in *Une pensée finie*). It captures powerfully the metaphor of writing that Heidegger employs to capture the manner in which a work of art draws out difference as a material relation of world and earth, but it also introduces in an important way the problematic of existence.

I note also that the link I have established between the notion of crucifixion and the theme of nailing is recognized in an important set of observations on Bacon's works by Jean-Claude Lebensztejn ("*Notes sur Francis Bacon*"), pp. 43–53. Unfortunately, this essay came to my attention only well after the initial publication of my own.

13. Deleuze, *Francis Bacon*, p. 67.

14. See, for example, "The Use-Value of D. A. F. de Sade" in *Visions of Excess*.

15. At a particularly poignant moment of the *Interviews*, and in the context of a discussion of his portrayal of coupled figures, Bacon alludes to new possibilities for painting the human body and remarks, "I can see now that I can start in another way altogether now, now that I feel exorcized—although one's never exorcized, because people say you forget about death, but you don't. After all, I've had a very unfortunate life, because all the people I've been really fond of have died. And you don't stop thinking about them; time does not heal. But you concentrate on something which was an obsession, and what you would have put into your obsession with the physical act you put into your work. Because one of the terrible things

about so-called love, certainly for an artist, I think, is the destruction. But I think without it they could probably never have . . . I absolutely don't know" (p. 76).

16. Sylvester, p. 56:

—Well, very often the involuntary marks are much more deeply suggestive than others, and those are the moments when you feel that anything can happen.
—You feel it while you're making those marks?
—No, the marks are made, and you survey the thing like you would a sort of graph. And you see within this graph the possibilities of all types of fact being planted. This is a difficult thing; I'm expressing it badly. But you see, for instance, if you think of a portrait, you maybe at one time have put the mouth somewhere, but you suddenly see through this graph that the mouth could go right across the face. And in a way you would love to be able in a portrait to make a Sahara of the appearance—to make it so like, yet seeming to have the distances of the Sahara.

17. Sylvester, p. 168:

—(FB) For me, it's just a jet of water.
—Perhaps I see it as something else as well because for me this picture, like the one of grass, has a sort of animal energy, not an elemental, macrocosmic energy but an energy that has an animal, even a human, scale.
—What I would like those things to be would be an essence, you might say, of landscape and an essence of water. That's what I would like them to be. Here is Bacon's very "Shakespearean" conclusion after Sylvester's evocation of another instance of such an essence: "Perhaps that is why painting is an old man's occupation, and perhaps, so long as one can work, one may be able to get nearer to a kind of essence of these things."

I regret very much that I was unable to include in this volume a reproduction of Bacon's triptych of March 1974, a painting whose central panel presents a beautiful example of the effort to which I believe he is pointing. Unfortunately, the image proved unattainable, trapped, as I learned after considerable difficulty, with portions of the archive in a commercial purgatory (somewhere between Soho and So Ho).

ANTIGONE'S FRIENDSHIP

1. My reading of *Antigone* is shaped by long familiarity with the translation by Elizabeth Wyckoff in *Sophocles 1*; I have cited it throughout these pages with only small alterations. I have also relied on the translation and commentary proposed by Sir Richard Jebb in the volume edited by E. S. Schuckburgh, and the translation by Hugh Lloyd-Jones. I want to thank Michael Naas and Mina Karavanta for their helpful comments on the work's translations.

For a more comprehensive treatment of the topic of *philia* in *Antigone* and in Sophocles' other works, see Mary Whitlock Blundell's *Helping Friends and Harming Enemies*. See also R. P. Winnington-Ingram, *Sophocles: An Interpretation*, pp. 129–41. I was able to attend to this critical work only after the initial formulation of these remarks for a conference on *Antigone* organized by Joan Copjec at Buffalo in April 1997, and was not surprised to discover that the general lines of my understanding of the play had already been traced in a nuanced fashion. But I believe that my more "speculative" approach supplements these earlier efforts in a significant way. Both of the authors I have cited recognize fully that Antigone's friendship extends to the dead; but I believe that one makes an additional step in arguing that this trait has something to do with the very essence of *philia* as she uses this term in the course of the play.

2. See Steiner, *Antigones*, pp. 206–11.

3. Benveniste, *Le Vocabulaire des institutions européennes*.

4. The disruptive instability of this figure (both for the determination of Antigone's feminine role and for the other *general* questions of intelligibility that have structured the play's reception) is brought forth powerfully by Carol Jacobs in "Dusting Antigone."

5. See Blanchot, *The Infinite Conversation*, pp. 187–93.

6. I refer to intriguing work on this topic (as yet unpublished) that Michael Naas has kindly shared with me.

7. Blundell gives: "My nature is to join not in enmity, but in *philia.*" She comments: "The primary reference, in the context with Kreon, is clearly to her dead brothers. She excludes herself from the hatred that divides them and abides by the claims of kinship-*philia* towards both. But her verb, 'it is my nature,' suggests a broader claim to *philia*" (*Helping Friends and Harming Enemies*, p. 113). Of this nature, Blundell remarks later, "she seems able to love only the dead" (p. 145).

8. "Die Gunst schenken"—a phrase Heidegger elaborates as follows: "We understand favor here in the sense of an originary allowing [*Gönnen*] and granting [*Gewähren*]. . . . To accord in an originary fashion is to grant what is due to the other because it belongs to this other's essence insofar as it bears this essence. Friendship, *philia*, is accordingly favor that is granted the essence of the other, which the other has inasmuch as through this granting the granted essence blossoms into its own freedom. In friendship, the reciprocally granted essence is released to itself. . . . *Philia* is the granting of favor that bestows something that fundamentally does not belong to it and yet for which it must give guarantee so that the other essence can remain in what is proper to it" (*Heraclitus*, pp. 128–29). The implications of these words merit the kind of lengthy meditation Jacques Derrida has accorded to them in "L'avoir, l'être, et l'autre: Tendre l'oreille, accorder ce

qu'on n'a pas" in *Politiques de l'amitié*, pp. 367–90. Here, I would simply underscore that the character of the gift made in Antigone's manner of serving the singular essence of the other (in his death) makes this gift necessarily irreversible and
non-reciprocal—for she serves, as I will argue, a "propriety" or "property" of the
other that the other cannot *own* and from which there is no return. (Derrida also
stresses the necessity of thinking a *philein* that would not answer to a law of reciprocity—even in the form of the "correspondence" Heidegger attributes to a
philosophia—and would be marked by the dissymmetry and incommensurability
of Antigone's "sovereign" act.) I would add, too, that Antigone's friendship, understood from this basis, also partakes of the essence of *usage* as Heidegger defines
it in "The Anaximander Fragment" and *What Is Called Thinking*. As we read in the
former text: "To use accordingly suggests: to let something present come to presence as such; *frui*, to brook, to use, usage means: to hand something over to its
own essence and to keep it in hand, preserving it as something present" (p. 53).
Since Heidegger understands the essence of *philia* from the play of concealing and
unconcealing proper to *physis* itself (once again: "physis kruptestai philei," which
Heidegger reads in "Aletheia (Heraclitus, Fragment B 16)" [p. 114] as a "mutual inclination," a "reciprocal favoring"), one might be prompted to understand "usage"
from *philia*. But the inverse would be more appropriately argued since the jointure
of the latter relation, as we learn in Heidegger's "The Anaximander Fragment" (I
refer specifically to the reading of Anaximander's "kata ton chreon"), is articulated
"according to usage." Heidegger does not link *philia* and "usage" (*der Brauch*, and
the forms of relation that enact the latter), but I will suggest here that Antigone's
act of friendship is perhaps best understood from this ground.

9. I note that Winnington-Ingram reads Antigone's reaction to her sister's
proposition much the same way as I do; see p. 134 of *Sophocles: An Interpretation*.
See also his emphasis on the motif of sharing (*koinonia*) on this same page.

10. In a reading of Heidegger's *An Introduction to Metaphysics* (*Heidegger:
Thought and Historicity*, pp. 117–30), I argued, some time ago, that the act to which
Heidegger refers is the act of suicide. But it is clear to me now that the suicide or
sacrifice to which Heidegger was referring must be understood in a very particular sense; I was thinking of Mallarmé ("modernizing" the act) when I should have
been thinking of Antigone herself. I should have known better, since I was also arguing that Heidegger understood something about friendship.

11. At this moment, Hölderlin writes, the tragic figure "Steht [sie] auch da am
offensten in seinem Charakter." Hölderlin, "Anmerkungen zur Äntigonä," pp. 784
and 785.

12. I have discussed Lacan's appeal to this notion in my "Between Ethics and
Aesthetics."

13. Humankind is *to deinotaton*, the strangest of all, Heidegger argues, in that it offers to *physis* a site for emergence through an intervention that represents a kind of mortal exposure, a passage to the limit of existence (we have seen something of what this means in Antigone's act of friendship).

14. To treat this with any precision, we would have to consider a number of passages from the seminar, including Lacan's reference to "the relation that puts man in the function of medium between the real and the signifier" (*The Ethics of Psychoanalysis*, p. 129 [trans. modified]). Elsewhere, he defines this as the place of evil in creationist thought. The Thing, he says, "maintains the presence of the human. It is a matter, in effect, of the Thing inasmuch as it is defined by the fact that it defines the human—though indeed, the human escapes us. At this point, what we are calling the human could not be defined otherwise than in the way I defined the Thing just now, namely, that which of the real suffers the signifier" (p. 124). Thus, when Lacan declares elsewhere in the text, "We can say that there is nothing between the organization in the signifying network . . . and the constitution in the real of the space or central place in which the field of the Thing presents itself to us" (p. 118), we have to add: nothing but the human that is the "medium" of this relation.

For the argument that I am summarizing in this paragraph, see p. 279.

ANONYMOUS FIGURES

1. The present essay is devoted essentially to a group of works presented at an exhibition organized by Liana Theodoratou at the A. S. Onassis Center for Hellenic Studies at New York University in the spring of 1995. Puglia entitled this exhibition "Abstracts (of Anamnesis)" and prepared the following statement for the occasion:

As Aristotle writes in his brief treatise "On Memory and Reminiscence," "the same effect occurs in thinking as in drawing a diagram," and "memory, even the memory of objects of thoughts, is not without an image."

Abstracts of anamnesis—or skeletal forms of reminiscence. Such forms must be more than one. No single formula could offer the ultimate image of the flotsam and jetsam of time, now that it is "out of joint." But a series of images could offer at least a hint of a possible world, one among others. And they must be abstracts: summarized, but also free from any specific instance. There is no supreme lesson or famous last word to be learned from the barely legible scrawls which haunt the pictorial surface.

Writing abstracts, conveys its graphic qualities apart from the object to which they belong. So does painting, in a way, gaining its own fantastic presence in this parting. So does thought—or so the Greeks said. Graphic, fantastic—two Greek words, describing operations of the human hand, which Aristotle called the "organ of organs." The image and the alphabet, *phantasia* and *grammata*, stand as the Scylla and Charybdis which define the straits the Greeks have left in their wake—with thought. But what would a painting look like if the presence of painting were precisely the quality it aimed to convey? How could it, at one stroke, accept the Greeks' legacy and question it? How could a legacy ever be shown, if not as a vanishing point? It is not so much a matter of memory. Rather, memories are at stake, as vestiges of memory: a recollection, or anamnesis, of anonymous bodies and sentences no one could sign now.

2. I refer to the indelible image of a wax tablet that has provided a constant reference for Puglia over the years and is perhaps repeated here in the etchings he practices on glass.

3. From "A travers l'image, contre l'image" (unpublished). I will also be quoting from Puglia's essay "Telegrams," also unpublished.

4. The form Bataille refers to as "la figure humaine" in a 1929 essay by that name from *Documents*. All of Puglia's group portraits implicitly cite this text.

5. Here I am referring principally to Heidegger's discussions in *What Is Called Thinking?* and "The Question of Technology" (especially his discussion of the "ambiguous" character of *Technik* and the human share in its unfolding). I have developed these issues in chapter 3 of *Language and Relation*.

6. One could well ask here whether this form of objectification and the "reproducibility" it brings forth can indeed address the present (the contemporary society of spectacle and cyberspace) from the basis of its own conditions for representation. I leave the question partially open in view of the speed and unevenness with which the contemporary structures of spectacle are evolving, but I note that I am inclined to answer in the affirmative by appealing to the meditations Walter Benjamin assembled for his Arcades Project. Like Benjamin, Puglia has turned insistently to the beginnings of the photo-graphic era, producing thereby an archaism that foregrounds some of the forgotten conditions of the technical project. Perhaps it would be most appropriate to say that the figures of *Uber die Schädelnerven* belong to a *pre-history* of the present; but I want to insist that they are nevertheless *of* the present era in their foregrounded reproducibility (a term that I use to evoke Benjamin's meditations on language and representation), and that an element of their "pre-historical" character inheres in a presence that escapes historical objectification and returns with the passive insistence of the *revenant*.

7. Agamben, *The Coming Community*: "The task of the portrait is grasping a unicity, but to grasp a whateverness one needs a photographic lens" (p. 49).

8. To be sure, Puglia's "ex-scription" diverges considerably from Francis Bacon's (see p. 31 above). But, like Bacon, he seeks to bring forward the material presence of the figure in such as a way as to remark an offering of absence (an offering

that is thought by Heidegger with the phrase *es gibt* and by Blanchot with the phrase *il y a*). Beyond Puglia's constant foregrounding of the materials of reproduction (photographic, x-ray, etc.) there is an effort to produce the equivalent of the sentence from "Abstracts (of Anamnesis)": "What would a painting look like if the presence of painting were precisely the quality it aimed to convey?" As Pierre Alféri recognized in an early (unpublished) statement, the *ethical* import of Puglia's work is inseparable from this effort to produce the aesthetic equivalent of a presentation of language itself (using "ethical" now in the sense of this term suggested by Wittgenstein in his "Lecture on Ethics": "ethical" being that language capable of conveying the fact that there is language).

9. Puglia refers in this respect to photographic images of a tortured Chinese man that fascinated Bataille for a number of years. In his essay "Telegram," Puglia asserts that every photograph shares a kinship with these images.

10. The phrase, once again, is from William Haver's volume by that name: *The Body of This Death: Historicity and Sociality in the Time of AIDS.* "Telegram" is, in fact, a long meditation on his tormented struggle with this body.

I would note here, too, that Puglia's "please, please don't" should recall to us Blanchot's discussion of the phrase from Camus's *L'homme révolté*: "I cannot." Blanchot's meditation on the phrase ends with the words: "'I cannot' is death speaking in person, an allusion that death formulates when, in the act of killing, it comes up against the evidence of the visage as though it were its own impossibility; a moment that is death's own drawing back before itself, the *delay* that is the site of speech, and where speech can take place" (*The Infinite Conversation*, p. 187).

Bibliography

Agamben, Giorgio. *The Coming Community*. Trans. Michael Hardt. Minneapolis: University of Minnesota Press, 1993.

———. *Infancy and History*. Trans. Liz Heron. London: Verso, 1993.

Anthelme, Robert. *L'espèce humaine*. Paris: Gallimard, 1978.

Bass, Bernard. *Le désir pur: Parcours philosophiques dans les parages de J. Lacan*. Louvain: Editions Peeters, 1992.

Bataille, Georges. "La figure humaine." In *Documents*. Paris: Mercure de France, 1968.

———. "Nietzschean Chronicle." In *Visions of Excess: Selected Writings, 1927–1939*. Trans. Allan Stoekl. Minneapolis: University of Minnesota Press, 1985.

———. *The Tears of Eros*. Trans. Peter Connor. San Francisco: City Lights Books, 1989.

———. *Visions of Excess: Selected Writings, 1927–1939*. Ed. Allan Stoekl, trans. Allan Stoekl, Carl Lovitt, and Donald M. Leslie Jr. Minneapolis: University of Minnesota Press, 1985.

Benveniste, Emile. *Le vocabulaire des institutions européennes*. Paris: Minuit, 1969.

Blanchot, Maurice. *Death Sentence*. Trans. Lydia Davis. Barrytown, N.Y.: Station Hill Press, 1978.

———. *The Infinite Conversation*. Trans. Susan Hanson. Minneapolis: University of Minnesota Press, 1993.

———. "Literature and the Right to Death." In *The Station Hill Blanchot Reader*. Ed. George Quasha, trans. Lydia Davis. Barrytown, N.Y.: Station Hill Press, 1999.

———. *The Madness of the Day*. Trans. Lydia Davis. Barrytown, N.Y.: Station Hill Press, 1981.

———. "Two Versions of the Imaginary." In *The Station Hill Blanchot Reader*. Ed. George Quasha, trans. Lydia Davis. Barrytown, N.Y.: Station Hill Press, 1999.

———. *The Unavowable Community.* Trans Pierre Joris. Barrytown, N.Y.: Station Hill Press, 1988.

———. *The Writing of the Disaster.* Trans. Ann Smock. Lincoln: The University of Nebraska Press, 1986. Originally published as *L'Ecriture du désastre* (Paris: Gallimard, 1996).

Blundell, Mary Whitlock. *Helping Friends and Harming Enemies.* Cambridge: Cambridge University Press, 1989.

Caruth, Cathy. *Unclaimed Experience.* Baltimore: Johns Hopkins University Press, 1994.

Celan, Paul. "Engführung." In *Sprachgitter.* Frankfurt am Main: S. Fisher Verlag, 1966.

Deleuze, Gilles. *Francis Bacon: Logique de la sensation.* Paris: Editions de la Différence, 1984.

———. *Nietzsche and Philosophy.* Trans. Hugh Tomlinson. New York: Columbia University Press, 1983.

De Man, Paul. "The Rhetoric of Temporality." In *Blindness and Insight.* Minneapolis: University of Minnesota Press, 1983.

Derrida, Jacques. "Nombre de oui." In *Psyché: Inventions de l'autre.* Paris: Galilée, 1987.

———. "Pas." In *Parages.* Paris: Galilée, 1986.

———. *Politiques de l'amitié.* Paris: Galilée, 1994.

———. "Sauver les phénomènes." *Contretemps,* no. 1 (spring 1995).

Felman, Shoshana, and Dori Laub, eds. *Testimony: Crises of Witnessing in Literature, Psychoanalysis, and History.* New York: Routledge, 1992.

Finkbeiner, Ann K. *After the Death of a Child.* New York: The Free Press, 1996.

Foucault, Michel. *The Use of Pleasure.* Vol. 2 of *The History of Sexuality.* Trans. Robert Hurley. New York: Vintage Books, 1990.

Freud, Sigmund. "A Child Is Being Beaten: A Contribution to the Study of the Origin of Sexual Perversions" (1929). In vol. 17 of *The Standard Edition of the Complete Psychological Works of Sigmund Freud.* Trans. and ed. James Strachey. London: The Hogarth Press, 1964.

———. "Formulations on the Two Principles of Mental Functioning" (1911). In vol. 12 of *The Standard Edition of the Complete Psychological Works of Sigmund Freud.* Trans. and ed. James Strachey. London: The Hogarth Press, 1964.

———. *The Interpretation of Dreams.* Vol. 5 of *The Standard Edition of the Complete Psychological Works of Sigmund Freud.* Trans. and ed. James Strachey. London: The Hogarth Press, 1964.

Fynsk, Christopher. "Between Ethics and Aesthetics." *L'esprit créateur* 25, no. 3, (fall 1995): 80–87.

———. "Community and the Limits of Theory." In *Community at Loose Ends*. Minneapolis: University of Minnesota Press, 1987.

———. *Heidegger: Thought and Historicity*. Ithaca: Cornell University Press, Expanded Edition, 1993.

———. *Language and Relation: . . . that there is language*. Stanford, Calif.: Stanford University Press, 1996.

Gallop, Jane. *Reading Lacan*. Ithaca, N.Y.: Cornell University Press, 1985.

Golding, Sue. *The Eight Technologies of Otherness*. London: Routledge, 1997.

Halperin, David. *Saint Foucault: Towards a Gay Hagiography*. New York: Oxford University Press, 1995.

Hamacher, Werner. *Premises: Essays on Philosophy and Literature from Kant to Celan*. Trans. Peter Fenves. Cambridge: Harvard University Press, 1996.

Haver, William. *The Body of This Death: Historicity and Sociality in the Time of AIDS*. Stanford, Calif.: Stanford University Press, 1996.

Heidegger, Martin. "The Anaximander Fragment." In *Early Greek Thinking*. Trans. David Farrell Krell and Frank A. Capuzzi. New York: Harper and Row, 1975.

———. *An Introduction to Metaphysics*. Trans. Ralph Manheim. New York: Doubleday, 1961.

———. *Being and Time*. Trans. John Macquarrie and Edward Robinson. New York: Harper and Row, 1962.

———. *Heraclitus*. Vol. 55 of *Gesamtausgabe*. Frankfurt am Main: Vittorio Klostermann, 1979.

———. *On the Way to Language*. Trans. Peter D. Hertz. New York: Harper and Row, 1971.

———. "The Question Concerning Technology." In *The Question Concerning Technology and Other Essays*. Trans. William Lovitt. New York: Harper and Row, 1977.

———. *Unterwegs zur Sprache*. Vol. 12 of *Gesamtausgabe*. Ed. Friedrich-Wilhelm von Hermann. Frankfurt am Main: Vittorio Klostermann, 1985.

———. *What Is Called Thinking?* Trans. J. Glenn Gray. New York: Harper and Row, 1968.

———. "What Is Metaphysics?" In *Basic Writings*. Trans. David Farrell Krell. New York: Harper Collins, 1993.

Hölderlin, Friedrich W. "Anmerkungen zur Antigonä." Vol. 2 of *Werke und Briefe*. Ed. Friedrich Beissner and Jochen Schmidt. Frankfurt am Main: Insel Verlag, 1969.

Jacobs, Carol. "Dusting Antigone." *Modern Language Notes* 3, no. 5 (December 1996): 889–917.

Jebb, Sir Richard, trans. *Antigone,* by Sophocles. Ed. E. S. Schuckburgh. Cambridge: Cambridge University Press, 1992.

Kinsch, Luc. "*Kindertotenlieder*—The Songs of the Dead Children: Childhood, History, Art." Ph.D. diss., Yale University, 1996.

Klarsfeld, Serge. *French Children of the Holocaust: A Memorial.* New York: New York University Press, 1996.

Lacan, Jacques. "The Agency of the Letter in the Unconscious, or Reason Since Freud." In *Ecrits.* Trans. Alan Sheridan. New York: W. W. Norton, 1977.

———. "Le désir et son interprétation (Compte rendu de J.-B. Pontalis)." *Bulletin de Psychologie* 13, no. 171 (January 1960): 263–72.

———. *Ecrits.* Trans. Alan Sheridan. New York: W. W. Norton, 1977.

———. *The Ethics of Psychoanalysis 1959–1960.* Vol. 7 of *The Seminar of Jacques Lacan.* Ed. Jacques-Alain Miller, trans. Dennis Porter. New York: W. W. Norton, 1986. Originally published as *Le séminaire de Jacques Lacan, Livre VII: L'éthique de la psychanalyse, 1959–1960* (Paris: Editions du Seuil, 1986).

———. *The Four Fundamental Concepts of Psychoanalysis.* Vol. 11 of *The Seminar of Jacques Lacan.* Ed. Jacques-Alain Miller, trans. Alan Sheridan. New York: W. W. Norton, 1978. Originally published as *Le séminaire de Jacques Lacan, Livre XI: Les quatre concepts fondamentaux de la psychanalyse, 1964* (Paris: Editions du Seuil, 1973).

———. "The Signification of the Phallus." In *Ecrits.* Trans. Alan Sheridan. New York: W. W. Norton, 1977.

Laplanche, Jean, and J.-B. Pontalis. "Fantasme originaire, fantasme des origines, origine du fantasme." *Les temps modernes* 215 (April 1964): 1850–68.

Lebensztejn, Jean-Claude. "Notes sur Francis Bacon." In *Francis Bacon.* Paris: Centre Georges Pompidou, 1996.

Leclaire, Serge. *A Child Is Being Killed: On Primary Narcissism and the Death Drive.* Trans. Marie-Claude Hays. Stanford, Calif.: Stanford University Press, 1997.

Leiris, Michel. *Francis Bacon, ou la vérité criante.* Montpellier: Fata Morgana, 1975.

Lerner, Lawrence. *Angels and Absences: Child Death in the Nineteenth Century.* Nashville, Tenn.: Vanderbilt University Press, 1997.

Levi, Primo. *Survival in Auschwitz.* Trans. Stuart Woolf. New York: Macmillan, 1986.

Levinas, Emmanuel. *Otherwise Than Being or Beyond Essence.* Trans. Alphonso Lingis. The Hague: Martinus Nijhoff, 1981.

Lloyd-Jones, Hugh, trans. *Antigone,* by Sophocles. In *Sophocles II.* Loeb Classical Library, 1994.

Lyotard, Jean-François. *Discours, figure.* Paris: Editions Klincksieck, 1974.

———. *Lectures d'enfance.* Paris: Galilée, 1991.

Mallarmé, Stéphane. *A Tomb for Anatole.* Trans. Paul Auster. San Francisco: North Point Press, 1983.

Nancy, Jean-Luc. "L'excrit." In *Une pensée finie.* Paris: Galilée, 1990.

———. "Notre probité." In *L'impératif catégorique.* Paris: Flammarion, 1983.

Nehemas, Alexander. *Nietzsche: Life as Literature.* Cambridge, Mass.: Harvard University Press, 1985.

Nietzsche, Friedrich. *Beyond Good and Evil.* Trans. Walter Kaufmann. New York: Random House, 1966.

———. *The Gay Science: With a Prelude in Rhymes and an Appendix of Songs.* Trans. Walter Kaufmann. New York: Random House, 1974.

———. *On the Genealogy of Morals and Ecce Homo.* Ed. Walter Kaufmann; trans. Walter Kaufmann and R. J. Hollingdale. New York: Random House, 1967.

Ragland-Sullivan, Ellie. *Essays on the Pleasures of Death: From Freud to Lacan.* New York: Routledge, 1995.

Schelling, F. W. J. "Letters on Dogmatism and Criticism." In *The Unconditional in Human Knowledge: Four Early Essays (1794–1796).* Trans. Fritz Marti. Lewisburg, Pa.: Bucknell University Press, 1978.

Steiner, George. *Antigones.* Oxford: Oxford University Press, 1986.

Sylvester, David. *The Brutality of Fact: Interviews with Francis Bacon.* New York: Thames and Hudson, 1981.

Weber, Elisabeth. *Meditating on the Shoah: Where Philosophy and Psychoanalysis Meet* (forthcoming).

Winnington-Ingram, R. P. *Sophocles: An Interpretation.* Cambridge: Cambridge University Press, 1980.

Wittgenstein, Ludwig. "Lecture on Ethics." *The Philosophical Review* 11, no. 74 (1965).

Wyckoff, Elizabeth, trans. *Antigone,* by Sophocles. In *Sophocles I.* Ed. David Grene and Richmond Lattimore. Chicago: University of Chicago Press, 1954.

Index of Names

Adorno, Theodor, 156
Aeschylus, 116
Agamben, Giorgio, 94–96, 171, 178n, 188n
Alféri, Pierre, 189n
Anaximander, 186n
Anthelme, Robert, 177–78n
Antigone, 7, 116, 118, 121, 122–24, 130, 131–43, 184n, 185n, 187n
Aristotle, 165
Artaud, Antonin, 17
Auster, Paul, 85

Bacon, Francis, 2, 8, 11–46, 116, 120, 156, 183n, 188n
Bacon, Lord, 11, 13
Bass, Bernard, 118, 128
Bataille, Georges, 17, 24, 30, 36, 44, 46, 112, 120, 133, 147, 170, 183n, 188n
Benjamin, Walter, 91, 188n
Benveniste, Émile, 95, 132, 185n
Blanchot, Maurice, 1–4, 6, 49–80, 90–91, 95, 112, 120, 123, 126, 127, 129, 131, 134, 137, 142, 172, 177n, 178n, 185n, 189n
Blundell, Mary Whitlock, 185n
Brinker-Gabler, Gisela, 88

Burger, Rodolphe, 152, 157
Byron, Lord, 37

Camus, Albert, 57, 189n
Caruth, Cathy, 90, 103, 105, 110–13, 178n
Celan, Paul, 46
Cézanne, P., 38
Chottin, Ariane, 154
Christ, 118, 121

Davies, Paul, 66
Degas, Edgar, 25
Deleuze, Gilles, 18–20, 30, 31, 34, 37, 39, 42, 181n, 182n, 183n
de Man, Paul, 89
Derrida, Jacques, 54, 130, 164, 185n, 186n
Dionysus, 14
Döblin, A., 161
Doillon, Jacques, 71

Erinyes, 22, 33
Eurydice, 91, 134

Felman, Shoshana, 178n
Finkbeiner, Anne, 96
Foucault, Michel, 14, 17, 46, 178n

197